HENRY Morford

Morford short-trip guide to America

HENRY Morford

Morford short-trip guide to America

ISBN/EAN: 9783337145293

Printed in Europe, USA, Canada, Australia, Japan

Cover: Foto ©Andreas Hilbeck / pixelio.de

More available books at **www.hansebooks.com**

MORFORD'S
SHORT-TRIP GUIDE

TO

AMERICA.

(*UNITED STATES AND DOMINION OF CANADA.*)

By HENRY MORFORD,

AUTHOR OF THE "SHORT-TRIP GUIDE TO EUROPE," "OVER-SEA,"
"PARIS IN '67," ETC:

NEW YORK:
CHARLES T. DILLINGHAM.

BOSTON:
LEE & SHEPARD.

LONDON:
TRÜBNER & CO.,
AND
W. H. SMITH & SON.

ADVERTISEMENT

TO THE SEVENTH EDITION.

In the preparation of the seventh edition of the "SHORT-TRIP GUIDE TO AMERICA," necessarily most of the features which had won it so much of commendation and success in previous editions, have been retained; though many variations have been found necessary, from the constant changes of routes, widening of space covered by railway transit, alterations and improvements in cities, &c. Some entirely new and important routes have been added, and completions of only less consequence made in others. Most of the very close particulars given last year with reference to the City of Philadelphia, have been retained as permanently useful; and especial attention has been paid to the very latest alterations in the City of New York. Southern and Western routes have also been materially remodeled and extended; and the various new railway connections with the main line crossing the Continent to the Pacific, will be found carefully noted, as well as the improvements and alterations made by the last three years in the strange City of the Golden Gate. It is believed that, taken all in all, the "SHORT-TRIP GUIDE" for 1877 will be found reasonably complete, and thoroughly welcome to the large body of native and foreign travelers to whose convenience it may minister.

NEW YORK AND LONDON,
June, 1877.

TABLE OF CONTENTS.

INDEX i
DISTANCES, TIME AND FARES xiv
COST AND TIME of Short American Trips. 7
PREPARATIONS for the Trip to America. 17
WHAT TO DO and Avoid on Shipboard 30
BELL-TIME at Sea 40
NEW YORK CITY, Harbor and Suburbs 42
ROUTE No. 1.—Northern—New York to Niagara and Canada 62
" No. 2.—Northern—New York to Niagara and Canada 83
" No. 3.—Northern—New York to Saratoga, Lake George, &c. 91
" No. 4.—Eastern—New York to Boston, by New Haven, Providence, &c. 103
" No. 5.—Eastern—Boston to Portland and Canada 124
" No. 6.—Northern and Eastern—Boston to White Mountains, &c. 129
" No. 7.—Northern and Eastern—New York to White Mountains, &c. 136
" No. 8.—Near Western—New York to Philadelphia 144
" No. 9.—Western and Southern—Philadelphia to Baltimore, Washington and Richmond 162
" No. 9½.—Special Virginian—Baltimore or Washington to Virginia Cities, Springs and Mountains. 189
" No. 9¾.—Western and South-Western—Washington or Baltimore, to Chicago and St. Louis. 189½
" No. 10.—South-Western—Richmond to Charleston, Savannah, New Orleans, &c. 196
" No. 11.—South-Western — Washington or Richmond to Nashville and New Orleans 195
" No. 11½.—Southern — Richmond to Charleston, Savannah, and Florida Resorts 196a
" No. 12.—Western—New York or Philadelphia to Cincinnati and Chicago 197
" No. 13.—Western—New York to Chicago, &c. 206
" No. 14.—Western—Cincinnati to Louisville, St. Louis and Chicago 217
" No. 15.—Northern and Western—Buffalo to Chicago, by Lake Shore 226
" No. 16.—Northern—New York or Philadelphia to Coal and Oil Regions 228
" No. 17.—Canadian and Western—Niagara to Detroit and Chicago 231
" No. 18.—North-Western—Chicago to St Paul and Lake Superior 237
" No. 19.—Canadian—Niagara to Toronto, Ottawa, Montreal, Quebec, &c. 241
" No. 20.—Canadian—Niagara to Toronto, Montreal and Quebec, by Steamers. 257
" No. 21.—Far Western—Chicago to Omaha, Salt Lake City and San Francisco. 261
OFF ROUTE and Minor Places. 277
STEAMSHIP LINES and Banking Houses .... —
AMERICAN HOTELS for Travellers. .... —
REMINDERS TO RAMBLERS .... —

INDEX.

[PLACES AND ROUTES. FOR PLACES THEMSELVES, SEE FIGURES IN HEAVY TYPE; FOR PLACES NOT FOUND IN THIS INDEX, SEE "OFF-ROUTE AND MINOR PLACES," PRECEDING.]

A

Acapulco, Mex., 273.
Adirondack Mountains, 97, 100.
Adrian, Mich., **227**, 235.
Akron, Ohio, 210.
Alameda (and Warm Springs), Cal., 271, 273.
ALBANY, N. Y., 70.
Albion, Mich., 235.
Albion, N. Y., 77.
Alexandria, Va., **183**, 185, 195.
Alkali, Neb., 269.
Allegheny City, Pa., 200.
Allegheny Mountains, 199.
Allegheny Springs, Va., 195.
Allentown, Pa., 208.
Alliance, O., 210.
Altoona, Pa., 199.
Alton Bay, N. H., 125, 129.
Alton, Ill., **224**, 239, 261, 263.
Alton, N. H., 129.
Amador, Cal., 274.
Amherst, Mass., 139.
Ammonoosuc Falls, N. H., 134.
Anchorage, Ky., 217.
Andover, North, Mass, 124.
Annapolis Junction, Md., 171.
ANNAPOLIS, Md., **168**, 171.
Ann Arbor, Mich., 235.
Appomattox, Va., 195.
Aquia Creek, Va., 183, 185.
Argenta, Nev., 272.
Arlington House, Va., 182.
Arnprior, Can., 243.
Arthabasca (Junction), Can., 128, 251.
Ashland, Iowa, 263.
Ashland, Ky., 217.
Aspen, Utah, 271.
Aspinwall, Cent. Amer., 273.
Athens, N. Y., 70.

Athens, O., 203.
Atlanta, Ga., 191.
Atlantic, Iowa, 264.
Atlantic City, N. J., 150, **160**.
Attleboro, Mass., 110.
Auburn, Cal., 273.
Auburn, N. Y., 76.
AUGUSTA, Ga., 191.
Augusta, Me., 127.
Au Sable River, N. Y., 100.
Austin, Iowa, 238, 261, 262.
Austin, Nev., 269.
Australia (to), 273.

B

Ballston Spa, N. Y., 91.
BALTIMORE, Md., **164**, 198, 201— Fort McHenry, 165 — Monuments, 165 — Streets, 165— Public Buildings, 166—Churches 166—Lit. Inst., 166—Theatres, 167—Hotels, 167—Cemeteries, 167—Excursions, 168 — Longer Excursions, 168, 169, 170.
Bangor, Me., 127.
Barrytown, N. Y., 68.
Batavia, N. Y., 77.
Bathurst, N. B., 260.
Battle Creek, Mich., 235.
Battle Mountain, Nev., 272.
Bay City, Mich., 240.
Beauport, Can., 253.
Beaverton, Can., 242.
Becancour, Can., 128.
Bedford Springs, Pa., **199**.
Bel-Air, Md , 168.
Belle Air, O., 202.
Belleville, Can., 243.
Bellows Falls, Vt., **140**.
Belmont, Mo., 220.
Belmont, Nev., 269.

INDEX.

Beloit, Wis., 238.
Berkeley Springs, Va.. 189a.
Bergen Tunnel, N. J., 83.
Berlin, Can., 232, 242.
Bethlehem, N. H., 134.
Bethlehem, Pa., 208.
Beverley, N. J., 150.
Biddeford, Me., 125.
Big Oak Flat Route, Cal., 276h.
Big Trees of Calaveras, Cal., 276a, 276h.
Big Trees of Mariposa, Cal., 276i.
Big Tunnel, Va , 195.
Binghamton, N. Y., 76, **87.**
Bird's Point, Mo., 221.
Birmingham, Pa., 200.
Bismarck, Mo., 221.
Bitter Creek, Wyo,, 271.
Black River, Can., 128.
Bladensburg, Md., 171.
Blairsville, Pa., 200.
Bloody Pond, N. Y., 95.
Bloomington, Ill., **224,** 261, 262, 263.
Bloomsbury, N. J., 207.
Boca. Cal., 273.
Boise City, Idaho, 208, 269.
Bonsack's, Va., 195.
Boone, Iowa, 262.
Boonton, N. J., 228.
Bordentown, N. J., 148, **150,** 160.
BOSTON, 107, 110, **115,** 251—Streets, 117—Public Grounds, 117 — Antiquities, 117 — Public Buildings, 118—Monuments, 119—Churches, 119—Libraries and Lit. Inst., 120—Theatres, 120—Hotels, 120—Excursions, 120—Harvard University, 120—Washington Head Quarters, 121—Mount Auburn Cemetery, 121—Longer Excursions, 121, 122.
Bothwell, Can., 232.
Bound Brook, N. J., 206.
Bowling Green, Ky., 219.
Bowmanville, Can , 242.
Bradford, Mass., 124.
Branch Intersection, Pa., 198.
Branchville, S. C., 191.
Brandywine Creek, Pa., 162.
Brattleboro, Vt , 140.
Breckenridge, Minn., 239.
Bridgeport, Ct., 103.
Bridgeton, N. J., 150, 159.
Brighton, Cal., 274.
Brighton, Mass., 107.

Bristol, Pa., 148.
Bristol, Tenn., 195.
Brockport, N. Y., 77
Brockville, Can., 245.
BROOKLYN connection with New York)—Streets, 47 — Churches, 50—Public Buildings, 51—Hotels 53—Theatres, 54—Churches for Service, 54—Public Grounds, 55, 57—Prospect Park, 57—Greenwood Cemetery, 57—Excursions 57, 58—Navy Yard, 58.
Brown's, Can., 246.
Brown University, 109.
Bryan, Wyo., 271.
Buckingham, Can., 246.
Bucyrus, O., 210.
Budd's Lake, N. J., 60, 228.
BUFFALO, N. Y., **89,** 232, 234, 240.
Buford, Wyo., 270.
Bull Run (Battle-field), Va., 183.
Bulstrode, Can., 128, 251.
Bureau, Ill., 263.
Burkeville (Junction), Va., 195.
Burlington, Iowa, 215, 238, 259, 261, 263, **264.**
Burlington, N. J., **150,** 160.
Burlington, Vt., **100,** 101, 140.
Bush River Bridge, Md., 164

C.

Cacouna, Can., 255.
Cairo, Ill., 194, 205, 216, **220.**
Caldwell, N. Y., 95.
Caledonia, N. Y., 77.
Caledonia Springs, Can., 246.
California Junction, Iowa, 264, 265.
Callicoon, N. Y., 86.
Calistoga (Springs), Cal., 276l.
Camden, N. J., 148, **150,** 159.
Camel's Hump Mountain, Vt., 100.
Canandaigua, N. Y., 77.
Canton, O., 210.
Cape Cod, Mass., 122.
Cape Elizabeth, Me., 125.
Cape May, N. J., 150. **160.**
Cape Rouge, Can., 253.
Cape Vincent, N. Y., 243.
Carbon, Wyo., 266.
Carbondale, Pa., 270.
Carillon, Can., 246.
Carleton Place, Can., 243, **245.**
Carlin, Nev., 272.
Carlisle, Pa , 198.
Carson, Nev., 269.

INDEX.   iii

Carter, Utah. 271.
Cascade Bridge, N. Y., 87.
Casey, Iowa, 264.
Castle Rock, Utah, 271.
Castleton, N. Y., 70.
Castleton, Vt., 101.
Catawissa, Pa., 209.
Catskill Landing, N. Y., 63.
Catskill Mountain House, 69.
Cave City, Ky., 218.
Cayuga, N. Y., 77.
Cedar Rapids, Iowa, 215, 238, **261**, 263.
Central City, Col., 266.
Centre Harbor, N. H., 102, **130**, 138.
Chambersburg, Pa., 183, 198.
Champaign, Ill., 224.
Charles City, Iowa, 238.
Charleston, Mo., 221.
CHARLESTON, S. C., 188, **189.**
Charlestown, Va., 189b.
Charlotte Town, P. E. I., 259.
Charlottesville, Va., **183,** 195.
Chatham, Can., 232.
Chattanooga, Tenn., 191, **196.**
Chaudiere Junction, Can., 128, 254, 255, 256.
Chaudiere Falls, Can., **244,** 253.
Chelsea, Mass., 122.
Chenoa, Ill., 224.
Cherry Valley, N. Y., 74.
Chester, N. J., 228.
Chester, Pa., 162.
Chester, Va., 186.
CHEYENNE, Wyo., 270, **274.**
CHICAGO, Ill., 201, 205, **212,** 220, 223, 225, 227, 234, 236. 238, 239.
Chicamauga, Tenn., 196.
China (to), 273.
Chinese Camp, Cal., 274.
CINCINNATI, O., 201, 202, **204,** 205, 210, 216, 221, 223, 227.
Claremont, Vt., 140.
Clearfield, Pa., 199.
Cleveland, O., 201, 202, 203, 205, 210, 216, **226,** 240.
Clinton, Iowa, 261.
Clyde, N. Y., 77.
Clyde, O., 227.
Coal Regions of Pennsylvania, 207, 208, 229.
Coatesville, Pa., 197.
Coburg, Can., 242.
Cohoes Falls, N. Y., 71.
Colborne, Can., 243.
Cold Spring, N. Y., 66.

Colfax, Cal., 273.
Collins' Bay, Can., 243.
Colmar, Iowa, 238.
Coloma, Cal., 270.
Columbia, Ind., 211.
Columbia, Pa., 198.
COLUMBIA, S. C., 188, **191.**
Columbia Springs (route to), 70.
Columbus, Ky., 220.
COLUMBUS, O., **202,** 210, 227.
Columbus, Neb., 269.
Communipaw, N. J., 206.
Como, Can., 247.
Coney Island, N. Y., 58.
Concord, Mass., **123,** 136.
CONCORD, N. H., 124, 125, **137.**
Conemaugh Station, Pa., 199.
Contra Costa, Cal., 273.
Conway, N. H., 102, 129, **131,** 138.
Conway Valley, N. H., 130.
Cooperstown, N. Y., 74.
Corinne, Utah, 272.
Corning, N. Y., 77, 8Sb.
Cornwall Landing, N. Y., 66.
Corry, Pa., 89, 198, 226, 230.
Coshocton, O., 202, 227.
Council Bluffs, Iowa, 262, 264.
Covington, Ky., 204, 217.
Coxsackie, N. Y., 70.
Coultersville Route, Cal., 276f.
Crawford House, N. H., 133.
C. esson, Pa., 199.
Crestline, O., 210.
Creston, Wyo., 271.
Crisfield, Md., 163.
Croton River, N. Y., 63.
Culpepper, Va., 183.
Cumberland, Md., 170, 201.

D.

Danvers, No., Mass., 124.
Danville, Can., 128.
Danville Junction, Me., 127.
Darien, Ct., 103.
Davenport, Iowa, 239, **263.**
Dayton, O., 204, 210, 211, 227.
Delaware Water Gap, **60,** 160, 207, 229.
Dennison, O., 202.
DENVER, Col., 274, **276**m.
Deposit, N. Y., 86.
DES MOINES, Iowa, 215, 262, **264.**
DETROIT, Mich., 210, 211, 216, 227, **233,** 240.
Devil's Gate, Utah, 271.

INDEX.

Dexter, Iowa, 264.
Dixon, Ill., 261.
Dobbs Ferry, N. Y., 63.
Dorsey, Md., 171.
Doucet's Landing, Can., 128.
DOVER, Del., 163.
Dover, N. J., 228.
Dover, N. H., **125**, 129, 137.
Downieville Cal., 270.
Downington, Pa., 197.
Drakesville, N. J., 228.
Dresden Junction, O., 202.
Dubuque, Iowa, 239, 261.
Duluth, Minn., 238, **240**.
Dundas, Can., 232.
Dunkirk, N. Y., 89, 226.
Dunleith, Iowa, 261.
Dunville, Can., 232.
Durham, N. H., 125.

E.

Easton, Pa., 160, **207**, 229.
East Penn. Junction, Pa., 208.
Eatontown, N. J., 59.
Ebensburg, Pa., 199.
Echo Canon (and City), Utah, 271.
Echo Lake, N. H., 141.
Effingham, Ind., 205b, 225.
Elgin, Ill., from Chicago, 212 to 216.
Elizabeth City, Va., 169.
Elizabeth, N. J., 59, **145**, 197, 206.
Elizabethport, N. J., 149, 206.
Elk Grove, Cal., 274.
Elkhart, Ind., 227.
Elkhorn, Neb., 268
Elkhorn, Wis., 237.
Elko, Nev., 272
Elkton, Md., 163.
Ellicott's Mills, Md., 170.
Ellis, Cal., 271.
Elmira, N. Y., **88**, 198.
Eminence, Ky., 217.
Emporium, Pa., 230.
Englewood, Ill., 262.
Erie Canal, 74.
Erie, Pa., 198, 201, **226**, 230, 240.
Essex Junction, Vt., 101.
Evanston, Utah, 271.
Evansville, Ind., 219.
Exeter, N. H., 125.

F.

Fairfax Court-House, Va., 183.
Fall River, Mass., 113, **114**.

Falls of the Ammonoosuc, N. H., 134.
Falls of the Chaudiere, Can., **244**, 253.
Falls of Cohoes, N. Y., 71.
Falls of the Genesee, N. Y., 77.
Falls, Glen Ellis, N. H., 131.
Falls, Glenn's, N. Y., 65.
Falls, Kauterskill, N. Y., 69.
Falls of Minnehaha, Minn., 239.
Falls of Niagara, 77, **78**, 242.
Falls, Passaic, 59, 84.
Falls of the Potomac, D. C., 182.
Falls, Rideau, Can., 244, 245.
Falls of the Sawkill, N. Y., 86.
Falls of St. Anne, Can., 247.
Falls of St. Anthony, Minn., 239.
Falls of Trenton, N. Y., 75.
Falls of the Yo Semite, Cal., 275.
Farmington, N. H., 129.
Fishkill Landing, N. Y., 66.
Fitchburg, Mass., 140.
Flemington, N. J., 207.
Florence, S. C., 189.
Florida Resorts, 196a, 196b
Flume, The (and House), N. H., 142.
Fonda, N. Y., 74.
Forest, O., 210.
Fort Bridger, Utah, 267.
Fort Dodge, Iowa, 262, 264
Fort Hamilton, N. Y., 58.
Fort Howard, Wis., 261.
Fort Massasauga, Can., 257.
Fort Niagara, N. Y., 257.
Fort Plain, N. Y., 74.
Fort Saunders, Wyo., 270.
Fort Schuyler, N. Y., 111.
Fort Sedgwick, Neb., 265.
Fort Snelling, Minn., 239.
Fort Washington, Va., 185.
Fort Wayne, Ind., 201, **211**, **224**, 227, 235, 262.
Fortress Monroe, Va., 169.
Four Lakes, Wis., 238.
Foxboro, Mass., 110.
Framingham, Mass., 107.
Franconia Notch, N. H., 134.
Frankford, Pa., 148.
Franklinton, Md., 168.
Frederick, Md., 170.
Fredericksburg, Va., 185.
Fredericton, N. B., 259.
Freehold, N. J., 149.
Freeport, Ill., 237, 261, 263.
Freeport, Pa., 200.
Fremont, O., 227.

INDEX.

Fremont, Neb., 268.
Frenchman's Bay, Can., 242.

G.

Galena, Ill., 239.
Galt, Cal., 276k.
Galveston, Texas, 192, 194.
Gananoque, Can., 243.
Garrison's Landing, N. Y., 64.
Gatineau River, Can., 245.
Genesee Falls, N. Y., 77.
Geneva, N. Y., 77.
Genoa, Ill., 237.
Georgetown, Cal., 270.
Georgetown, D. C., 152.
Georgetown, Mass., 124.
Germantown, Pa., 159.
Geysers, The, Cal., 276k, 276l.
Girard, Pa., 226.
Glen Allen, Mo., 221.
Glencoe, Can., 232.
Glen Cove, L. I., 61.
Glen Ellis Falls, N. H., 131.
Glen House, N. H., 131.
Glenn's Falls, N. Y., 95.
Goderich, Can., 232. 240.
Golden City, Cal., 266.
Gold Hill, Nev., 269.
Goshen, Va., 189d, 189e.
Gordonsville, Va., 183. 186. 189g.
Gorham, N. H., 102, 127, 251.
Gosport Navy Yard, Va., 169.
Grafton, Mass., 107.
Grand Haven, Mich., 227, 235.
Grand Island, Neb., 269.
Grand Junction, Iowa, 262.
Grand Rapids, Mich., 235.
Granger, Utah, 267.
Granite Canon, Wyo., 270.
Grass Valley, Cal., 270.
Great American Desert, 268.
Great Bend, N. Y., 87, 229.
Great Falls, N. H., 125.
Great Nevada Sandy Desert, 269.
Great Salt Lake, Utah, 268.
Green Bay, Wis., 215, 261.
Greenbush, N. Y., 70.
Greenfield, Mass., 140.
Greenport, L. I., 61.
Green River, Wyo., 271.
Greensboro, N. C., 188.
Greensburg, Pa., 200.
Greenwich, East, R. I., 109.
Greenwood Lake, N. Y., 85.
Grenville, Can., 246.

Greycourt, N. Y., 85.
Grimsby, Can., 231.
Grinnell, Iowa, 263.
Groton, Ct., 108.
Groton Junction, Mass., 136, 140.
Grout's Corners, Mass., 140.
Guelph, Can., 232, 242.
Gunpowder River Bridge, Md., 164

H.

Hackettstown, N. J., 60, 228.
Ha Ha Bay, Can., 256.
HALIFAX, N. S., 250, 259.
Hamilton, Can., 231, 241.
Hamilton, O., 210.
Hampton Junction. N. J., 207, 228.
Hampton, N. H., 125.
Hamptou and Roads), Va , 169.
Hancock, N. Y., 86.
Hannibal, Mo., 239.
Hanover, Md., 171.
Hanover, Va., 163.
Harper's Ferry, W. Va., 170, 171. 183, 189, 201.
HARTFORD, Ct., 105.
Harrisonburg, Va., 189c.
HARRISBURG, Pa., 160, 163, 198, 209.
Harvard University, 120.
Haverhill., Mass., 124.
Havana, Cuba, 194.
Havre de Grace, Md., 162, 163.
Hawkesbury, Can., 246.
Hazard, Wyo., 270.
Hazleton, Pa., 209.
Helena, Nev., 268.
Henderson, Ky., 219.
Herkimer, N. Y., 74.
Hermitage, the, Tenn., 219.
Hickford Junction, Va., 189.
Highlands of Navesink, 59.
Highlands of the Hudson, 63.
Hightstown, N. J., 150.
Hillsdale, Mich., 227.
Hillsdale, Wyo., 270.
Hoboken, N. J., 58.
Homewood, Pa., 210.
Honesdale, Pa., 229.
Hoosic Tunnel, Mass., 136.
Horicon, Wis., 237.
Hornellsville, N. Y., 89.
Hudson, Can., 247.
Hudson, N. Y., 70.
Hyannis, Mass., 122.
Hyde Park, N. Y., 67.

I.

Indiana, Pa., 200.
India (to), 273.
INDIANOPOLIS, Ind., 205a. 218, 223.
Ione City, Cal., 274.
Iowa City, Iowa, 263.
Island Pond, 127, 251, 253, 255.
Isle of Shoals, N. H., 125.
Iron Mountain, Mo., 221.
Ironton, Mo , 221.
Irvineton, Pa., 230.
Ithaca, N. Y., 88.

J.

Jackson, Cal , 274.
Jackson, Mich., 235.
JACKSON, Miss., 194.
Jacksonville, Ill., 224.
Jamaica, L. I., 61.
Jamesburg, N. J., 149.
Jamestown (ruins), Va., 169.
Janesville, Wis., 215, 237.
Japan (to), 273.
Jefferson City, Mo., 223.
Jeffersonville, Ind , 218
Jersey City, N. J., 144, 197.
Johnsonville, Tenn., 220.
Johnstown, Pa., 199.
Joliet, Ill., 224, 262.
Jonesville, Mich., 227.
Julesburg, Neb., 269.

K.

Kalamazoo, Mich., 227, 234, 235.
Kauterskill Falls, 60.
Kearney (and Fort) Neb., 269.
Keene, N. H., 140.
Keeseville, N. Y., 100.
Kelton, Utah, 272.
Kenosha, Wis., 237.
Kennebunk, Me., 125.
Kensington, Pa., 148.
Keokuk, Iowa, 239, 261, 262, 264.
Kinderhook, N. Y., 70.
Kingston, Can., 243, 257.
Kingston, N. Y., 67.
Kingsville, S. C., 191.
Kittery, Maine, 125.
Knoxville, Tenn., 188, 195, 219.
Komoka, Can., 232.

L.

Lachine, Can., 247.
Lachine Rapids, Can., 250.

Lackawaxen, N. Y., 86.
La Crosse, Wis., 239.
Lafayette, Ind., 211.
Lafayette College, 208.
Lagrange, Ky., 217.
Lake Champlain, 99.
Lake Donner, Cal., 276f.
Lake George, 95.
Lake Hopatcong, 60, 223.
Lake Mahopac, 60.
Lake Memphremagog, Can., 127, 138, 140.
Lake Pepin, Minn., 239.
Lake Ponchartrain, La., 194.
Lake Simcoe, Can., 242.
Lake St. Charles, Can., 253, 254.
Lake St. Clair, 233.
Lake St. Louis, Can., 247.
Lake St. Peter, Can., 128.
Lake Superior, 215, 240.
Lake Superior Copper Regions, 240.
Lake Superior Iron Regions, 240.
Lake Tahoe, Cal., 276f.
Lake Winnepesaukie, 125, 129.
Lake of the Two Mountains, Can., 247.
Lambertville, N. J., 207.
Lamokin Junction, Pa., 162.
Lancaster, Pa., 160, 197.
L'Ance a l'Eau, Can., 255.
Lanesborough, N. Y., 87.
LANSING, Mich., 235.
Lansingburgh, N. Y., 71.
Laporte, Ind., 227.
La Prairie, Can., 100.
Laramie, Wyo., 270.
La Salle, Ill., 263.
Lathrop, Cal., 273, 276a.
Laurel, Md., 171.
Lawrence, Mass., 122, 124, 136
Lawrenceville, Pa , 200.
Lawton, Mich., 236.
Lazaretto, The, Pa., 162.
Lebanon, Pa., 198, 209.
Lebanon Springs, N. Y., 70.
Leesburg, Va., 183.
Leetonia, O., 210.
Lennoxville, Can., 135.
Le Roy, N. Y., 77.
Lewes, Del., 163.
Lewiston, N. Y., 242, 257.
Lewiston, Pa., 199.
Lexington, Ky., 217.
Lexington, Va., 189f.
Lima, O., 211, 227.
LINCOLN, Neb., 262.

INDEX. vii

L'Islet, Can., 254.
Little Falls, N. Y., 74.
Little Rock, Ark., 220.
Littleton, N. H., 102, **139**, 140.
Lock Haven, Pa., 199, **230.**
Lockport, N. Y., 77.
Logansport, Ind., 211, 224, 227.
London, Can., 232.
London, O., 203.
Long Branch, N. J., **59**, 149, 150, 161.
Long Sault Rapids, Can., 246.
Lookout Mountain, 196.
Lorette, Can., 253.
L'Original, Can., 246.
LOUISVILLE, Ky., 211, **217**, 221.
Loveland, O., 204.
Lowell, Mass., **121**, 134, 136.
Lundy's Lane, Can., 81.
Lyme, Ct., 108.
Lyme, E. & S., Ct., 108.
Lynn, Mass., 121, 122.
Lynchburgh, Va., 189*g*, 195.
Lyons, N. Y., 77.

M.

Macon, Ga., 191.
Madison, N. J., 228.
MADISON, Wis., 215, **237**, 261.
Major's, Can , 246.
Malden, N, Y., 68.
Malden (So.) Mass., 122.
Mallory Town, Can., 243.
Mammoth Cave of Kentucky, 218.
Manassas Junction, Va., 183, 195.
Manchester, N. H., 124, **137.**
Mankato, Minn , 238.
Mansfield, Mass., 110.
Mansfield, O., 210.
Mantua Junction, Pa., 197.
Manunkachunk, N. J,, 228, 229.
Marietta, O., 204.
Mariposa Route, Cal., 276*K*.
Marshall, Iowa, 262.
Marshall, Mich., 235.
Martinsburg, Va., 189*a*.
Martha's Vineyard, Mass., 123.
Marquette, Lake Superior, 240.
Marysville, Cal., 270, 273.
Mason City, Iowa, 262, 263.
Massillon, O., 210.
Mast Hope, N. Y., 86.
McGregor, Iowa, 238.
McKenzie, Tenn., 220.
McPherson (and Fort), Neb., 269.
Medford, Mass., 124.

Medina, N. Y., 77.
Memphis Junction, Ky., 219.
Memphis, Tenn., 194, 196, 219, 220.
Mendota, Ill., 263.
Mendota Junction, Minn., 238.
Meredith Village, N. H., 101, 138.
Meriden, Ct., 105.
Meridian, Miss., 196.
Merrimac River and Valley, 136.
Michigan City, Mich., 236.
Middlebury, Vt., 101.
Middletown, N. Y., 85. [104, 108.
Middletown, (and Portland), Ct.,
Milford, Va., 186.
Millville, N. J., 150.
Milton, Pa., 229.
Millboro, Va., 189*e*.
Milroy, Pa., 199.
Milwaukie, Wis., 215, **237**, 239, 261.
Mineral Point, Mo., 221.
Mingo Junction, O., 202.
Minneapolis, Minn., 238.
Minnehaha, Min., 238.
Mississippi, Mouths of, 194.
Missouri Valley Junction, Iowa, 262.
Mobile, Ala., 192, 196.
Modesta, Cal., 275.
Mohawk Valley, N. Y., 73.
Mokelumne Hill, Cal., 276*K*.
Monmouth Junction, N. J., 149.
Monocacy (and Valley), Md., 170.
Monroeville, O., 227.
Monson, Mass., 139.
Monterey, Cal., 273.
MONTGOMERY, Ala., **191**, 196, 220.
Monticello, Va., 183.
Montmorenci, Falls of, Can., 253.
Montpelier, Vt., 140.
MONTREAL, Can., 138, 242, 243, 244, 245, **247**, 253, 255, 257.
Moosehead Lake, 127.
Moreau Station, N. Y., 95.
Morrison, Ill., 261.
Morristown, N. J., 60, **228.**
Morrow, O., 204.
Moscow, Iowa, 263.
Mound City, Ill., 220.
Mount Holly, N. J., 150.
Mount Hope, R. I., 113, 114.
Mt. Joy, Pa., 198.
Mt. Lafayette, N. H., 141, 143.
Mt. Mansfield, Vt., 100.
Mountain of Rigaud, The, Can., 246.

Mount Vernon, Va., **184, 185**.
Mount Washington, N. H., 131, 132.
Mount Webster, N. H., 133.
Mount Willard, N. H., 133.
Murray Bay, Can., 254.
Muscatine, Iowa, 263.
Mystic, Ct., 109.

N.

Nahant, Mass, 121.
Napanee, Can., 243.
Narrowsburg, N. Y., 86.
NASHVILLE, Tenn., 191, **219**.
Nashua, Mass., 122, 124.
Natick, Mass., 107.
Natural Bridge, Va., 189f, 195.
Nauvoo, Ill., 239.
Nebraska City, Neb., 262.
Nevada, Cal, 270.
New Almaden Mines, Cal., 273.
NEWARK, N. J., 59, **144**, 197, 228.
Newark, O., 202.
New Baltimore, N. Y., 70.
New Bedford, Mass., 122.
New Brighton, S. I., 59.
NEW BRUNSWICK, N. J., **146**, 197.
New Buffalo, Mich., 236.
Newburgh, N. Y., 67.
Newburyport, Mass., 124.
Newcastle (and Junction), Del., 163.
Newcastle, Pa., 210.
New Durham, N. H., 129.
NEW HAVEN, Ct., **104**, 107.
New Lisbon, O., 210.
NEW LONDON, Ct., **108**, 114, 136, 139.
Newmarket Junction, N. H., 125.
Newmarket, N. H., 125.
NEW ORLEANS, La., **192**, 196, 223, 239.
Newport, Ky. 204.
NEWPORT, R. I., 111.
Newport, Vt., 138, 140.
Newton, N J., 228.
NEW YORK CITY, 42—Harbor, 43—Streets, 47—Museums, 48—Libraries, 48—Public Galleries, 48—Educational Institutions, 49—Monuments, 50—Antiquities, 50—Churches, 51—Public Buildings. 52—Commercial Buildings, 53—Private Dwellings. 54—Hotel Buildings (Hotels), 54—Theatres,

55—Churches for Service, 56—Public Grounds, 57—Ferries, 57—Street-Car Routes, 58—Central Park, 60—Prospect Park, 61—Greenwood, 61a—Excursions, 61b to 61f.
Niagara Falls, 77, **78**, 242.
Niagara (Village), N. Y., 257.
Niles, Cal., 273.
Niles, Mich., 236.
Norfolk, Va., 163 168.
Norristown, Pa., 160.
North Adams, Mass., 140.
North Bend, Neb., 268.
North Platte, Neb., 269.
Norwalk, Ct., 103.
Norwich, Ct., **114**, 136, 139.

O.

Oak Hill, N. Y., 68.
Oakland, Cal, 273, **276a**.
Oakville, Can., 241.
Oberlin, O., 227.
Ogallala, Neb, 269.
OGDEN, Utah, 272, **275**.
Ogdensburgh, N. Y., 76, 244, 245 258.
Oil City, Pa., 201, 230.
Oil Regions, Pa., 89, 201, 226. 230.
Old Man of the Mountain, N. H., 141.
Old Point Comfort, Va, 169.
Oleopolis, Pa., 230.
Omaha, Neb., 216, 223, 262, **265**, 273.
Ontonagon, Lake Superior, 240.
Orange Court House, Va., 183.
Orange, N. J., 228.
Oregon City, Oregon, 273.
Orient, L. I., 61.
Orleans, Island of, Can., 254.
Oroville, Cal., 273.
Orville, O., 210.
Osino, Nev., 272.
Oswego, N. Y., 76.
Otsego Lake, N. Y., 74.
OTTAWA, Can., 243, **244**, 250, 258.
Ottumwa, Iowa, 262, 264.
Overlook Mountain House, 67.
Owatona, Minn., 238.
Owego, N. Y., 88.

P.

Paducah (and Junction), Ky., 220
Painesville, Pa. 226.

Palatine Bridge, N. Y., 74.
Palisade, Nev., 272.
Palisades, the Hudson, 63.
Palmer, Mass., 106, 139.
Palmyra, N. Y., 77.
Panama, Cent. Amer., 273.
Paradise, Idaho, 269.
Paris, Can., 232.
Parma, Mich., 235.
Passaic Falls. 59. **84.**
Paterson, N. J., 58, **83.**
Pawtucket, R. I., 110.
.Peaks of Otter, Va., 195.
Pekin, Ill., 224.
Pemberton, N. J., 150.
Pensacola, Fla., 192.
Peoria, Ill., 211, 224, 263.
Pequop, Nev., 272.
Percy, Wyo., 270.
Perth Amboy, N. J., 149.
Peterboro, Can., 243.
Petersburg, Va., 189.
Petrolia, Can., 232.
PHILADELPHIA, Pa., **151**-Streets.
152—Public Buildings, 153—Antiquities, 154—Public Grounds, 155—Fairmount. 155 — Centennial Grounds, 156 — Churches, 159 — Libraries, 160 — Theatres, etc., 160—Hotels, 161--Routes to Places of Interest. 161—Excursions, 161d—Navy Yard, 161d—Arsenals, 161d — Laurel Hill Cemetery, 161d—The Wissahickon, 161e—Germantown, 161e—Valley Forge, &c., 161f—Longer Excursions, 161g.
Philipsburg, N. J., 207.
Pictou, N. S., 260.
Pictured Rocks, Lake Superior, 240.
Piermont, N. Y., 63.
Pike's Peak, Col., 266.
Pilot Knob., Mo., 221.
Pine Bluffs, Neb., 270.
Pinkham Notch, N. H., 131.
Pithole (and Creek) Pa., 230.
PITTSBURG, Pa., 170, **200,** 202, 226, 262.
Pittsfield, Mass., 139.
Pittston, Pa., 208, 229.
Placerville, Cal., 270.
Plainfield, Ct. 115.
Plainfield N. J., 206.
Plattsburg, N. Y., 99.
Plum Creek, Neb., 269.
Plymouth, Ind., 211.

Plymouth, Mass., 122.
Plymouth, N. H., 138.
Plymouth, Wis., 238.
Pointe-aux-Anglais, Can., 247.
Point Levi, Can., 128, 251, 254.
Point of Rocks, Md., 170, 189.
Point St. Charles, Can., 249, 250.
Pollard, Ala., 192.
Pond Creek, Ill., 263.
Portage City, Wis, 237.
Portage, N. Y., 80.
Port Deposit, Md., 162.
Port Hope, Can., 242.
Port Huron, Mich., 234.
Port Jervis, N. Y., 85.
PORTLAND, Me., 102, **126,** 250, 251, 253, 255.
PORTLAND, Oregon. 268, 273.
Port Sarnia, Can. 232.
Portsmouth, N. H., 125, 137.
Portsmouth, Va., (Naval Depot), 169.
Port Stanley, Can., 232.
Potomac Falls, D. C., 182.
Potosi, Mo., 221.
Poughkeepsie, N. Y., 67.
Prairie du Chien, Wis., 215, **238,** 239.
Prescott, Can., **243,** 245, 258.
Princeton, N. J., 147.
Profile House, N. H., 134, 139, 140, 141.
Promontory Point, Utah, 272.
PROVIDENCE, R. I., 109, 115.
Put-in-Bay Islands, (Lake Erie), 234.
Putnam, Ct., 115.

Q.

QUEBEC, Can., 128, 138, 250, **251,** 255, 256.
Queenston, Can., 81, 257.
Quincy, Ill, 224, 263

R.

Racine, Wis., 237.
Rahway, N. J., 146, 197.
RALEIGH, N. C., 189.
Ramapo Gap and Valley, N. J., 85.
Ramsey, Minn., 238.
Reading, Mass., 124.
Reading, Pa., 197, 198, 208, **209,** 229.
Readville, Mass., 110.

x INDEX.

Red Bank, N. J., 59.
Red Wing, Minn., 239.
Reno, Nev., 273.
Renova, Pa., 230.
Rhinebeck, N. Y., 67.
Rice Lake, Can., 243.
Richmond, Can., 128, 251, 253, 235.
Richmond, O., 204.
RICHMOND, Va., 169, 183, **186,** 205.
Rideau Falls, Can., 244, 245.
Ridgeway Junction. N. C., 180.
Riviere du Loup, Can., 128, 251, 253, **254,** 256.
Rochester, N. H., 125, 129.
Rochester, N. Y., 77.
Rochester, Pa., 202, 210.
Rockaway, N. J., 228.
Rockbridge Springs and Baths, Va., 189*e*, 189*f*.
Rock Island, Ill., 225, 239, 261, **263.**
Rockland Lake, 63.
Rome, N. Y., 76.
Rondout, N. Y., 67.
Rouse's Point, Vt., **100,** 140, 244, 250.

ROUTES:

No. 1.—Northern. New York to West Point, Catskill, Albany, Troy, Utica, Trenton Falls, Rochester and Niagara Falls—62 to 82.

No. 2.—Northern. New York to Paterson, Upper Delaware, Upper Susquehanna, Binghamton, Elmira, Buffalo and Niagara Falls (Erie Railway)—83 to 90.

No. 3.—Northern. New York to Albany, Saratoga, Lake George, Adirondack Mountains, Lake Champlain, Vermont cities, and Montreal—91 to 103.

No. 4.—Eastern. New York to New Haven, Hartford. Springfield, Providence. Newport, New London, Stonington and Boston (options)—103 to 123.

No. 5.—Eastern. Boston to Portsmouth, Portland, White Mountains, Quebec, or Montreal—124 to 128.

No. 6.—Northern and Eastern. Boston to Lake Winnepesaukie, White Mountains, Portland and Canadian cities—129 to 135.

No. 7.—Northern and Eastern. New York to New London, Norwich, Worcester, New Hampshire cities, Lake Winnepesaukie and the White Mountains—136 to 143.

No. 8.—Near Western New York to New Jersey cities and Philadelphia—144 to 161.

No. 9.—Western and Southern. Philadelphia to Wilm'n (Del.), Balt., Wash'n and Richm'd—162 to 188.

No. 9½.—Special Virginian. Balt. or Wash'n to Virginia Springs, Mountains, &c., to Lynchburg and Richm'd—189 to 189*g*.

No. 9¾.—Western and South-Western. Wash'n or Balt. to Cumberland, Graft'n and Wheeling and Chicago and St. Louis.

No. 10.—South-Western, Richm'd to Raleigh, Wilm'n (N. C.), Charleston, Atlanta, Montg, Mobile and N. O—189*l* to 194.

No. 11.—South-Western. Richmond to Lynchburg, Knoxville, Chattanooga, Mobile and New Orleans—195 to 196.

No. 11½.—Southern. Richmond to Charleston or Savannah, and to Jacksonville, St. Augustine and Florida Resorts—196*a*, 196*b*.

No. 12.—Western. New York or Philadelphia to Harrisburg, Pittsburg, Wheeling, Columbus, Cincinnati, St. Louis or Chicago, (Penn. R.R.) 197 to 205.

No. 13.—Western. New York to Plainfield, Somerville, Easton, Allentown, Harrisburg, Pittsburg, Fort Wayne and Chicago, (Allentown Route)—206 to 216.

No. 14.—Western. Cincinnati to Louisville, Mammoth Cave of Ky., Nashville, Cairo, St. Louis, and Chicago—217 to 225.

No. 15.—Northern and Western. Buffalo to Erie, Cleveland, Toledo and other Ohio cities, Cincinnati or Chicago—226 to 227.

No. 16.—Northern. New York or Phila. to Dover, Morristown, Del. Water-Gap, Coal, Lumber and Oil Regions, &c.,—228 to 230.

No. 17.—Canadian and Western. Niagara Falls to St. Catherine's, Hamilton, Paris, London, Canada, Oil Regions, Detroit, Ann Arbor, Kalamazoo and Chicago—231 to 236.

No. 18.—North-Western, Chicago to Racine, Milwaukee, Madison,

INDEX. xi

Prairie du Chien, St. Paul, and Falls of Minnehaha and St. Anthony, (with optional return by the Mississippi or Lake Superior)—237 to 240.
No. 19.—Canadian. Niagara Falls to St. Catherine's, Hamilton, Toronto, Kingston, Prescott, Ottawa, Montreal, Quebec and the Saguenay River—241 to 256.
No. 20.—Canadian. Niagara Falls to Toronto, Kingston, Thousand Islands, Rapids of the St. Lawrence, Montreal and Quebec, by steamers; and to Halifax, St. John, Fredericton, Windsor, Sidney, Shediac, Charlotte-Town, Pictou and Bathurst.— 257 to 260.
No. 21.—Far Western. Chicago to Council Bluffs, Omaha, Cheyenne, Ogden Salt Lake City, Sacramento, San Francisco, the Big Trees, Yosemite Valley, &c. —261 to 276*j*.
Rupert, Pa., 229.
Rutland, Vt., **101,** 140.
Rye Beach, N. H., 125.

S.

SACRAMENTO, Cal., 273, **276***a*.

Saginaw, Mich., 234.
Saguenay River, Can., 255.
Salamanca, Pa., 89, 226, 230.
Salem, Mass., 122.
Salem, O., 210.
Salisbury, Md., 163.
Salmon Falls, N. H., 125.
Salmon-Trout Lake, Can., 243.
SALT LAKE CITY, Utah, 216, 223, 275, **276***d*.
San Antonio, Cal , 273.
Sandusky, O., 202, 205, 210, 227.
Sandwich Islands, 273.
Sandy Hook, 59.
SAN FRANCISCO, Cal., 273, **276***a*.
—Streets, 276*b*.—Public Buildings, 276*b*.—Churches, 276*b*.—Theatres, 276*b*.—Hotels, 276*b*.—Excursions, 276*c*.—Lone Mountain Cemetery, 276*c*.—Cliff House 276*c*.—Mission Dolores, 276*c*.—Presidio and Fort Point, 276*c*.—Longer Excursions, 276*c*.
San Jose, Cal., 273, **276***a*.

San Luis, Cal., 273.
San Quentin, Cal., 273.
Santa Barbara, Cal., 273.
Santa Fe, New Mex., 266.
Saranac Lakes, N. Y., 100.
Saratoga Springs, 91, **92,** 140.
Saucelito, Cal., 273.
Sault St. Marie, 240.
Savage, Md., 171.
Savannah, Ga., 190.
Saybrook (and Junction), Ct., 108.
Schenectady, N. Y., 74.
Schooley's Mountain, N.J., **60,** 228.
Schroon Lake, N. Y., 96
Schuyler, Neb., 269.
Scranton, Pa., 207, 208, **229.**
Seconnet (Point), R. I., 112.
Sexton's Junction, Va , 186.
Sharon Springs (route to), 74.
Shasta (and Butte), Cal., 273.
Shawangunk Mt., N. Y., 85.
Shediac, N. B., 259.
Shelbyville, Ky., 217.
Sherbrooke, Can., 127.
Sherman, Wyo., 270.
Shohola, N. Y., 86.
Sidney, C. B., 259.
Sidney, Neb., 270.
Silver City, Idaho, 269.
Sing Sing, N. Y., 63.
Sioux City, Iowa, 262, 264.
Skowhegan, Me., 127.
Sloatsburg, N. Y., 85.
South Amboy, N. J., 149.
South Bend, Ind., 227, 235.
South Berwick Junction, Me., **125.**
South Pass, Wyo., 267.
South Reading (Junction), Mass., 124.
South Trenton, N. Y., 75.
South Vernon, Vt., 140.
Somerville, Mass., 122.
Somerville, N. J., 207.
Sonora, Cal., 274.
Sparta, Ky., 217.
Spotswood, N. J., 149.
SPRINGFIELD, Ill., **224,** 227, 261, 263.
Springfield, Mass., 106.
Springfield, O., from Xenia, 203.
Stafford, Ct., 139.
St. Albans, Vt., **101,** 244.
Stamford, Ct., 10?
Stanhope, N. J., 228.
St. Anne's, Can., 247, **254.**
Staunton, Va., 189*d*.
Staustead, Can., 127.

St. Anthony (and Falls of), Minn., 215, **239.**
Starrucn Viaduct, N. Y., 87.
Staten Island, 59.
Staunton, Va., 186, 195.
St. Catharine's, Can., **231,** 241.
St. Clair River and Lake, 240.
St. Cloud, Minn., 239.
Steubenville, O., **202,** 210.
Stevenson, Ala., 219.
St. Gregoire, Can., 251.
St. Hyacinthe, St. Brune, St. Hilaire, St. Lambert, Can., 128, 250.
St. John, Can., 100.
St. John, N. B., 259.
St. Joseph, Mo., 223, 262, 264.
St. Lawrence Rapids, 258.
St. Lawrence River, 258.
ST. LOUIS, Mo., 194, 201, 205, 216, 220, **221,** 227, 239, 261, 263.
St. Mary's, Can., 232.
St. Mary's, Wyo., 270.
Stockton, Cal., 273, **276**a, 276h.
Stonington, Ct., **109,** 115.
Stony Point, N. Y., 63.
St. Paul Junction, Minn., 238.
ST. PAUL, Minn., 215, **238,** 262.
St. Peter, Minn., 238, 239.
Strasburg, Va., 183, 189c.
Stroudsburg, Pa., 229.
St. Thomas, Can., 254.
Sturgis, Mich., 227.
Stuyvesant, N. Y., 70.
Suffern's, N. J., 84.
Summit Station, Cal., 273.
Summit, Va., 183.
Sunbury, Pa., 199.
Susquehanna, N. Y., 87.
Swampscott, Mass., 122.
Sweetwater Mining Region, Wyo., 267.
Syracuse, N. Y., 76.

T.

Tadoussac, Can., 255.
Tallahassee, Fla, 190.
Tarrytown, N. Y., 63.
Terre Haute, Ind., 205a.
Thorold Can., 231, 241.
Thousand Islands (and Lake), St Lawrence River, 258.
Three Rivers, Can., 128, 251.
Throg's Neck, N. Y., 111.
Thurso, Can., 246.
Ticonderoga, N. Y., 93.

Tidcoute, Pa., 230.
Titusville, Pa., 230.
Tiverton, R. I., 114.
Toano, Nev., 272.
Toledo, O., 203, 205, 210, 211, 216, **227,** 235, 240.
Tolland, Ct., 139.
TOPEKA, Kas., 223, 264, 276n.
TORONTO, Can., 232, **241,** 249 250, 257.
Townsend, Md., 163.
Towsontown, Md., 168.
Trenton, Can., 243.
Trenton Falls, 75.
TRENTON, N. J., **147,** 150, 197.
TROY, N. Y., 71.
Truckee, Cal., 273, 276.
Tuscaloosa, Ala., 196.
Tyrone, Pa., 199.

U.

Uintah, Utah, 271.
Union City, Tenn., 220.
Union College (Schenectady, N. Y), 74.
Unionville, N. H., 129.
University of Virginia, 183.
Urbana, O., from Xenia, 203.
UTICA, N. Y., 74.

V.

Valparaiso, Ill., 211.
Vandalia, Ind., 205b, 225.
Venango, Pa, 201.
Victoria Bridge, Can., 249, 250.
Vincennes, Ind., 205, 220.
Vineland, N. J., 160.
Virginia City, Nev., 269.
Virginia, Nev., 268.
Visalia, Cal., 273.
Vallejo, Cal., 276a, 276k.

W.

Wadsworth, Nev., 273.
Walla Walla, Oregon, 268.
Wallingford, Ct., 105.
Walton, Ky., 217.
Wanatah, Ind., 211.
Warrenton (and Junction), Va., 183.
Warsaw, Ind., 211, 224.
Wasatch, Utah, 271.
WASHINGTON, D. C., **172,**201-Location, 172, 173—The Capitol

INDEX. xiii

174—President's House, 178,
—Patent Office, 178 — Departments, 178, 179—Smithsonian Institute, 180—Public Grounds, 180—Churches, 181 — Theatres, 181—Hotels, 181—Excursions, 181—Soldiers' Home, 181—Navy Yard, 181—Congressional Cemetery, 181—Longer Excursions, 181, 182.
Washington Junction, D. C., 171.
Washington, Iowa, 263.
Washington (Junction), N. J., 228.
Washington, N. J. 149.
Washoe, Nev., 269.
Waterford, Ct., 108.
Waterloo, Iowa, 261.
Waterloo, Ind., 211.
Waterloo, N. J., 228.
Watertown, N. Y., 76, **243**.
Watkins Glen, N. Y., 88*a*.
Waukegan, Ill., 237.
Waverley, Tenn., 220.
Waynesburg, Pa., 197.
Weber Canon, (and Station and River), Utah, 271.
Webster, Mass., 115.
Weir's Landing, N. H., 137.
Weldon, N. C., 188.
Wells (and Humboldt W.) Nev., 272.
Wells, Me., 125.
Wells River, Vt., 101, **138**, 140.
Wenona, Mich., 234.
Westerley, R. I., 109.
West Island, R. I., 112.
West Liberty, Iowa, 263.
West Newton, Mass., 107.
West Point, N. Y., 61, 62, **65**,
West Scarboro, Me., 125.
Weyer's Cave, Va., 189*c*, 189*d*.
Wethersfield, Ct., 105.
Wheeling, W. Va., **201**, 210, 227.
Whitehall, N. Y., **101**, 140.
White House, Va., 188.
White Mountain House, N. H., 134.
White Mountains, 125, 127, 130 to 133, 137, 141 to 143.
White Oak Bottom, Md., 171.
White Pigeon, Mich., 227.
White Pine, Nev., 268.
White River Junction, Vt., 102, 138, **140**.
White Sulphur Springs, Va., **184**, 186, **189***e*, 195.
Wickford, R. I., 109.

Wilcox, Pa., 230.
Wilkesbarre, Pa., 229.
Willey House, N. H., 133.
William-and-Mary College, **Va.**, from Richmond, 186.
William's Bridge, N. Y., 103.
Williamsburg, Va., from Richmond, 186.
Williamsport, Pa., 198, **229**.
Willimantic, Ct., 139.
Wilmington, Del., **163**, 197.
Wilmington Junction, Mass., 124.
Wilmington, N. C., 188, **189**.
Wilton, Iowa, 263.
Winchester, Va., 183, 189*b*.
Windsor (and Locks), Ct., 105.
Windsor, Can., 233.
Windsor, N. S., 259.
Windsor, Vt., 140.
Winnemucca, Nev., 272.
Wolfboro, N. H., 129, 138.
WORCESTER, Mass., **106**, **115**, 136.
Wyandotte, Kas., 264.
Wyoming, Nev., 269.

X.

Xenia, O., 203.

Y.

Yale College, 104.
Yarmouth Junction, N. H., **102**, 127.
Yarmouth, Mass., 122.
Yonkers, N. Y., 63.
York, Pa., 198.
Yorktown, Va., from Richmond, 186.
Yo Semite Valley, Cal., 276*a*, 276*i*
Ypsilanti, Mich., 234.

Z.

Zanesville, O., 202, 210, **227**.

The Short-Trip Guide to America.

COST AND TIME OF SHORT AMERICAN TRIPS.

SEVERAL important questions are involved, with Europeans, and especially with Englishmen, in the calculations preceding a trip to America: so that *Whether to go?* precedes the corresponding queries, *How to go?* and *Where to go?* The distance is known to be great, between the Old and New Worlds, though it is really only about one-eighth of that around the globe.

With many men *Time* is the great object, and the want of it the great hindrance; though they may annually spend quite as much of it as would be necessary for a Summer tour across the Atlantic, in lingering about home watering-places and sea-shore resorts, re-visiting the often-seen Lake Country, the Welsh, Irish and Scottish Mountains, etc., or repeating old experiences on the Rhine, among the Swiss Alps or the Pyrenees. This, too, at a time when the great Continent of the West has been made so much more broadly accessible, and so much more closely linked to that of Europe, by the Pacific Railroad, the Atlantic Cable, and other enterprises—when the late great civil war in the United States has necessarily left many fields worth visiting and relics worth gathering — and when steam-transit between the two Continents has become so rapid and reliable that the ocean-passage is little more than that of a ferry. This false idea of *Time* is, as already said, the bugbear which hinders many of those who have comparatively-liberal means and a fair proportion of leisure; but with a far greater number of those who love Nature in her varying moods and wide differences, and who desire to see the different peoples of the world, at *home*,—*Money* is the anxiety, the want of it the hindrance, and the belief that a mint is necessary for anything in the shape of transatlantic travel, the great bugbear which confines them to one continent.

A large proportion of this is a mistake, originally induced by want of intelligent inquiry, and materially added to by the exaggerations, not to call them falsehoods, of some of those who have been over the desired routes. While "going to America" was principally confined to the wealthy few or those driven by business demands, it was at once an easy and a tempting thing to do, to add to the supposed importance of what had been done, by overstating the cost as well as enlarging on the personal adventure and peril; and, truth to say, the habit has not yet quite died out, now, when the many follow in the track of the few and detection is so much easier. Many a man, of quite the average integrity, but who supplies (as he believes) the center at home of an admiring circle, not many members of which are likely to follow him abroad—cannot resist the temptation to show, when he returns, that he has been doing, in the way of cost, what *they* had better not attempt if they do not wish to fail miserably; and it is just possible that there have been members of the opposite sex, guilty of adding to the misunderstanding by corresponding exaggerations of their own elevation above the untraveled, and, consequently, the easily-deceived.

Travelers tell "travelers' stories," in a pecuniary as well as an adventurous point of view: that is the truth, briefly stated; and those stories frighten away many who would else enlarge their knowledge of life by seeing other continents than their own.

Now it is the fact that the European can spend much money in America, within a very brief period and without going over any wonderful space, if he will; just as in travels on the Continent, years ago, the average Englishman spent twice as much, under the same circumstances, as any man of any other nation, creating in different minds the impression of his being a "prince" and a "fool"—until the American became first his rival and then his admitted superior, in the detail of lavish and tasteless expenditure, and the Englishman who made any pretensions to common sense, taking a lesson from the example, comparatively abandoned the field of extravagance. The lavish and the reckless may still pave their very way with gold, if they will—as evidenced by the fact that a certain well-known Englishman, spending less than three months in the United States, drew upon his London bankers during his absence, for nearly £3,000 : the expenditure all the more notable, because the tourist, a markedly free liver and entertainer, made no purchases of consequence for preservation, did not play, and never indulged in what are called the "costly vices." Others have followed, in different approximations, ranging between £300 and £800 the month of absence; though it is to the credit of the national wisdom, to say that these instances of what must be considered wasteful expenditure for any one not in possession of a princely patrimony or a great banking-house, are somewhat rare.

So much for what may be spent in very brief tours, by those who can afford plenty of money, or think that they can do so : now for what may be saved, or rather for the question upon how little these brief tours may really be made, without discomfort or painful compromise of position.

Even in the steerage, on some of the best-appointed lines, passages may be made with much less discomfort than most stay-at-home people suppose; and it is not at all certain that thousands of hardy persons, limited in means, who spend the requisite amounts of time and money on very questionable home-amusements, approaching to vices, might not do well to tempt a little rugged life in the forward parts of the ships that carry over their wealthy brothers in the saloon-cabins. For on the best lines the discomforts, inconveniences and unhealthiness of steerage-passage, have all been materially ameliorated within the past three or four years : the sleeping accommodations on many of them are endurable if no more ; the food is almost always plentiful and generally excellent; the amount of amusement enjoyed is always greater than that attainable by the better-lodged people at the stern ; and the safety to person is necessarily the same except under circumstances of gross carelessness.

Let us see, for the benefit of those very limited in means and still desirous to see a little fragment of the New World—what would be the absolute cost of doing what emigrants of both sexes and all countries very often do for the sake of spending a few days with friends in the places of nativity. Say that six weeks' time is attainable, and let the cost of that six weeks be measured as carefully and yet as liberally as possible.

Steerage passage to New York, £6 10s.—return, £6 10s.; total, £13. Time not on board ship, about three weeks; board, for that time, average of £1 15s. per week, £5 5s. Expenses of sight-seeing about New York, Boston and Philadelphia, with conveyance to each, during that period, £5. Occasional necessary conveyance, the feet being principally trusted to, £3. Incidental expenses, liberally calculated, £4. Total, £32. £10 to £12 more would enable the cheap tourist to visit Niagara Falls, greatest of American natural curiosities, and see at least one or two cities of the Queen's dominions in Canada. Grand total, with that included, £42 to £45; with a certainty that any economical person, in good health and temper, could come within the smaller sum named, and even reduce it, without other inconvenience than carefully adhering to the cheaper rates of conveyance corresponding to that of the ocean transit.

How many comparatively-poor men are there with longing and hopeless desires after seeing other countries than their own, who never make any calculation or effort to such an end, and yet who could and would compass it if they fairly understood the comparative trifle for which so much might be enjoyed!

One of the greatest of American travelers, Mr. Bayard Taylor, made his first European excursion under circumstances quite as illiberal as anything here indicated—"did" Great Britain and a very considerable portion of the Continent on foot, except with rare instances of riding, and remained abroad something like two years, his whole expenditure being only about $500 (say £105), and the fortunate result of his travel that successful volume "Views-a-foot; or, Europe seen with Knapsack and Staff." And it is very doubtful whether in any portion of his later experience, in all descriptions of traveling "state," up to that of Secretary of Legation at St. Petersburg, he has ever enjoyed his wanderings better than when making that first essay as a poor boy. As a pleasant pendant to which, the writer recalls having met, not many months ago, in the streets of New York, an English workman from Sheffield, spending a little of his moderate surplus-earnings in seeing what he called "a tidy bit of the New World," and one of the most intelligent of travelers on many subjects of interest and enquiry —whose expenditure, as given by himself, would not reach within ten per cent. of the figures above given, while he was healthy, happy and entirely comfortable in what his saving expenditure allowed him to secure and enjoy.

But the figures already given represent, of course, the minimum possibility of travel in any desirable part of America, compatible with even the decencies of life, without too many of its comforts; and, it is, equally of course, with that class of people standing midway between the possible steerage-passenger and the traveler *en prince*, that we have next and principally to do. The most important question of this paper is — *What need be the expenses and the time consumed for a certain round, of a traveler going first-class and demanding all the comforts, and yet indisposed to waste money on costly luxuries?*

To answer that question, then, as intelligibly as may be consistent with brevity.

For six to seven weeks' absence from home, visiting New York, Boston, Philadelphia, Baltimore, Washington, one or two of the most noted watering-places, Niagara Falls, and one or two of the cities of Canada—only

Ticket to New York and return, £36 to £60—say an average of £48, for which all necessary comfort and quite sufficient "style" can be secured. Average board of the three weeks off-ship, £3 to £4 per week —say £10 10s. Traveling expenses, railway and carriage fares, etc., £30. Maps, pictures, curiosities, etc., (not at all necessary, but inevitable), £10. Incidental expenses, for which no name can be given; money to guides, beggars, stewards and servants; money lost and wasted, with an occasional indulgence in a luxury, *not* including costly wines or "society," gambling or other vices—£15. Total, £113 10s. £12 to £15 or possibly £18, may easily be saved from this, by a *very* careful person, leaving the expenditure about £100; and a person at all the reverse of careful may quite as easily *add* a corresponding sum, making the expenditure, with no greater amount of travel or sight-seeing, £125 to £130.

For ten weeks' absence, an estimate of £50 additional may safely be made, bringing the total outlay up to say £160 10s; and this will secure, in addition to the round already named, an extension of the tour through the White and Green Mountains of the north-east, with Saratoga, Lake George, and Lake Winnepisaukie; or it will add the great Coal Regions of Pennsylvania, Cincinnati, and other cities of Ohio, with Chicago, and glimpses of the Mississippi and the Great Lakes.

For three months' (thirteen or fourteen weeks)

absence, another £50 may be added, bringing the amount up to say £200 or £210; and with this all the foregoing may be done, with the addition of the "North-West," now found in the States bordering the Upper Missouri, with the Lake Superior region, and a much more extended visit to the cities of Canada, and the natural curiosities of the Dominion; or, it will enable the tourist (if the season should be a proper one for Southern travel) to go southward from Washington to Richmond, Charleston, Savannah and New Orleans, with their intermediate towns and a general view of what is technically known in the United States as "the South."

Four months will add to this £50 to £60 of expenditure, bringing up the outlay to £260 or £280, and permitting the pursuance of some of the routes named, more at leisure, as well as the addition of others of the watering-places, if the visit is paid in the proper season. And within the same time may even be managed a run over the Pacific Railroad, to Salt Lake City, San Francisco, and the great natural curiosities of California, with a view of the Pacific —though five months would be a more rational calculation for the whole time of absence. With the California route added, the expenditure will be found materially increased from all the previous calculations—say £100 additional for that alone; the amount necessary for the four-to-five-months trip, with Pacific excursion crowning it, being somewhere within the range from £360 to £380 or £400, and half of the continent travelled over in that time and at that cost.

At this point the phrase "short-trip" may be said to be exhausted; for only people of liberal means and abundant leisure are likely to go far beyond in any one visit, and to them these calculations possess only limited interest; though even they may find a certain advantage in bestowing that slight amount of study on the subject, necessary to secure a proper knowledge of time to be spent and money used to the best purpose.

PREPARATIONS FOR THE TRIP TO AMERICA.

The following paper, like some of the others to come after it, is especially intended for those who have never before crossed the Atlantic; and, consequently, some of the advice tendered in it may seem very primitive to those who have already taken their degree, however low a one, in the academy of traveling experience. The suggestion may properly be added, however, that even some of those who have taken that degree may find themselves none the worse for reading over these hints, even if they do so to dissent from them. An apology may need to be made, too, for the direct and conversational style adopted in this and some other papers: the aim of the writer is, in this regard, to come as near as possible to the words and manner that would be used in a personal conversation, with one of the parties doing much more than half of the talking.

It may be proper, too, with reference to this paper and those succeeding, to say that the writer speaks almost entirely from personal experience—and that where that experience has failed, it has been eked out, not often through the means of books, but from the personal hints and relations of frequent and experienced travelers. For himself, the writer, in repeated and extended travel on both continents, has made, first and last, nearly all the mistakes against which in the present instance he attempts to guard others, and felt the necessity for some instruction like that which he now endeavors to impart, on almost every point touched upon. So much said, the promise of the paper must be kept, in a brief but comprehensive list of rules connected with the preparation for transatlantic voyages, and especially for those *first* voyages which more or less imitate Columbus.

1st. Decide whether you can afford time and money to go at all, taking into consideration the before-urged opportunities for economy. Also, decide whether, in going, you leave too much of anxiety, personal or pecuniary, for fair enjoyment; for there is an old adage about the absentee who "drags with each remove a lengthening chain," and there are not charms enough, even in the natural scenery and odd character-studies of the New World, to make such a trip "pay," when the heart or the business-powers must be left at home. So much decided, and in the affirmative, then

2nd. Having made up your mind, stick to the resolution. Arrange your time of going, and make everything work to accommodate *that*—not leave that to accommodate itself to everything. Generally, in this as in everything else in life, too long anticipation is not the healthiest or the most profitable, and a voyage not canvassed over for five years

PREPARATIONS. 19

in advance is likely to yield more pleasure than one submitted to that length of speculation. Above all things never boast that you are going, when you have merely *thought of going* and made no definite decision; as unpleasant consequences may often result, in the event of the projected voyage being abandoned, and the suspicion may sometimes creep into the minds of acquaintances, either that there was "bounce" in the original statement, or that some heart-failure at the last moment has induced the abandonment.

3d. Having resolved upon time of going and probable duration of trip, and selected the line of steamers by which the outward voyage is to be made, do not permit the paltry folly of wishing to keep a certain number of pounds for a few days longer in pocket, to prevent the early taking of a passage. The best state-rooms of any favorite steamship are likely to be first taken up; and even in the event of any unexpected hindrance occurring, there is rarely any difficulty in disposing of a well-located berth, while most of the companies, at any time before the "eleventh hour," will transfer the passenger from one steamer to a later one, if a change of time is all the deviation from the original plan rendered necessary.

4th. If suddenly-occurring events happen to have changed the calculation in the other direction, and the plan of going is formed almost at the very moment when some favorite steamer is about to sail, never heed the stories so likely to be told, that "the steamer is full and you cannot get a place!" There is nearly always room for "one passenger more," as there is in most land conveyances; and if the worst comes to the worst, it is a very rare case when some of the officers of the ship cannot be found ready to give up a room for the run, at the inducement of no-very-large addition to the price of the passage-ticket. These are suggestions for extreme cases, however: as before said, passage had much better be taken early, whenever possible, for reasons already stated or about to be.

5th. In selecting berths, when a good opportunity for choice remains, always aim to get as near as possible to the midships of the vessel—a consideration of not much consequence to old voyagers with strong nerves, but of great importance to landsmen, as every foot of distance from the waist increases the amount of motion in a heavy sea; and not only is the danger of sea-sickness less amidships, but the chances of having sleep broken by the "pitch" of a "head" or "following" sea are proportionably decreased when so located. The same principle applies, in a less degree, to the question of outside or inside rooms (those inside or outside of the alleyways). There is much less effect from the "roll," in a "beam" sea, for those occupying inner berths; but there is always much less light for reading or any other purpose, and the one advantage will probably balance the other, except in winter passages, when the inner rooms are altogether preferable.

6th. No guide-book, until very la'ely, ever contained a hint of the advice to be embodied in this paragraph; and yet there is no word of counsel, of the whole, more important. Unless that miserable being, a "man of letters," and thus compelled to be always reading—there are few intending voyagers, male or female, who will not be the better for a little "reading up" as to any country about to be visited. A fresh glance at the Atlas, to see how the different sections lie and the relation which they bear to each other, is almost indispensable, even to some of us who flatter ourselves (before we think the second time) that we learned our geography in early life, and have kept pretty well up with it ever since. This rule, as already hinted, applies to travel and to travelers in all countries, but to no other geographical division of the earth's surface with the same force as to the New World, and especially to that covered by the Great Republic of the West, where change seems the rule, and where the alterations of boundaries and names, within the past few years, have been almost as startling as those effected in political status and society. Upon the relative positions of different States, the names of their capitals and chief cities, their rivers and natural wonders, and even their commercial and industrial features, it is exceedingly profitable to be as well as possible freshened in advance; and the same remark obviously applies with equal force to the main facts of history and the more important points in established or current literature. And to the latter suggestion a few words of particulars may be added. Exactly as a man from the New World would find more than half his possible pleasure lacking, visiting Great Britain without possessing any comprehensive knowledge of Shakspeare, Scott, Burns, Thackeray, Moore, Tennyson, etc., or France with no acquaintance with Rousseau, Voltaire, Lamartine, Beranger, Victor Hugo, Dumas, etc.—so the visitor from the Old World to the New must be lacking in many of the opportunities for observation, social life and popularity, who fails to know something of Cooper, Irving, Hawthorne, Longfellow, Whittier, Bret Harte, Mark Twain, and (especially for New England travel) Holmes, Emerson and Lowell.

7th. Another "rubbing up" is advisable though not absolutely indispensable. Thousands of questions about native land, its physical appearance, wealth, working of government, industrial aspects, etc., are constantly asked of all persons on their travels, supposed to be of the average intelligence, by foreigners whom they chance to meet; and it is decidedly pleasant as well as proper, not to be three or four thousand miles from home, unable to answer the simplest questions with reference to things occurring at our own doors. The more we know about our own land, the more intelligent and agreeable travelers we shall make; and, in this connection,

8th. Throw overboard two false impressions, together, before leaving Europe. Overboard with the idea, at once, that the land you are leaving is better than all others in every regard, so that nothing can be learned abroad: and with it give the go-by to the alternative impression that you have nothing worth asserting and even boasting about, and that what you are to learn abroad will stand in place of the previous experience and pride of a life. Each of the leading European countries possesses, at this day, many things unequaled by the rest of the world and matters of legitimate pride to her citizens; but she is almost equally sure to have errors and deficiencies which may well be corrected by observations among other, if not necessarily wiser, people. Every tourist going abroad should carry with h m all practical knowledge of his own land, and all well-founded pride in it; and, at the same time, he should travel with eyes and ears open and power to divest himself of ridiculous national vain-glory prejudicially shutting away all beyond.

And now to a few minor particulars belonging to the very eve of starting, and still important enough to deserve place and number:

9th. Start with a confident expectation of returning, and yet leave property-interests disposed of as if no return was likely to be made. There is really less danger, in a given number of days, in going over-sea than in most railway-travel; but absences thus involved are necessarily much longer and demand additional forethought in at least one or two particulars. "No man dies the sooner for making his will," they say; and certainly no man travels less comfortably for leaving affairs at home in such a shape, that, if he does not return, his absence will cause the least possible inconvenience to those left behind. And, in this connection, again,

10th. There is nothing wiser for the departing "family-man," whatever the status of those dependent upon him, than an investment in a moderate *life-assurance*, with an additional *assurance against accident*. Nothing of an earthly character (the religious questions will naturally suggest themselves) adds more comfort in a storm at sea, or danger in some distant land, than the reflection that there would be, at least, one benefit from the risk terminating unfavorably: *the dear ones at home would be pecuniarily the gainers by it.*

11th. Arrange baggage compactly, and not too extensively. For each person (male—the ladies *will* make rules for themselves, applying what hints may chance to suit them)—one stout leather or wood-and-leather trunk of 30 to 36 inches by 16 to 20 inches, and one convenient valise for carrying in the hand, are always sufficient, for anything less than carrying over the whole personal effects with a view to residence. The trunk for deposit in the great cities, in the event of expecting to return along the same line—if not, unavoidably to be carried along. The valise for short excursions from those great centers having this advantage—that it can be carried in the railway-carriage or cab, while the trunk must be looked after, with trouble and expense. Both trunk and valise should be plainly marked with name and residence—initials not always enough for either safety or convenience. If the trunk is small enough, for the sea-voyage, to find place in the state-room, all the better; if not, care must be taken that, before it goes into the hold, all articles are taken out from it that will be needed before landing on the other side. The valise will always find place in the state-room, of course. And this brings

12th. The important question of Clothing, with reference to which a few general suggestions may be found valuable. The point of view here taken is especially for the male sex, but the female will find it easily varied to their requirements. For crossing the North Atlantic, to return in two or three months, the first requirement is a suit of thick clothes, so old and valueless that one can lounge upon the deck in them, with no fear of damage. (Dandyism is at a discount at sea—a lesson quickly and surely learned.) Clothing thick, because sea air is nearly always damp, and generally cold. Then as thick an overcoat and gloves as can well be procured, the use of which will become patent, either off the Irish coast or among the fogs and possible icebergs of the Banks of Newfoundland. A thick blanket, rug, or heavy robe, to make lounging upon deck the easier and warmer. For summer travel in the Northern, Middle and Western States, or Canada, a neat traveling-suit of Melton, with one of flannel for proceeding further southward, and for very hot weather in even the States named. A summer-overcoat or wrap of waterproof Melton or *aqua-scutum*—not so regularly or often needed as in the British Islands, but indispensable. Heavy-wool under-clothing for sea use, with courage enough to double it if necessary; for American hot weather, on land, lighter under-clothing of merino, silk, or zephyr. A dress-suit, if entrance into "society" is intended, or if there is plenty of room in the trunks; as clothing is somewhat high in America, while exceptionally tasteful and well made—though, candidly, in hurried trips of this character, the traveling-suit is seldom shaken off. Figured or colored-wool overshirts, with high throat, collar and wristbands, for time at sea, or for any temporary "camping-out" or "roughing-it" among woods or mountains. Plenty of linen and white goods, to avoid being at the mercy of the washerwoman at times of sudden transit, and because all these, as well as all hosiery and under-clothing, cost more in the United States than in England. Stout-soled shoes—of calf, best. Low-crowned tourist-hat, of felt (dress-hat to be bought, if necessary); umbrella, of late years almost as indispensable on the western side of the Atlantic as the eastern; a good opera-glass, necessary for catching views rapidly and correctly, both by sea

PREPARATIONS.

and land, and more convenient if not too large for the pocket and not necessitating the *prononcé* strap.

13th. Make such arrangements, if possible, that a little longer absence than that contemplated will not work serious business or other inconvenience, as the best calculator cannot always be quite sure of non-detention through some influence or action beyond himself.

14th. Arrange (as before suggested) to take a little more money abroad than is supposed to be necessary for either time or distance; but

15th. Carry in actual money, (English gold, or Bank of England notes, with a trifle of silver) only so much as will pay expenses on ship-board and last during the few days that may happen to elapse before reaching the point at which the first draft is made payable. All beyond this should be taken either in bills-of-exchange on bankers in one or more of the more important cities to be visited, or in circular letters-of-credit to corresponding houses in those cities. It is scarcely necessary to say that only the very first-class of banking houses, at home, should be dealt with, in procuring exchange or letters-of-credit, if the painful possibility of finding oneself abroad without funds, is to be avoided.

16th. Take some letters of introduction, when tendered, and to the *right persons;* but depend very little upon them, except in some business point of view. The fact is that, without any discourtesy to givers being intended, letters of introduction go for less in America and secure less consideration additional to the deportment and standing of the bearer, than in any other part of the civilized globe: and they should be understood and rated accordingly. Added to which may be set down that in no other country is the best society of any given region so accessible, the letter of introduction being thus rendered little else than commercial or useless.

17th. Avoid attempting to carry over, among baggage, anything that can be construed as beyond necessary personal use, as the American administration of the customs, of late years, is stringent to oppressiveness, and a misunderstanding on that point may be more easily avoided than removed. (Articles most watched for and guarded against are clothing, [new and in undue quantity,] silks, linens, laces, watches, jewelry and precious stones).

18th. Create as little impression as possible, on the verge of departure, of feeling that some event, moving half the world, is taking place in your first leaving your native land. A sea-voyage, now, no further than America, is about equivalent to a trip from London to Edinburgh or Dundee, fifteen years ago —and not much more than was the transit across the channel to France, at the distance back of thirty or fifty years; and the observing world is generally coming to regard it in that light.

19th and last. If possible, go on board before the last moment of sailing, and have any heavy luggage on board even earlier. Also, if possible, make any extended tender farewells earlier and elsewhere than on the crowded deck of a steamer, at the last moment, when everybody is in the way of everybody else, when the officers naturally wish to throw overboard all the whiners, and when there is a probability of the grief of departure being added to by the worry of having wife, sister, child or friend tumbled into the river at the landing-stage, or dropped over between tender and steamer as the two separate.

WHAT TO DO AND AVOID ON SHIPBOARD.

THE advice in this paper, too, will be set down didactically, and much of it will be considered as very elementary by those who have once or oftener crossed the Atlantic. In the meantime, not even to some of them will the maxims be found unprofitable, if attended to—judging by the very large number of habitual travelers who seem to happen upon the very conditions of discomfort and imprudence, as if seeking them.

1st. Perhaps the first condition of comfort in a sea-voyage, is to avoid making up the mind as to any positive time at which the voyage must be concluded. To look across the three thousand miles of the Atlantic, and think over the days necessary to traverse it, even on the swiftest vessel, is rather discouraging than the reverse, to people of rapid thought and active habit; but by simply avoiding any definite calculation, and considering the ship and her officers and crew as doing their "day's work," the amount of impatience may be very considerably reduced. Creeping ahead a little every day, the whole voyage will soon be accomplished: that is enough to know and enough to feel, no matter what anxieties may be at the end.

2d. Perhaps the next desideratum is to avoid any

considerable anxiety as to the voyage being a prosperous one, by first remembering that more than an hundred runs are made without a single accident, and more than five hundred without the total loss of a vessel—and then falling back upon that pleasant recollection that you have not the affair in charge, any way—that (Providence over all, and always to be remembered, of course,) the officers and crew of the ship have their duty to do and are very likely to do it, for the sake of their own lives and the property committed to their skill. It may be straining a point, perhaps, but there is really some philosophy in getting into the state of mind of the droll fellow who demonstrated to one of the "anxious," in a storm at sea, that, having paid their passage, and the company having consequently contracted to take them across, the question of the ship's foundering was really something with which they (the passengers) had nothing to do! This may not have much reassured the frightened man, but it certainly silenced him; and there no doubt was more than a grain of earnest in the old traveler's philosophy of *remembering that he did not steer the ship*, as there was undoubtedly comfortable indolence in it.

3d. It is not wise to expect too much on shipboard, either in the way of luxury, or even of positive comfort. Ships, at the largest, are small as compared with hotels, and at the steadiest are "shaky," as compared to private dwellings, except when the latter have the rarity of earthquakes to throw them off the perpendicular. Plenty of good food, respectable though confined sleeping-quarters, and attendance fair, but by no means that of a first-class hotel —these are all that ought to be expected; and a very little philosophy makes them enough. It has before been said that "dandyism is at a discount, at sea;" so is, or ought to be, *finickiness.* What if neither shaving, nor dressing, nor any of the other offices of civilized life, can be done quite as well as at home? Nobody notices whether they are scrupulously performed, or not; and some of the neatest of men when on shore, when they have become old travelers, consent to be slovenly for those few days without serious suffering. The golden rule, on going to sea, is: *Expect very little, and be prepared to bear good-humoredly with it;* then, if "all the modern conveniences" should happen to present themselves, as is not at all likely, they will afford double enjoyment; and the want of them will not entail misery.

4th. Determine to be as jolly as health will allow, and as companionable as is at all consistent with the temperament. Join in all practical harmless amusements and exercises, with the result of making your own days less tedious, and producing the same effect on those of others. One jolly fellow, sometimes, seems to leaven up a whole ship-load; one or two glum faces act like a wet-blanket on all concerned. There is a comradery in sea-going, scarcely second to that of the army; and some of the pleasantest friendships of years originate on the deck filled with comparative strangers. Quoits, shovelboard, chess, draughts, backgammon, social games at cards, all these supply amusement to those who will take part in them; and there is room for any amount of table sociability at meals, not marred but rather increased by the little accidents to which breakfasting or dining in rough weather is certainly subject.

5th. Make friends, early, with the captain and other officers of the ship, so far as they will permit; but take no liberties with them, and carefully avoid compromising any one of them who may have shown any peculiar favor, by speaking of it to others of the ship's company or passengers. Strictly observe those cardinal rules which forbid going upon the bridge, talking with the officers when on duty, or distracting the attention of the quarter-masters at the wheel. Avoid getting in the way of the officers at the compass, or hindering them when engaged in that most important event of the day—"taking an observation." Obey them, quietly and respectfully, when they give a direction calculated to secure your safety or prevent accident—even if the reason of the order should not be fully evident to a landsman. Don't inquire any oftener than is unavoidable, where the ship is at any particular moment, what a certain movement on deck means, what kind of weather it is going to be during the next twenty-four hours;

and don't ask the men, when they are heaving the log, how many miles an hour the ship is going, or don't expect them to tell the truth if you do! Don't get in the way when hawsers are being overhauled or yards braced; and don't wonder if, getting in the way when some evolution of hauling the ropes is going on, you occasionally trip and so learn what times and places are dangerous. Don't attempt to "help," at any time, except in the rare event of an accident; and thus "keeping out of the way," without losing any chance of observation and enjoyment, secure the friendship of the officers, the respect of the crew, and the gratitude of all concerned.

6th. Make friends with the stewards, at once, not only by treating them respectfully, but by speaking to the two in charge of your particular table and state-room—requesting their attention and promising them the due *douceur* at the end of the voyage. Half a sovereign each to the saloon and lower-saloon stewards, and say a crown to the "boots," with half-a-crown for beer to the captain of the watch who first "chalks" you when you break the rules of the ship by going forward, and perhaps half a dozen shillings to persons who do errands for you during the run—this, reaching not much more than thirty shillings altogether, is quite sufficient to grease the wheels of service and make welcome then and afterwards.

7th. Avoid attempting to read much, at sea, however interest may tempt in that direction. There is a motion and jar of the vessel, making the letters swim and damaging head and optic-nerves to a degree needing days for recovery. Some persons can read steadily, almost without injury; others cannot: it is never best to try the experiment when it can be avoided. And there is rarely much occasion: it is a poor passage-list in which more amusement cannot be found than in books, for the short period consumed in crossing the Atlantic.

8th. Keep on deck, all that is possible. Half the charm of going to sea lies in the pure, fresh air, except in very stormy weather. The air of lower-cabins and state-rooms is necessarily more or less confined, and consequently unhealthy; while the healthiest atmosphere in the world comes fresh to the lungs from blue water. There is far less danger of sea-sickness, too, on deck than below, when actual illness does not enforce confinement to the berth; and the thousand sights and sounds of sea-life—sunrises, sunsets, moonlight, storm-waves, whales, porpoise-shoals, passing vessels, observations, log and lead heaving, making and taking in sail, signalling, etc., are only to be enjoyed by those who keep the deck as persistently as possible. And this is even additionally true at times of leaving or making land; approaching port, etc., opportunities for remark and study, lost during which periods, may be and probably will be lost forever.

9th. Dress warmly—quite as warmly as comfort demands, and err on the safe side if at all. Sea-air, though healthy, is damp and deceptive as to temperature. Never mind the appearance; put on the clothes.

10th. Take much exercise. Want of occupation induces long sitting at table and hearty eating; and the system must be a strong one which can endure this for days, without exercise, and yet suffer no injury. When there is not too much sea to make it possible, at least a mile or two should be walked every morning, and a corresponding space in the afternoon—the long cleared decks, or the alleyways, of most of the best steamers, rendering this *amusement of exercise* easy and convenient.

11th. Aid the direction last named, by eating moderately as usual habits will allow—either by abridging the quantity of each meal, or by avoiding some of the number. Four meals per day are usually provided—breakfast, lunch, dinner and tea: very often, and especially when there is any tendency to inactivity of the system, and fever, two of the four may be profitably omitted.

12th. Put confidence in the ship; believe, for the time being, that the ship is the best afloat. If you go down into the fire-room (which, by the way, is quite as well kept out of), don't fall into the fancy that so large a mass of fire in the midst of a vessel must inevitably burn her; vessels are especially constructed to guard against that danger, and iron does not take fire easily. Don't be alarmed at the noises continually coming from the fire-room, or think that some calamity has happened there: firemen are normally noisy as well as grimy, and they need to speak loudly to make themselves heard. Don't fancy, in short, that everything will go wrong unless you attend to it, except in one particular; and that is,

13th. Join the fire-police of the ship, and stick to the organization. Take no combustible materials below in your baggage—neither matches nor dangerous chemicals; take no light of any kind below the decks, for better reason than because there is a severe punishment for any proceeding of the kind—the all-powerful reason that such an act may destroy your own life and the lives of others. On this point, watch your own conduct and that of others, and no harm is likely to result from the close surveillance; though any discovery made should always be communicated quietly to some person in charge, and not shouted through the ship so as to create a panic among the passengers.

14th. Never go forward when the ship is pitching into a heavy sea: there is always danger of injury, in such an experiment by a landsman, and very often of being swept overboard, at times when even sailors can scarcely keep footing on the wet and slippery decks. Never stand at or very near the taffrail (extreme stern) in correspondingly heavy weather, as there is always danger of the ship "jumping out from under you"—an accident which sometimes happens to experienced seamen who stand unguardedly in that dangerous position. Never climb upon the bulwarks, however calm the sea; for there is no knowing at what moment there may be *one* roll—enough to finish the individual voyage very unpleasantly.

15th. Never attempt to go up or down one of the companion-ways (stairs), or along one of the gangways, or the decks, when the sea is heavy, without making as much use of the hands as the feet—holding on firmly to the nearest convenient rail. Broken ribs or limbs are sometimes the consequence of forgetfulness or bravado, on this point.

16th. In the event of illness (other than sea-sickness), don't take nostrums, or trust to anything in your private "medicine-chest." There is always one surgeon, or more, on each ship; they are paid for attending to the health of passengers, without charge except for costly medicine; they are particularly familiar with the treatment prudent at sea; and it is very often the case that medicines upon which dependence can be placed when on the more stable element, prove injurious in the abnormal condition of never being entirely quiet.

17th. If sea-sick, don't fancy the disease is a mortal one. Few people die of it, though many (it is to be feared) are rendered vastly uncomfortable. Keep the bravest heart and the strongest determination possible, against the great foe; and above all, do not join the noble army of those who ask to be mercifully " thrown overboard" as a means of escaping the torture. Nobody dares obey the request—not even your worst enemy, who wishes that he could; and if it *should* be obeyed, the chances are ten to one that before you had gone down ten fathoms in blue water the cry might be a different one.

18th. Berths, in sea-going ships, are mostly single; and yet it is best, especially in heavy weather, to have a *bed-fellow*. This is easily found in the valise or well-filled carpet bag, which packed closely in against the side-board, the would-be sleeper lying on the side in the inner part of the berth, will generally enable him to lie without rolling, even when the ship is doing her worst in that direction, and secure sleep when it would be otherwise impossible from the constantly-waking motion. An alternative arrangement of almost equal excellence in rough weather, though not always practicable—is to use a broad luggage-strap, fastened to any stanchion at the back of the berth and then buckled around the breast of the would-be sleeper.

19th—and more important than any of the preceding. Remember, oftener than when the service is read on Sabbath morning, that there is a Hand, wiser and stronger than that of any officer of the ship, ruling not only the vessel, but the waves upon which she rides and the winds and other elements which may place her in peril.

BELL-TIME AT SEA.

PASSENGERS by any of the transatlantic steamers, or on any other extended route involving the continual change of longitude, should never risk injuring their time-pieces by setting them slower or faster, but quietly allow them to run down immediately after starting, and keep them in that condition, though carrying them in the ordinary upright position, until the end of the voyage. They will be obliged, meanwhile, to depend upon the ship's bell, with occasional glimpses of the saloon-clock, for the requisite knowledge of the flight of time during each day, to prevent a mental vacuum on that subject, and enable them to make proper preparation for meals.

A little experience of the use of the bell, however, is necessary for putting this advice into ready practice; and the following brief table of "bell-time at sea" will be found worth an hour or two of study, to that end; one fact being always borne in mind: that the farther eastward the faster the time, and, the farther westward, the slower; so that a steamer of ordinary speed loses about half an hour per day of the running time with which she is charged, in going eastward, and gains a corresponding amount of time in going westward.

BELL TIME AT SEA.

Commencing the day at sea, with the half-hour succeeding midnight, the following explanation of the "bells" (*i. e., strokes of the bell*) will be found easily understood and quite sufficient for practical use, if one aid to the memory is employed—the recollection that the odd numbers of strokes are always half-hours, that the even numbers are always hours, and that those hours which can be divided by 4 are always represented by numbers which can also be divided by 4.

1 bell	½ o'clock, A. M.			1 bell	½ o'clock, P. M.	
2 bells	1	"	"	2 bells	1	"	"
3 "	1½	"	"	3 "	1½	"	"
4 "	2	"	"	4 "	2	"	"
5 "	2½	"	"	5 "	2½	"	"
6 "	3	"	"	6 "	3	"	"
7 "	3½	"	"	7 "	3½	"	"
8 "	4	"	"	8 "	4	"	"
1 bell	4½	"	"	1 "	4½	"	"
2 bells	5	"	"	2 "	5	"	"
3 "	5½	"	"	3 "	5½	"	"
4 "	6	"	"	4 "	6	"	"
5 "	6½	"	"	1* bell	6½	"	"
6 "	7	"	"	2 bells	7	"	"
7 "	7½	"	"	3 "	7½	"	"
8 "	8	"	"	4 "	8	"	"
1 bell	8½	"	"	1 bell	8½	"	"
2 bells	9	"	"	2 bells	9	"	"
3 "	9½	"	"	3 "	9½	"	"
4 "	10	"	"	4 "	10	"	"
5 "	10½	"	"	5 "	10½	"	"
6 "	11	"	"	6 "	11	"	"
7 "	11½	"	"	7 "	11½	"	"
8 "	12	noon.		8 "	12	midnight.	

* From 4 P. M. to 8 P. M. instead of presenting an unbroken succession of bells from 1 to 8, is divided into two "Dog Watches"—4 to 6 (" first dog-watch") and 6 to 8 ("second dog-watch")—in order to prevent the larboard and starboard watches of sailors being on duty during the same hours, one day after another—as they would be if they were continually and only changed once every four hours.

NEW YORK CITY, HARBOR AND SUBURBS.

APPROACH AND HARBOR.

Land is generally made, approaching the harbor of New York, from any vessel coming down the "Great Circle," at some point on the Long Island coast, at starboard or right of the ship; and the time may be anywhere from four to ten hours (in clear weather) before crossing the bar at Sandy Hook, the entrance of the Lower Bay of New York. After first sighting, this land will keep in sight—low and uninteresting, the course of the vessel being nearly parallel with the shore, and at a few miles distance. Pilots are taken on board from small schooners, at distances varying from a few miles from the coast to two or even three hundred—as disasters from want of pilotage off this port, many years ago, have induced much activity and competition, of late years.

Two or three hours from Sandy Hook, for ships coming down the Long Island coast, and as a first sight for those crossing from the south, are made the *Highlands of Navesink*, fine bold headlands approaching the sea, and forming one point of the eastern coast of New Jersey. These hills show to excellent advantage on a nearer approach, and are very imposing when the Bar at Sandy Hook is being crossed; two square-tower light-houses showing on the Highlands, behind the long, low point of wooded sand forming the Hook, on which are to be seen one light-house and two beacons, with a formidable line of government fortifications in progress, near the outer or northern end, very near to which the ship necessarily passes the channel.

Passing the Bar and running up the Lower Bay, the New Jersey Highlands continue ahead and to the left, sloping away toward Long Branch a few miles southward ; on the right continues *Long Island*, with the still lower and sandier *Coney Island* adjoining it in front ; still ahead and to the left rise the hills of *Staten Island*, with an opening between it and Long Island marking the *Narrows*, through which entrance is made from the Lower or Raritan Bay into the Upper or Bay of New York proper.

At the left, four or five miles below the Narrows, is passed (if there is no occasion to make its nearer acquaintance) the *New York Quarantine* — ranges of low buildings on two artificial islands built within the last few years on a shoal known as the West Bank of Romer. Passing the Narrows, the fine fortification to the right, on Long Island, is *Fort Hamilton*, with the ruins of the once celebrated *Fort Lafayette* standing in the water at some distance below it—while to the left rises the corresponding bluff of Staten Island, crowned with a light-house and fortifications, with a strong new structure, *Fort Richmond*, standing below at near the water's edge.

The view of *New York Bay*, after passing the Narrows, is considered one of the finest of its character in the world, and should never be lost by the traveler enjoying the opportunity for the first time. On the right, passing up, will be observed the Long Island shore, handsomely shaded, and dotted with the residences of well-to-do citizens or suburbans; and on the left Staten Island presents much higher ground, landings and thriving villages near the shore, and the sides of the hills in like manner well shaded and dotted with tasteful residences. Some six miles above the Narrows, at the immediate right, the monuments of *Greenwood Cemetery* may be seen covering and crowning one of the Long Island hills near the shore; still to the right, but ahead, the *City of Brooklyn* shows its many spires and wilderness of buildings; immediately ahead rises *Governor's Island*, with its round fort, *Castle William*, and its long ranges of barracks and officers'-quarters; and as Governor's Island is passed, still directly ahead, the *City of New York* is seen, stretching right and left, from its lowest point at the Battery, up the East and North rivers (Long Island Sound and the Hudson), each line showing a perfect forest of the masts of shipping, and the marked deficiency of commanding spires partially relieved by the nearness and grace of that of Trinity

Church and the height of several of the new buildings now overtopping the city, especially the Western Union Telegraph Building, New Post Office, *Tribune* Office, *Evening Post* Office, Equitable and Mutual Insurance Buildings, &c.

From this point, which also best shows the Brooklyn Bridge, Brooklyn lies a little behind, at the right; Staten Island has fallen away to a much greater distance behind and at the left; the Hudson River stretches northward, immediately ahead, Long Island Sound branching away eastward at an acute angle; the other two islands of the harbor, so far unnamed, *Bedloe's* and *Ellis'*, lie at some distance to the left; and behind them, to the left and ahead, on the west or New Jersey side of the river, may be prominently seen the towns of *Jersey City* and *Hoboken*, continual high lands rising up-river from the latter, along the Hudson, towards Fort Lee and the Palisades.

It is also at this point that the traveler visiting the New World for the first time from the Old, will find one of the most marked of sensations in observing not only the immense variety of shipping and the flags of all nations at the wharves and in the stream, but the many particulars in which the American river and ferry craft differ from those of any other nation—the prevailing color being white, and both strength and grace often sacrificed to speed and temporary convenience.

NEW YORK CITY AND BROOKLYN.

As will already have been observed, the City of New York lies at the junction of the North or Hudson River and Long Island Sound (familiarly called the East River), having thus the best of opportunities for cleanliness and health, which are by no means always embraced with due diligence and faithfulness—the city being always ineffectually cleaned, in comparison with the cost to the people, and often disgracefully dirty. In effect, Brooklyn, immediately opposite on the southeast, and connected with it by half-a-dozen or more well-managed steam-ferries, is a part of the same city, though lying in another county, and bearing a different name; while nearly the same may be said of both Jersey City and Hoboken, on the New Jersey shore, and reached in the same manner by ferry.

Before proceeding to explore the city or suburbs, it should be noted that carriage-service in New York is very high and very bad; cab-service better and improving, though by no means up to the European standard—so that the first should be almost entirely avoided, and the latter much oftener foregone in favor of the public conveyances than they would be in any city of the Old World. The ferries should be used freely, not only for necessary crossings, but as an additional means of studying the topography of the harbor, and the excellence of the system. For most directions the street horse-cars [see directions for those cars, different lines, pp. 58 and 59, and following] run regularly and well, and are comfortable, except at morning and evening hours, bringing too great crowds; and the Elevated Railroad, from South Ferry, and omnibuses from the Brooklyn Ferries, are available and respectable.

Of the Streets, the best worth noting is *Broadway*, which should be driven, in open carriage if convenient, from its commencement at the Battery (harbor side) to its virtual termination at Madison Square, many of the best commercial buildings being thus seen, and a succession of splendid business erections observed, not equalled, perhaps, in any other city of either continent. Thence *Fifth avenue* should be taken, to the Central Park, and on return *Madison avenue*, views being caught, in the two, of many of the most fashionable private erections of the city. Much of the leading fashion of the city may be found gathered in the streets running out from Fifth avenue, from Fourteenth to Sixtieth street—notably on *Twenty-third, Thirty-fourth, Forty-second* streets, &c. The *Bowery* may be noted as the people's or east-side Broadway. *Greenwich street* will be found filling a somewhat similar position on the west side; *Third, Sixth* and *Eighth avenues* may be taken as fair types of prosperous commonalty and bustle; *West street* (Hudson River side) will be found to supply a jam quite worthy of the Strand at its worst hours;

and still further down town, *Wall street, Broad* and *New streets* command attention as the centres of the moneyed interest. In BROOKLYN, the most notable streets are *Montague* and *Clinton*, for fashion; *Fulton* and *Court streets, Atlantic* and *Myrtle avenues*, &c., for business activity; *Third street, Union street, Fourth avenue*, &c., as drives; *Clinton, Washington, Bedford, Grand* and other *avenues*, for suburban beauty.

Of Wharves, New York has never had any deserving the name, though a fine water front is now presented at the Battery, and arrangements are in progress to supply well-built docks along both rivers. Of Markets, the *Washington*, foot of Vesey street, Hudson River side, and the *Fulton*, foot of Fulton street, East River side, will be found among the best supplied in the world, though the buildings are very old and badly kept. Newer and better erections are the *Metropolitan*, foot of Thirty-fourth street, North River, and the *Tompkins*, Third avenue and Seventh street. Of Museums, the *Metropolitan Museum of Art*, Fourteenth street, near Sixth avenue; one at Central Park; and a small but unique one (naval) at the Brooklyn Navy Yard. Of Libraries, the *Astor*, Lafayette Place; the *Mercantile, Lenox, Society, Law, American Institute, Historical, Printers', Woman's*, &c. Of Public Galleries, that of the *Metropolitan Museum of Art*, (above named); the *Lenox*, Fifth avenue; those of the picture-dealers, *Goupil* (*Knoedler*, successor),

Somerville, Snedecor, Schaus, &c., with annual exhibitions of the *Academy of Design* (Twenty-third street and Fourth avenue); and the Private Galleries of some of the wealthy citizens and merchant-princes, of taste and liberality, are very creditable, and sometimes exhibited to the public. Large collections of national and celebrity portraits are to be seen in the great photograph galleries of *Kurtz, Fredricks, Rockwood, Bogardus, Sarony, Mora*, and several others. Of Hospitals, the leading are the *Bellevue*, Twenty-sixth street and East River; *New York*, Fifth avenue; *St. Luke's, St. Vincent's, German, Mt. Sinai, Woman's, Seamen's*,—their locations popularly well known, and easily ascertained by any visitor for use or curiosity.

Of Educational Institutions and the structures connected, the following are most notable: *Columbia College* (an institution of moderate age but reputation and usefulness, and with Law and Mining Schools attached), East Forty-ninth street; *New York University* (collegiate, but making no pretence to fill the European use of the word), Washington Square; *New York College* (formerly the New York Free Academy), Twenty-third street and Lexington avenue; *College of Physicians and Surgeons*, East Twenty-third street and Fourth avenue; *University Medical College*, Worth street; *Rutgers Female College*, Fifth avenue; *Union Theological Seminary*, University Place; *New York Law*

Institute, Chambers street ; *Protestant Episcopal Theological Seminary;* new *Normal College,* &c., &c. In connection with educational facilities it should be added, that the Common Schools of the City of New York are the best in the world, in handsome and commodious buildings, free to all, numerously attended, and worth observation by any visitor.

Of Monuments, New York has as follows: In Central Park : *Shakspeare, Sir Walter Scott, Humboldt, Schiller, Webster, Halleck, Seventh Regiment,* &c. In Union Square, equestrian statue of *Washington,* statues of *Lafayette* and *Lincoln.* In Madison Square, monument obelisk to *General Worth* and statue of *Wm. H. Seward.* In Trinity Churchyard, *Martyrs' Memorial* (handsome Gothic structure in honor of revolutionary patriots who died on the prison-ships); monument to *Captain Lawrence,* who fell on the Chesapeake; the horizontal slab over the remains of the heroine of the romance of the same name, *Charlotte Temple.* In St. Paul's Churchyard, shaft to Robert Emmett, the Irish patriot; monument to *Gen. Montgomery;* one (back of church) to *George Frederick Cooke,* the actor. In Printing House Square, bronze statue of *Franklin.*

Of antiquities, the city may be said to have literally none, the hand of "improvement" having lately been very busy with the few remaining. The two most interesting old buildings existing, are the *Old Walton House,* Pearl Street, most fashionable residence of the past century, now decayed; and the *Washington Hotel*, Broadway and Battery Place, once the residence of Gen. Washington, of Sir Guy Carleton, &c.

Of Churches, few command any attention architecturally, though there is no deficiency as to number. The two oldest were the *North Dutch*, Fulton and William streets, not long since demolished, and the *Middle Dutch*, used as a pr'son by the British during the War of the Revolution, and late the City Post Office—Nassau, Liberty and Cedar streets. *St. Paul's*, Broadway (where the pew of General Washington, when President, still remains), and *St. John's*, Varick street, best deserve present notice, from age and unpretending grace; and *Trinity*, Broadway, as the most respectable finished Gothic erection on the Continent—though *St. Patrick's Cathedral*, Fifth avenue and Fiftieth street, will eventually dwarf it and all others. Those remaining, best repaying visits of curiosity, are *St. George's*, Rutherford Place; *Grace Church*, Broadway; *St. Paul's* and *All Souls*, Fourth avenue; *St. Thomas'*, Fifth avenue; *Holy Trinity*, Madison avenue; *St. Mark's* (old), Stuyvesant street; the *Tabernacle*, Sixth avenue; *St. Stephen's*, Twenty-eighth street; *Dr. Chapin's*, Fifth avenue; *Dr. Hepworth's*, Madison avenue. In BROOKLYN, the most notable are the *Holy Trinity* and *St. Ann's-on-the Heights*, both on Clinton street; *Baptist*, Strong Place; *Dr. Eddy's*, Pierrepont street; *Church of* the *Pilgrims*, Henry street; the *Tabernacle*, Schermerhorn street; *St. Charles Borromeo* (Catholic), Sidney Place.

Of Public Buildings, the most interesting, from one cause or another, will be found the *City Hall*, City Hall Park (with a collection of civic and hero‘c portraits of some interest, in the "Governor's Room"); the *New Court House* (unfinished, but with many handsome rooms) same place; the *City Prison* ("Tombs"), Centre street; the *Custom House* and *Sub-Treasury*, Wall street; the *Cooper Institute*, junction of Third and Fourth avenues; the *Bible House*, opposite the preceding, above; the *Academy of Music*, Fourteenth street; the *Academy of Design* and *Christian Association* buildings, Fourth avenue and Twenty-third street; *Booth's Theatre*, Twenty-third street; the *Grand Opera House*, Eighth avenue; *Tammany Hall*, Fourteenth street; the *Central Police Station*, Mulberry street; *Hudson River Railroad Freight Depot*, Hudson street (with colossal bronze of much oddity and a certain merit, on the principal front, in honor of Cornelius Vanderbilt); new *Grand Central Depot*, of the N. Y. Central, Harlem, and New Haven Railroads, Fourth avenue and Forty-second street; *Post Office*, City Hall Park; *Methodist Book Concern*, Broadway and Eleventh street; *Masonic Hall*, Twenty-third street and Sixth avenue; *Stock Exchange* (new), Broad street; *N. Y. Historical Society*, University Place; *Produce Exchange*, Whitehall st.

In BROOKLYN, the *City Hall* and *County Court House*, Court and Fulton streets; *Academy of Music*, Montague street; *Mercantile Library*, and *Art Association Building*, same street; *Athenœum*, Atlantic avenue, &c.

New York has many Commercial Buildings of great cost and splendor—no other city in the world having more of what may be designated as "palaces," devoted to money or trade. The lead is taken among purely financial buildings, by the *Park Bank*, Broadway. No less than three structures devoted to Life Assurance command much attention—those of the *Equitable Society*, at Broadway and Cedar street; of the *Mutual Company*, Broadway and Liberty street; and of the *New York Company*, Broadway and Leonard street; while the *Western Union Telegraph* building, Broadway and Dey street, the *Drexel Banking House*, Wall and Broad streets, the *Bennett Building*, Nassau, Fulton and Ann streets, and others command attention. The most prominent among what are called the "business palaces," are those of *A. T. Stewart & Co.*, Broadway and Chambers street, and Broadway and Ninth street; of *Lord & Taylor*, Broadway and Twentieth street; of *Arnold & Constable*, Broadway and Nineteenth street; of *Tiffany*, Union Square and Fifteenth street; of the *Domestic Sewing Machine Company*, Broadway and Fourteenth street; of the *Wheeler & Wilson Sewing Machine Company*, Union Square; of

Appletons, Broadway; of *Brooks Brothers*, Broadway; *Harpers'*, Franklin Square; *Frank Leslie*, Pearl st., *Brewster's*, Fifth avenue, &c.

There are many private dwellings of great cost, splendor, and varying architectural taste, on Fifth avenue and the more fashionable streets on Murray Hill; the first among them being the palace of the lately deceased *A. T. Stewart*, at Fifth avenue and Thirty-fourth street, of which the details, without and within, are of the most lavish magnificence, while the picture collection is very rich and valuable. Closely following, are those of *Mr. Geo. Opdyke*, *Mr. W. H. Vanderbilt*, *Messrs. Astor*, *Judge Hilton*, *Mr. Lenox*, *Mrs. Stevens*, *Mrs. Coles*, *Mr. Morgan*, &c., all on Fifth avenue; *Miss Wolf*, *Messrs. Phelps* and *Dodge*, Madison avenue, &c. Of Club Houses, among the most prominent are the *New York*, *Travelers'*, *Knickerbocker*, *Lotos*, *Manhattan*, &c., Fifth avenue; the *Union League*, Madison avenue, &c.

Of Hotel Buildings (also Hotels), New York has many of great size and fine architecture, prominent among them being the *Windsor*, Fifth avenue and Forty-seventh street; *Fifth Avenue*, Fifth avenue, Broadway and Twenty-fourth street; *Rossmore*, Broadway and Forty-second street; *Buckingham*, Fifth avenue and Fiftieth street; *Grand Central*, Broadway opposite Bond street; *Brevoort*, Fifth avenue near Washington Park; *Astor House*, Broadway and Barclay street; *St. Nicholas*, Broadway and Spring street ; *Metropolitan,* Broadway and Prince street ; *Westminster,* Irving Place and Sixteenth street ; *Grand Hotel,* Broadway and Thirtieth street ; *St. Cloud,* Broadway and Forty-second street ; *Gilsey,* Broadway and Twenty-ninth street ; *Sturtevant,* Broadway and Twenty-eighth street ; *St. James,* Broadway and Twenty-sixth street ; *Hoffman,* Broadway and Twenty-fourth street ; *Coleman,* Broadway and Twenty-seventh street ; *Everett,* Union Square; *Clarendon,* Fourth avenue ; *Delmonico's,* Fifth avenue ; *Berkeley,* Fifth avenue and Ninth street ; *New York,* Broadway and Fourth street; *Earle's,* Canal street ; *Merchants'* (mercantile), Cortlandt street, &c. In BROOKLYN, the *Pierrepont House,* Montague street, and the *Mansion House,* Hicks street. Several Newspaper Offices of mark are to be noticed in New York, those of the *Evening Post,* Broadway and Fulton street; the *Tribune,* Printing House Square; the *Herald,* Broadway and Ann street; the *Times,* and the *Staats Zeitung,* Printing House Square.

The principal Theatres of New York City proper are *Wallack's,* Broadway and Thirteenth street ; the *Olympic,* Broadway near Bleecker street; *Niblo's,* Broadway near Prince street ; *Booth's,* Twenty-third street and Sixth avenue ; the *Grand Opera House,* Eighth avenue and Twenty-third street ; *Daly's New Fifth Avenue,* Twenty-eighth street, near Broadway; the *Lyceum,* Fourteenth street; *Park,* Broadway and Twenty-second street ; *New*

Broadway, Broadway and Thirtieth street ; *Union Square Theatre*, Union Square; *Twenty-third Street*, street of that name; *Eagle*, Broadway and Thirty-third street; *Germania* (German), Fourteenth street; and the *Bowery*, street of that name. Opera House, the *Academy of Music*, Fourteenth street. Aquarium, the *New York*, Broadway and Thirty-fifth street. Ethiopian Minstrel Houses and Varieties, *Tony Pastor's*, the *San Francisco Minstrels*, &c. BROOKLYN has several excellent places of amusement, in the *Academy of Music*, Montague street; *Brooklyn Theatre*, Washington street; *Park Theatre*, Fulton street; *Hooley's Opera House*, Court street; the *Atheneum*, Atlantic avenue, &c.

Most popular Churches (for service), *Trinity*, Broadway (Episcopalian); *Grace*, Broadway and Tenth street (Epis.); the *Tabernacle*, Sixth avenue and Thirty-fourth street (Cong.) ; *Dr. Chapin's*, Fifth avenue and Forty-fifth street (Univ.); *St. Thomas'*, Fifth avenue (Epis.); *Dr. Tyng's*, Rutherford Place (Epis.); *Fifth Avenue*, Fifth avenue and Nineteenth street (Pres.) ; *Dr. Hepworth's*, Madison ave. and E. Forty-fifth st. (Cong.) ; *St. Paul's*, Fourth ave. and Twenty-second street (Methodist Episcop.) ; and in BROOKLYN, *Plymouth* (Rev. Henry Ward Beecher's), Orange street (Cong.) ; *St. Ann's on-the-Heights* and the *Holy Trinity* (Epis.), both on Clinton st. ; *First Baptist*, Nassau street ; *Strong Place* (Bapt.), Strong Place ; *Dr. Talmage's Tabernacle*, Schermerhorn st. Present Catholic Cathedral in New York, *St. Patrick's*, Mulberry and Houston streets ;. with other leading. Catholic Churches — *St. Stephen's*, Twenty-eighth street, near Third avenue (noted for fine music), and *St. Francis Xavier's,* Sixteenth street, near Fifth avenue.

Public Grounds—*Central Park,* (see "Excursions," following); *Washington, Madison* and *Union Squares,* and *Battery* and *City Hall Parks,* most of limited dimensions, but all assuming attractive shapes, and most of them being provided with music on certain evenings of the week, during the warm season; and *Jones' Wood,* lying on the eastern side of the Island, on the river, opposite the lower end of the Central Park, for many years frequented and famous as a place for great outdoor gatherings, including the German and Irish festivals and the Scottish annual games; *Jerome Park,* Westchester (also see "Excursions"); and in BROOKLYN, *Prospect Park* (also see "Excursions"), *Prospect Park Fair Grounds, Lefferts Park,* &c.

Principal Ferries: To *Brooklyn,* from foot Fulton street, foot Wall street, foot Catharine street, Peck Slip, foot Whitehall street; to *Jersey City* (and Cunard Docks, and Pennsylvania Railroad), foot Cortlandt street, and foot Desbrosses street; to *Communipaw* (and New Jersey Central Railroad), foot Liberty street; to *Hoboken* (and Bremen and Hamburg steamers, and Morris and Essex Railroad), foot Barclay street and foot Christopher street; to *Pavonia* (and passenger-depot of the Erie Railway), foot Chambers street and foot Twenty-third street; to *Staten Island,* foot Whitehall street and foot Dey street; to *Hunter's Point* (and Long Island Railroad), James Slip and foot Thirty-fourth street.

PRINCIPAL STREET (HORSE) RAILROADS.

Second Avenue Line.—Cars leave Peck Slip (East River, near Fulton Ferry), run through South, Oliver, Bowery, Grand and Christie streets, and Second avenue to One Hundred and Twenty-eighth street, Harlem. Branch from Broadway at Worth street to Bowery, and thence same route. *Third Avenue Line.*—Cars leave Broadway, opposite Astor House, run through Park Row, Chatham street, Bowery, Third avenue to One Hundred and Thirtieth street, Harlem. *Fourth Avenue Line.*—Cars leave Broadway, opposite Astor House, run through Park Row, Centre and Grand streets, Bowery and Fourth avenue to Forty-second street, (Grand Central Depot.) *Broadway Line.*—Cars leave Broadway corner Barclay street, run through Barclay, Church and Greene streets, Clinton and University Places, Broadway and Seventh avenue to Fifty-ninth street (Central Park). Branch of this road, from Broadway at Broome street, through Broome street to Greene street, and as above. *Sixth Avenue Line.*—Cars leave Broadway, corner Vesey street, run through Vesey, Church and Chambers streets, West Broadway, Canal, Varick and Carmine streets, and Sixth avenue to Fifty-ninth street (Central Park). *Seventh Avenue Line.*—Cars leave Broadway, corner Park Place, run through Park Place, Church, Canal, Sullivan and Macdougal streets, Clinton place, Greenwich and Seventh avenues to Fifty-ninth street (Central Park). *Eighth Avenue Line.*—Cars leave Broadway, corner Vesey street, run through Vesey, Church and Chambers streets, West Broadway, Canal and Hudson streets, and Eighth avenue to Fifty-ninth street (Central Park). Branch of this road, from Broadway at Canal street, through Canal to Hudson street, and as above, with continuation to Manhattanville. *Ninth Avenue Line.*—Cars leave Broadway, corner Fulton street, run through Fulton and Greenwich streets and Ninth avenue to Fifty-fourth street. *Lexington Avenue Line.*—Cars leave Broadway opposite Astor House, run through Park Row, Chatham street, Bowery, Third Avenue, Thirty-fifth street, Lexington avenue to Forty-second street and Fourth avenue (Grand Central Depot). *Bleecker Street Line.*—Cars leave Fulton ferry (East River), run through Fulton, William and Ann streets, Park Row, Centre, Leonard, Elm, Howard, Crosby, Bleecker, Macdougal, West Fourth, West Thirteenth, Hudson, West Fourteenth streets and Tenth avenue to Twenty-third street. *Belt Line.*—(Eastern division): Cars leave South ferry (Battery), run through Front street, Old Slip, South, Montgomery, South, Corlaers, Grand, Goerck and East Houston streets, Avenue D, East Fourteenth street, Avenue A, East Twenty third street, First avenue and East Fifty ninth street to Fifth avenue at Central Park. (Western division): Cars leave South ferry (Battery), run through Whitehall street and Battery Place, West street, Tenth avenue and West Fifty-ninth street to Fifth avenue at Central Park—the two forming perfect connection round the city. *Dry Dock Line.*—Cars leave Broadway, opposite Astor House, run through Park Row, Chatham street, East Broadway, Grand and Columbia streets, Avenue D, East Eleventh street and Avenue B, to foot East Fourteenth street. *East Broadway Line.*—Cars leave Broadway, corner Ann street, run through Park Row, Chatham street, East Broadway, Clinton street, Avenue B, East Fourteenth street, Avenue A, East Twenty-third street, First avenue to Twenty-third street ferry. *Grand and Cortlandt Line.*—Cars leave Jersey City ferry, foot Cortlandt street, run through Cortlandt, Greenwich, Beach, Lispenard and Canal streets, East Broadway and Grand street to Grand street ferry (East River). *Cross-Town Line.*—Cars leave West Forty-second street at Tenth avenue, run through Tenth avenue, Thirty-fourth street, Broadway, Twenty third street, Fourth avenue, Fourteenth street, and east side minor streets to foot of Grand street, East River. *Church Street Line.*—Cars leave Astor House (Vesey street), run through New Church street, Battery Place and Whitehall street to South ferry. *Elevated Railway.*—(Steam)—Cars leave station at the South Ferry, (extreme lower end of Broadway) every few minutes, through or rather *over* Greenwich street and Ninth avenue, to Central Park, with stopping-places at very short intervals, and many extensions projected. There are several other and minor roads, cross-town lines, &c., besides those here given; but all the more important have been enumerated, and the least instructed visitor will have little difficulty, with the foregoing directions, in making full use of these great conveniences. It will be noted that, with a single exception, the up routes of all these lines have been given, as most intelligible; some of them make slight variations in return or down routes, but when so, only to a small distance. *Omnibuses*, up Broadway to various points, leave South, Wall street and Fulton ferries, conspicuously lettered as to destinations.

Other objects of interest to those making longer sojourn; the *East River Bridge*, now building between New York and Brooklyn, and promising to be one of the master-works of its class in the world; the many large *Ocean and River Steamers* at their wharves; *Views over the City*, from high buildings; *Governor's Island*, head-quarters of the military department (reached by boat from South ferry); the *Navy Yard*, Brooklyn (cars from Fulton Ferry); the Penal and Charitable Institutions on *Blackwell's*, *Randall's* and *Ward's Islands* (under control of Commissioners of Charities and Correction—building, Third avenue and Eleventh street); and a variety of *Asylums* for orphans and the afflicted.

SUBURBS, DRIVES AND EXCURSIONS.

Of Drives and Short Excursions (by carriage), the first favorite is that to the

CENTRAL PARK, a large and admirable public ground, occupying nearly the centre of the Island, extending in width from Fifth to Eighth avenue, and in length from Fifty-ninth to One-Hundred and Tenth street, handsomely laid out, shaded and ornamented, with fine roads and costly bridges, and lacking only age to be equal to any public ground in Europe. It has a *Lake*, with boats (service); a *Museum*, with Zoological collection and many other curiosities; a *Casino*, on the European plan; *Public Carriages*, making the round of the Park at short intervals, for trifling fare: *Statues* of Shakspeare, Humboldt, Schiller, Morse, Scott, Webster, Halleck, &c. ; statuary groups of the "Hunter and his Dog," "Auld Lang Syne;" and presents the feature of Music by a fine band every Saturday afternoon during the warm season, attracting immense concourses of people. In connection are also to be seen the *Croton Receiving Reservoirs*, alleged to be of size enough, and to contain water enough, to float the navies of the world. [*Central Park* may also be reached by horse-cars from the City Hall, or from most of the ferries (Belt road along either river), by the Elevated Railroad, &c.] Beyond, the drive by carriage is often and profitably extended to the *Harlem* and *Bloomingdale Roads*, or to HIGH BRIDGE, an aqueduct Bridge over the Harlem River, of great height and solidity; or to *Jerome Park*, new and handsome trotting and racing ground of the American Jockey Club, beyond the Harlem River, in Westchester. Another scarcely less fashionable drive is to

PROSPECT PARK, the new but very handsome public ground of Brooklyn, which bids fair to rival if not to excel the Central, has a *Lake*, a *Dairy Cottage* and *Barn*, a fine stretch of natural forest, an elevated drive (the "Ocean Parkway,") statue of

President Lincoln (at entrance), busts of Washington Irving, John Howard Payne, &c. Music by a fine band, Saturday afternoons. [May also be reached from New York by Fulton ferry and by horse-cars of Flatbush avenue line.] Near Prospect Park is to be visited

Greenwood Cemetery, one of the largest and handsomest Cities of the Dead on the globe, with lakes, rising grounds, fine shades, costly monuments, and all the other melancholy attractions possible to be flung around places of burial. Among the leading features are the handsome sculptured Entrance Way; the Firemen's, Pilots', Old Sea Captain's, Canda, Scribner, J. G. Bennett, Greely and Clarke monuments; the tombs of William E. Burton, the comedian, Lola Montez (with inscription, "Eliza Gilbert"), Crawford Livingston, &c.; the vaults of Stephen Whitney, William Niblo, &c. Most beautiful point that at and around "Sylvan Water;" finest views, those from "Ocean Hill" and "Battle Hill." [May also be reached from New York by Fulton Ferry and horse-cars of the Greenwood or Fifth avenue lines.] Service-carriages for going through the cemetery, may always be found at the entrance. Beyond Greenwood and Prospect Park, the same drive may be profitably extended to *Prospect Park Race Course*, and by grand new Ocean Parkway, to

Coney Island,—fine sea-beach, with excellent bathing and great and improving popularity as a riding and sailing resort for visitors. [May also be reached from New York by Fulton ferry, and by Smith and Jay street horse-cars; or by either of the horse-car lines to Greenwood, thence by steam to the beach; or by steamer from New York, several times daily during season.]

Other Short Excursions will be those to the *Brooklyn Navy Yard*, with extensive Dry Dock, Museum of Marine Curiosities, and much of general interest [horse-cars from Fulton ferry, "Navy Yard"]; to *Fort Hamilton*, at the Narrows, junction of the Upper and Lower bays, with fortifications and very fine sea-view [drive, or may be reached by Fulton or Hamilton ferry, and horse-cars]; to *Evergreen Cemetery*, East New York [drive, or Fulton ferry and Fulton avenue horse-cars]; to *Rockaway Beach* and *Far Rockaway*, picturesque line of coast on the South side of Long Island, celebrated for sailing, fishing, and as a resort always cool even in the hottest weather, owing to the breezes caused by peninsular position, and once made famous by the song commencing:

> "On old Long Island's sea girt shore,
> Many an hour I've whiled away,
> Listening to the breakers' roar,
> That washed the beach of Rockaway."

[Ferry from James Slip or Thirty-fourth street to Hunter's Point for Long Island Railroad; or ferry from foot of Grand street, East River, for South-Side Railroad; or horse-cars to East New York from

Fulton or South ferries, steam-cars to *Canarsie* and boat to beach; or, daily excursion boat from New York]; to *Hoboken*, great base-ball and cricket grounds, and favorite German resort, across the Hudson, in New Jersey [ferry from Barclay street or Christopher street]; to *Bergen Point*, [drive or horse-car from Jersey City, or train on New Jersey Central Railroad, from foot Liberty street]; to *Paterson* and *Passaic Falls* [train on Erie Railway, foot Chambers or Twenty-third street: see route North by Erie Railway]; to *Newark*, largest and most thriving city in New Jersey [train on Pennsylvania Railroad, foot of Cortlandt street; see route New York to Philadelphia; or Newark and New York Railroad, foot Liberty street]; to *Elizabeth*, New Jersey [train on Pennsylvania Railroad, foot Cortlandt street, or New Jersey Central, foot Liberty street;] to *Staten Island*, [New Brighton, Sailors' Snug Harbor, Port Richmond, Elm Park, &c., by the North Shore boats, from the Battery every hour; and Vanderbilt's, Quarantine, Tompkinsville, Clifton, &c., by the East Shore boats, from Battery or foot Dey street.

Longer excursions of interest, conveniently made from New York, those to (1)

LONG BRANCH, great sea-shore resort on the New Jersey coast, with several miles of the bluff, bold surf-bathing, admired sea-view, splendid drives and excursions, and an immense number of summer hotels, capable of accommodating fifteen to twenty thousand visitors (among the principal the *Ocean Hotel, West End, Mansion House, United States, Brighton, Howland, Pavilion,* &c.), and a present popularity making it the most generally sought and notable place on the American sea-coast. It supplied the summer residence of President Grant, and has many cottages of the wealthy. Near it are *Eatontown* (with *Monmouth Park Race Ground* in the immediate neighborhood), *Red Bank, Deal,* and other villages of New Jersey. [Reached by boats of the New Jersey Southern Railroad, to *Sandy Hook* (with government fortifications and entrance to the Lower Bay); thence rail, by the *Highlands of Navesink* (fine elevation, with splendid sea-air and view, and summer-boarding place of merit and popularity—hotels, *Thompson's, Jenkinson's*), *Seabright,* &c., [the whole distance within sight of the sea.] Or, by the new All-Rail Route from New York, from foot of Liberty st., by Central Railroad of New Jersey (Communipaw ferry), and Rahway, to Perth Amboy, Keyport, Middletown, Red Bank, &c., to Long Branch. [From Long Branch railway connection to *Freehold,* and thence to Trenton and other cities of West New Jersey; or train may be taken for *Manchester, Tom's River,* and towns of New Jersey further southward; to *Atlantic City* or PHILADELPHIA.] To (2)

LAKE MAHOPAC, pleasant and very popular minor watering-place, with handsome quiet wooded scenery, islands, fine boating, sailing, fishing and other attractions. Reached by Harlem Railroad, in a few hours, through the very fine scenery of that line, at the lower edge of the Hudson Highlands. Hotels, the *Gregory House, Baldwin House,* &c. To (3)

SCHOOLEY'S MOUNTAIN (*Heath House*), mineral springs and popular summer resort, with fine air and charming scenery, in the minor mountains of New Jersey; reached by the Morris and Essex Railroad, from foot of Barclay street, by *Morristown*, one of the handsomest towns and most popular residences in the State, to *Hackettstown*, whence short ride by stage-coach. Also, *Budd's Lake*, within a few miles of the preceding, and reached by same conveyances—with many attractions of boating, fishing, &c. Also, *Lake Hopatcong*, with similar attractions to the place last named, reached by the same railroad to Stanhope or Dover, thence carriage or boat to destination. To (4)

THE DELAWARE WATER GAP (*Kittatinny* and *Water Gap Houses*) lying at one of the finest passes of the Upper Delaware, through and among the mountains dividing Pennsylvania and New Jersey, and with superb mountain and river scenery, pure and healthful air, and much popularity as a place of summer resort. Has many features of especial wood and beauty, in *Rebecca's Well, Venus' Bath* and *Eureka Falls*, views from *Prospect Rock, Fox Hill,* &c. [From the Water Gap, continuing by rail, may be reached *Stroudsburg* and the Lackawanna Coal Regions of Pennsylvania; or, southward, *Easton,* PHILADELPHIA, &c.] To (5)

Greenport, Orient, Babylon, Fire Island, &c., minor watering-places at the east end of Long Island ; and to *Jamaica* and other places nearer. [Reached by Long Island Railroad.] Also, to *Glen Cove* and other near places on that Island, by boat. To (6)

WEST POINT, by evening or morning boat or Hudson River railroad. [See route to West Point, Catskills, Albany, &c., Route No. 1.] To (7)

NEW HAVEN, Conn. [See Route No. 4, p. 104. By rail on that route, or daily boat on the Sound, leaving Peck Slip every afternoon for that place direct.] To (8)

Bridgeport, Norwalk, and other towns of Connecticut. [Rail as in Route No. 4.] To (9)

HARTFORD, capital of Conn. [Rail as in Route No. 4, or by daily boat direct.]

ROUTE No. 1.—NORTHERN.

NEW YORK TO NIAGARA FALLS AND CANADA, BY HUDSON RIVER, NEW YORK CENTRAL RAILWAY AND CONNECTIONS.

Division A.

NEW YORK TO AND AT WEST POINT AND HUDSON HIGHLANDS.

The transit from New York to West Point and the Highlands may be made in from two to four hours, by (1) Hudson River Railroad to Garrison's, thence ferry to West Point; or by (2) morning boat on the river, to West Point direct; or (3) evening boat on the river, also direct. Either of the latter is preferable to the former, for reasons hereafter to be given.

By Rail.

Leaving New York by rail, on Hudson River Railroad, the first object of special interest, except the high lands at and about Fort Washington, studded with fine residences,—is the crossing from New York island to the main land of Westchester, at Kingsbridge or *Spuytenduyvel;* and on the opposite or western side of the river, commence, at about the same point,

THE PALISADES, immense almost perpendicular masses of rock, rising sheer from the river on that side, in shape suggesting the name, and continuing at various heights of hundreds of feet, for some ten miles, where they break away into rugged hills.

Beyond Spuytenduyvel, the first place of importance passed through is the handsome small town of *Yonkers;* then *Dobbs Ferry,* with the long wharf of the Erie Railway opposite, at *Piermont,* and a ferry between; then *Tarrytown* (where the laying over of a train may be well compensated in visiting "Sunny-side," the late residence of Washington Irving, the Major Andre Monument, &c., in the immediate neighborhood); then *Sing-Sing,* with its strong State-prison buildings, and on the opposite bank of the river a view of the gorge running back to the celebrated *Rockland Lake,* from which so much of the best ice is derived. After leaving Sing-Sing, very soon is crossed the *Croton River,* from works on which and the lake of the same name, the New York supply of water is derived. Shortly after crossing the Croton, a mass of rocks, rising conically and crowned with a light-house, on the other or west side of the river, marks *Stony Point,* celebrated for the reckless courage displayed in its capture by Gen. Wayne, during the Revolutionary War. The next stopping-place of importance is *Peekskill,* on leaving which the

HIGHLANDS OF THE HUDSON are entered, presenting their heavy and picturesque masses on both sides of the river, and enchanting the eye with the continual changes, appearances and disappearances made inevitable by the course of the railway through them. The disembarkation from the railway is made at *Garrison's Landing*, whence ferry-boat and omnibus to the Military Academy or one of the hotels at West Point.

By Steamboat.

Precisely the same features as those indicated by rail, will be enjoyed by boat, with the advantage of both sides of the river being seen in lieu of one, and the additional escaping of the noise inevitable in riding by rail along rocky passes. When entering the Highlands, however, the advantage of the boat is even more manifest, as there is scarcely a river or lake approach in the world, so magnificent as that through the Highlands proper, from Peekskill to West Point—fine as any one point of the Rhine, and forcibly reminding the tourist of the middle and upper portions of Loch Lomond, approaching and above Inversnaid. It is from boat on the river, especially, that the alternating wild beauty and rugged grandeur of the giants of the range, their feet at the very water's edge, can best be appreciated.

Morning boats, making this voyage, and then going on up the Hudson to Albany, leave New York every morning, at an early hour; and evening boats, passing through the Highlands before nightfall, leave every afternoon.

Disembarkation, from either, is made at Cozzens'

or the Military Academy docks, at West Point; thence to the hotels by omnibus.

At and near West Point.

One of the principal attractions at West Point, consists in the admirable views which can be enjoyed either from *Cozzens'*, the fashionable hotel and summer resort, on the high cliffs below the Military Academy, the *Parry House*, in the same vicinity, or the *West Point*, above it, making quiet lounging a continued luxury. This is not true of one direction alone, but of all, the elevation being high and the reaches of the river, above and below, singularly beautiful. Of excursions, the most notable is to

Old Fort Putnam, ruins, with some portions of solid wall remaining, lying on a hill westward from the Academy. This fort must always retain its interest, as the "Key of the Highlands" during the Revolutionary War, and the scene of Arnold's intended treason. The views from it, in all directions, too, are the very finest to be enjoyed in any portion of the Highlands. An early visit will, of course, be paid to the

United States Military Academy, which gives the place its peculiar importance, and which ranks among the first of military institutions, with some features of severity attracting peculiar attention. [Information as to modes and forms of visiting can always be obtained at the leading hotels.] In connection with the Academy comes the interesting spectacle,

Parade of the Cadets (morning and evening)—which should not be missed—the evening especially, by any who desire to see the perpendicular in carriage, the angular in motion, and the sharp in discipline.

Pleasant excursions may also be made to *Buttermilk Falls*, in the neighborhood; and across the river to *Cold Spring*, and to the *Robinson House*, standing four or five miles south from it, where Arnold resided at the time of his treason. Near Cold Spring may also be seen *Undercliff*, residence of the late Gen. Geo. P. Morris, the poet.

Division B.

WEST POINT TO AND AT THE CATSKILL MOUNTAINS.

Northward from West Point, by steamboat on the way towards Albany, from the wharf; or rail from Garrison's Station, opposite. Assuming that the boat will be taken, and remembering that if proceeding by rail the variation of scene will be very slight—the following will be the most important features, beyond West Point. Emerging from the Highlands proper, and passing "Cro'nest" and "Storm King," the largest hills of the range, and also *Cornwall Landing* on the left, with much beauty and picturesque scenery in the neighborhood (among other attractions, *Idlewild*, residence of the late N. P. Willis), and *Fishkill Landing* on the right, is shortly reached, on the left,

ROUTE NO. 1.—NORTHERN.

NEWBURGH, very slopingly situated on the high bank, with large river-trade, an important railway connection westward to the Erie road, and one feature of great importance on the bluff below: *Washington's Head-Quarters*, a revolutionary relic of prominence, with many reminders of the struggle. Chief Hotel, the *United States*. Above Newburgh, though the river is fine, there is no feature of marked interest, until, at the right, is reached

POUGHKEEPSIE, a large town with some picturesqueness of location, and a triple distinction compounded of its heavy river-trade in agricultural products, the manufacture of ale, and the proximity of the noted *Vassar Female College*.

Within a few miles after leaving Poughkeepsie, the rough scenery is supplemented and completed by the breaking into view, far ahead and to the left, of the

Catskill Mountain Range, which thenceforth scarcely leaves the eye of the tourist until arrival —so graceful is the outline, and so beautifully blue the general aspect. Minor landings of *Hyde Park*, etc., are passed, to

Rhinebeck, on the right, where landing is made for *Rondout* and *Kingston*, on the opposite side (connection by ferry), and for

The Overlook Mountain (House burned, but very soon to be re-erected) at great height on the southern portion of the Catskills, and commanding a most magnificent view, especially eastward and southward. Also with many attractive features in the neighborhood, in the *Devil's Kitchen, Cleft in the Rocks, Pulpit Rock, Overlook Cliff, &c.* Also, at a little distance, *Shoe Lake*, a beautiful and attractive sheet of water. [Reached from Rhinebeck by ferry to *Rondout*, thence by rail to *West Hurley*; thence by stage-coach, by the Sawkill Creek and Woodstock, to destination. May also be reached by evening boat, direct from New York to Rondout, thence as before.]

Beyond Rhinebeck are passed *Barrytown* and other landings on the right, *Malden* and others on the left, to

Catskill Landing, point of disembarkation for the Mountains, and of crossing from *Oak Hill Station*, for those who have come up by the rail. Also, popular summer resort, at the *Prospect Park House*, immediately above, with fine grounds and admirable view; at the *Powell House* (posting-house for the mountains, on the wharf) &c. [Catskill Landing may also be reached by evening boat from New York direct, and direct connection made for the mountains.]

From Catskill Landing by stage-coach, always in waiting for boats and trains, by *Catskill Village*, the *Half-Way House*, and at one-third distance of the ascent of the Mountains proper, the *Rip Van-Winkle House*, with a broad flat rock beside it, on which tradition alleges the sleep of Irving's hero to have taken place. Views over the Hudson Valley are very fine, before reaching the

Catskill Mountain House, among the highest of all American places of eastern sojourn, and in many regards the superior of all others on the continent, as to situation. The view from the house, over the Hudson river and valley, is wonderfully extensive and beautiful; and *Sunrise*, as seen from the piazza, is scarcely second to the same spectacle from the famous Swiss Rhigi. Of excursions, there are many and most pleasing. The most interesting (longer ones by carriage, always in readiness) follow. To

Kauterskill Falls, wild and romantic basin, with two cascades, of 180 and 80 feet, and picturesque in every aspect, above and below, besides being surrounded by wild and grand mountain and ravine scenery, and views of *High Peak* and *Round Top*, the two giants of the range, obtainable from different points. (The *Laurel House*, a popular place of sojourn, standing at near the verge of the falls, affords residence to the many who wish to study the splendid scenery in this immediate neighborhood). To the *Lakes*, small sheets of water, lying in primeval wildness; short walk from the Mountain House, or on the way to the Falls. Through the *Clove*, one of the most remarkable mountain clefts in the world, from *Palensville* towards *Hunter*, with views of the beautiful *Fawn's Leap Fall*. To *Plauterkill* and *Stony Cloves*. To *Parker's Ledge*, overlooking the Clove. To *Moses'* and *Sunset Rocks*. To the tops of the *South Mountain, North Mountain*, etc. To the top of *High Peak*, laborious ascent, but with magnificent view, etc.

Division C.

CATSKILL MOUNTAINS TO AND AT ALBANY AND TROY.

Leave Catskill by rail from Oak Hill Station; or by boat from New York from Catskill Landing; making landing at

HUDSON, on the east side of the river, a large and thriving town, with considerable manufactures. [Point of departure for *Lebanon Springs* and the Shaker Village connected with them; as also for *Columbia Springs;* both minor watering-places of salubrious situation and increasing popularity. Also, railway connection east for Boston.] From Hudson, through scenery much tamer than along the Lower Hudson—past *Athens* (whence there is a railway to Albany), *Coxsackie, New Baltimore,* etc., on the left; and *Stuyvesant, Kinderhook* (residence of the late President Martin Van Buren), *Castleton,* etc., on the right—to

ALBANY, Capital of the State of New York, somewhat picturesquely situated on rising ground, on the west bank of the Hudson, with *Greenbush* opposite; the river spanned by a railway-bridge of recent erection and a certain celebrity on account of the opposition made to it by the residents of Troy, higher up the stream. It has great commercial importance, as the virtual head of sailing-vessel navigation northward; as a heavy lumber and timber depot; and especially as the point at which the immense carrying-trade of the Erie and Champlain Canals enters the Hudson.

The buildings best worth a visit and observation are the *Capitol* (now being replaced by a much finer erection), with the Senate and Assembly Chambers (legislative sessions from 1st January to 1st April); the *State Library*, adjoining; the *State House*, with government offices; the *Dudley Observatory*, rapidly assuming position as one of the first institutions of the kind in the country; the *State Arsenal;* the *University;* the *Medical College* (with Museum); the *City Hall; State Normal School*, &c. Rides from Albany are many and attractive—especially to the *Cemetery* (one of the handsomest in the State), to *Cohoes Falls, Lansingburgh*, and other handsome and thriving villages at practicable distance, and to some one of the *Shaker Villages* lying northward—at the latter of which (as at Lebanon), the most odd and peculiar of all forms of worship may be encountered. Leading hotels at Albany, the *Delavan, Stanwix Hall, Congress Hall*, &c.

From Albany, by street-car, omnibus or boat to

TROY, some eight miles up the rapidly-diminishing river from the Capital, where will be found nearly a rival of the latter in size and population, its superior in beauty of location, and not only a flourishing town in general manufactures, but one of the most extensive lumber and timber depots in the world. It lies on both sides of the river—the eastern portion called by the common name, and the western, *West*

Troy. There is much manufacturing, of various heavy kinds in both divisions, but especially in West Troy, where street-cars, stoves and oilcloths are among the principal articles, while at the *Watervliet Arsenal* (United States government) the founding of small arms and munitions of war is carried on very extensively. Troy has also additional prominence from the junction of the Northern, Western and Eastern lines of railway, here occurring; it has some churches of prominence (*St. John* and *St. Paul*, the principal)—the *Rensselaer Polytechnic Institute*, and the *Female Seminary*, both popular in management and extensive in influence. Two slight eminences, near the town, bear the ridiculously classical names of *Mt. Ida* and *Mt. Olympus;* and there are two pretty cemeteries—*Oakwood* and *Mount Ida.* From Troy, also, may be conveniently reached, by carriage or other conveyance, Cohoes, Lansingburgh, &c.

Division D.

NEW YORK TO ALBANY OR TROY BY NIGHT-BOAT.

Those who have before made the passage of the Hudson from New York to Albany by daylight; or those who intend to return by some day-route, and so do not wish to consume time or experience fatigue on the route northward before reaching Albany—will be able to make the transit, so far as the latter place, by night-steamers on the Hudson, leaving

ROUTE NO. 1.—NORTHERN.

New York at 6 P. M., finding luxurious accommodation for eating and sleeping, on board, and reaching Albany or Troy at so early an hour in the morning as to ensure connection with the trains for either the Northern, Western or Eastern routes.

For this transit two lines present themselves : the People's Line (New Jersey Steamboat Company), in the very large and splendid boats of which the full luxury of American river-navigation is seen; and the Citizens' Line (the Troy Citizens' Steamboat Company), displaying less splendor though supplying strong and efficient boats, and making a specialty of reduced prices as compared with the People's Line.

Going by either of these lines, in the long days of midsummer, a considerable portion of the scenery of the lower Hudson is passed through before the disappearance of daylight; and if time at or near the full moon can be chosen, the sail under such circumstances through the Hudson Highlands affords aspects of peculiar beauty not otherwise attainable.

Division E.

ALBANY OR TROY TO AND AT TRENTON FALLS.

The New York Central Railroad will be taken at either Albany or Troy, bending westward, up the very handsome though narrow

Valley of the Mohawk, considered one of the finest in America for tracts of quiet beauty in scenery;

and often within sight of that wonderful enterprise in original construction and present capacity of conveyance, the

Erie Canal, which crosses the whole State between Lake Erie, at Buffalo, and the Hudson, at Albany;—by *Schenectady,* a quiet little old town, principally celebrated as having been the scene of a dreadful conflagration and massacre by the Indians, during the Revolutionary War. [Railway branches here for Saratoga, Lake George, Lake Champlain and Montreal, for those who prefer.] From Schenectady, by minor stations of *Fonda ; Palatine Bridge* [point of disembarkation for *Sharon Springs,* reached hence by coach]; *Fort Plain* [whence coach conveyance to *Otsego Lake, Cooperstown* (residence of the late Fenimore Cooper) and *Cherry Valley*]; *Little Falls* (where particular attention is due to the wondrous river-and-rock scenery of the pass on the left); and *Herkimer*—to

UTICA, one of the flourishing large towns of Central New York, and Capital of Oneida County. It is pleasantly situated on rising ground on the south side of the Mohawk River, and is surrounded by very fertile lands, from which proceeds, at the hands of the Welsh and other residents, one of the principal cheese-manufactures of the country. The town stands on the site of old Fort Schuyler, of Revolutionary fame; is an entrepot of both the New York Central Railroad and Erie Canal; and has a peculiar though melancholy attraction in the large and well-managed

State Lunatic Asylum. Drives around Utica are numerous and excellent. Prominent hotels at Utica, *Baggs'* and the *American.*

Lay over at Utica one day or more, and proceed, either by carriage direct, or by cars of the Utica and Black River Railroad to *South Trenton* and *Trenton Falls Station* (thence by omnibus), to

TRENTON FALLS, on West Canada Creek, branch of the Mohawk River—a series of cascades unexcelled in the world for picturesque beauty. The principal falls are five in number, successively, passing up the stream, the *Sherman Fall, High Fall, Mill-Dam Fall, Alhambra Fall* and *Rocky Heart.* To appreciate and enjoy them thoroughly, the tourist needs to descend the bank, by stairway, to the rocky level at the bottom, as far as practicable, and pass up along the left bank, on an irregular line of shelf-path, easily found, and presenting little difficulty and no danger to the careful. The rock-strata of this remarkable gorge will excite mingled wonder and admiration,—as will the really unique collection of fossils and crystals found in the neigborhood and kept on view at *Moore's Hotel,* near the Falls. Returning from the extreme point reached, to below the Mill-Dam Fall, the stairway should be ascended, to the *Rural Retreat,* to view the High Fall from above—and way taken back to the Hotel through the fine woods. Return to Utica for pursuance of route northward.

Division F.

TRENTON FALLS AND UTICA TO NIAGARA FALLS.

Leave Utica by rail on New York Central Railroad, to

ROME, a thriving town, also on the Mohawk River and the Erie Canal. [Here, those who wish to proceed more directly to the St. Lawrence and Canada, may take Rome, Watertown and Ogdensburgh Railroad, to *Watertown,* for crossing to Kingston and the Grand Trunk Line in either direction— or to *Ogdensburgh,* for crossing to Prescott and nearest route to Ottawa]. Rome, continuing by New York Central, to

SYRACUSE, large and flourishing town of Onondaga County, at the junction of the Erie and Oswego Canals, with an immense production of salt from the Salt-wells, and the peculiar celebrity of having long been the favorite place for political conventions. It is pleasantly situated at the south end of Onondaga Lake. [Railway connection, here, southward by the Syracuse and Binghamton Railroad, to *Binghamton* and the Erie Railway; and northward to *Oswego,* on the shore of Lake Ontario, with steamer connection to Canadian ports and down the St. Lawrence. Branch line of the New York Central may also be taken, at Syracuse, direct to *Buffalo,* by

AUBURN, flourishing town on Cayuga Lake, and capital of Cayuga County, where one of the New

York State Prisons is located, and where Secretary Seward has long resided—by *Cayuga, Geneva, Canandaigua* (whence branch lines to *Rochester* and southward to the Erie Railway at *Elmira*), *Caledonia, LeRoy* and *Batavia*.]

By main line, from Syracuse, by *Clyde, Lyons* and *Palmyra*, to

ROCHESTER, on the Genesee River, one of the largest towns of Northern New York, and one of the most prosperous. It has a great natural curiosity, in *Genesee Falls*, a single cataract of eminence, in jumping from which "Sam Patch," the leaper, lost his life, many years ago. Artificially, its leading attractions are the great *Erie Canal Aqueduct* over the Genesee; the *Rochester University* and *Theological Seminary; Mount Hope Cemetery; St. Mary's Hospital*, etc. [Railway connection southward to the Erie Railway, at *Corning;* also by rail to *Charlotte*, on the lake shore, whence boats to all points on Lake Ontario]. Leading hotels, the *Osborn, Congress, Brackett*, &c.

From Rochester, by New York Central, by *Brockport, Albion, Medina*, and *Lockport* (point of entrance into the Erie Canal, from Lake Erie), to *Niagara* (village), and

NIAGARA FALLS, first natural curiosity of America and admittedly among the first in the world.

Division G.

AT AND ABOUT NIAGARA.

Most students of geography, even those who have never traveled, know that the Falls of Niagara lie between the State of New York, and Canada, and that they are formed by the rushing through the comparatively narrow pass of the Niagara River, over a curved shelf of uneven rocks, of all the mighty mass of water going eastward from Lake Erie to Lake Ontario; and to a smaller number of non-visitors are known the additional facts that the *Horse-Shoe Fall* (Canadian side) is 1,800 feet across; that *Goat Island*, separating the two, is 500 feet in width; that the *American Fall* is only 900 feet in width; that the average depth of descent is estimated to be about 160 feet; and that the enormous amount of 100,000,000 tons of water is believed to pass over the ledge every hour—nearly 1,500,000 tons every minute, and about 25,000 tons every second or beat of the pulse! Beyond this, no additional statistics need be given, except that the banks of the river, below the falls, have a perpendicular height of about 180 feet, and that the mass of water, below, all the way to the *Whirlpool*, is compressed into an average space of about 480 feet of width.

It is scarcely necessary to say that days of sojourn at the Falls are desirable, to see them in all their varying aspect and become fully acquainted with their beauty (often underrated) as well their grandeur. The short-trip traveler, however, will be better served than otherwise, with a brief statement of the points of view most absolutely necessary and most conveniently attained. Of these are (1) that

Over the Rapids—view caught in passing from the neighborhood of the Cataract House, by the fragile-looking but perfectly-secure bridge, to Goat Island. It is doubtful whether the cataract itself is more impressive than this mad rush of waters, threatening to sweep away the beholder at any instant, and suggesting all the images of beautiful rage and fury. (2),

From Goat Island, over the Canadian Fall, the Canada shore and the lower rapids—with the shape of the horseshoe fully defined, and the rainbow almost constant during fine weather. (3),

From *New Observatory,* below the American Fall, and near the *Inclined Railway,* with stained glass for effects, &c. Reached from *Prospect Park,* in rear of International House. From Inclined Railway, *Ferry to Canada side.* (4),

From Prospect Point, (within the *Prospect Park,*) on the American side, giving the American Fall almost at the feet, and the Canadian Fall and shore broadly opposite. (5),

From under the American Fall, down-river side, reaching that point by descent of steps or *Inclined Railway,* from Prospect Point. From no other point of view can the impression of the broken bright water really falling from the clouds, be caught in such enchanting perfection. (6),

From the River, crossing the lower rapids by boat, and looking up to the Falls from the greatest attainable depth below them. (7),

From the Suspension Bridges, especially the upper and smaller one, near the Falls. (8),

From the Clifton Ledge, in front of the Clifton House, on the Canadian side—the American Fall being seen from this point to perhaps even better advantage, and the whole ensemble of the Falls better caught, than even in the view (9),

From Table Rock, higher up on the Canadian side, immediately at the verge and edge of the Horse-Shoe Fall, always a favorite with experienced visitors, and from which point the view in Church's great picture was taken. Descent

Under the Falls may be made, by those who have taste for that style of adventure—either by going down the Biddle Staircase, from Goat Island (under American Fall and to the *Cave of the Winds*), or the staircase at Table Rock (under Canadian Fall, to *Termination Rock*). Neither of these descents should be made, however, without due preparation of waterproof clothing (kept on hand at both points named), and the services of a capital guide.

Lunar Island, joined by a bridge to Goat Island on the right, should be visited, in sunlight to see the *Rainbow* of the Falls in greatest perfection and, in moonlight, if the time of visit so serves, in the chance of seeing that most wonderful of spectacles, the *Lunar rainbow*.

The *Sister Islands* (three) are now connected with Goat Island and with each other, by strong and handsome suspension-bridges; and no visitor to the Falls should fail to go out on each of them, for the unequalled view of the Upper Rapids thus to be obtained. That from the extreme outward one is perhaps the finest of all.

The *Whirlpool* and *Whirlpool Rapids*, three miles below the Falls, on the American side (elevator to descend to the river-side, at the latter), show some of the most terrible rushes of water in the world, and also the outlet, beyond, into the deep-banked river.

Other Spots to be profitably visited at and near the Falls, may be named

Grand Island, very large island, above (reached by ferry) notable as the spot where Major Mordecai M. Noah, of New York, some fifty years ago commenced to build what he believed to be the City of Restoration of the Jews. (Monument commemorative, still remaining);

Burning Spring, within a short walk above the Falls, on the Canada side, showing some rare phenomena in liquid combustion;

Lundy's Lane (Canada side—carriage), scene of the Battle of Chippewa (1812), with observatories and many stories of that battle;

Queenston and Lewiston, opposite towns on the Niagara River, seven or eight miles below the Falls; the former (Canada side) with a handsome monument to the English General Brock, who fell here in 1812. Prominent hotels at Niagara, the *International*, *Cataract* and *Park Place*, on the American side ; and the *Clifton*, on the Canada side.

[From Niagara (Suspension Bridge) through Canada, by Great Western Railway, to Detroit, Chicago, and the West (including California); or, Niagara to Buffalo, and West by the Lake Shore Railroad; or, by the Grand Trunk, to Toronto, Ottawa, Montreal, and other Canadian cities; or, rail to Kingston, and thence boat to and down the River St. Lawrence to Montreal, etc. [See Canadian routes.]

ROUTE NO. 2.—NORTHERN.

NEW YORK TO BUFFALO, NIAGARA FALLS AND CANADA, BY THE ERIE RAILWAY.

Leave New York (by morning train, for enjoyment of Delaware and Susquehanna scenery) by ferry from foot Chambers St., or foot 23d St., to *Long Dock* at Pavonia (New Jersey), midway between the towns of Hoboken and Jersey City—the immense range of wharf commanding admiration for the enterprize which has created the whole from tide-water and useless marsh; and its importance for a short time added to, as the site of the piers and houses of the White Star Line of Steamers to Liverpool, now removed.

From Long Dock, by rail, on the Erie Railway; the first point of interest after departure being the

Bergen Tunnel, through the West Bergen Hills, reached within a few moments after leaving the wharf, three-quarter mile in length, and considered a most costly and elaborate piece of engineering, until dwarfed by recent examples in the same line. Beyond, the first town of any importance passed through, is

PATERSON, New Jersey, capital of Passaic County, in that State; the town presenting many interesting features in manufactures and industry. Paper, cotton, silk and other fabrics are extensively produced; and iron and steel working have even more prominence. The Ivanhoe Paper Mills, here, are the most extensive in the country; Paterson foundries boast of being able to produce steamship-shafts and other heavy irons, of greater size than any others in America; and two of the most successful and notable of the establishments for the manufacture of locomotive engines, in the world, are located here—those of Grant, and of the Rogers Co., of whom the former won the great gold medal at the French Exposition of 1867, for the splendid locomotive "America." Within the boundaries of the town are also to be seen the

Passaic Falls, on the river of the same name—well worthy the tourist's attention, from the peculiar character of the chasm into which the river leaps, and the rock-scenery in the vicinity. Beyond Paterson, the scenery, which has so far been tame, roughens and becomes better worthy of notice, as the hills of Orange County begin to break into view; and thenceforth, for a long distance, it may be said that the Erie road is one of the most picturesque in America—a marvel of wild natural beauty in surroundings, as well as of enterprize in engineering. At

Suffern's Station [junction with the old road, now used for freight only, to Piermont, on the Hudson], commences the fine scenery of the

Ramapo Mountains, Gap and *Valley,* scene of many of General Washington's warlike operations; and the country around and beyond, entering Orange County, in the State of New York, equally celebrated for the wonderful richness of its dairy products—the noted *Orange County milk and butter.*

At *Sloatsburg,* stage may be taken to *Greenwood Lake,* a rural summer resort of much beauty and some popularity.

At *Greycourt* occurs the junction with another and now more important branch of the line—that to Newburgh, on the Hudson. Also, connection to favorite watering-place, Greenwood Lake. At

Goshen, connection with Montgomery and Walkill Valley Branch, for Kingston and Rondout. Soon after is reached

Middletown, largest town of Orange Co., with much industry, extensive iron-works, an academy, and a surrounding country at once fertile and picturesque. Beyond Middletown soon comes into view the magnificent scenery and bold engineering operations connected with the great

Shawangunk Mountain, the passage around which, by railway, was once deemed impossible. From this point, alternate rock cuttings of great depth and length, and magnificent views over the Neversink Valley and into the wild gorges of the Upper Delaware (river), of which the first comprehensive views are caught shortly before reaching

Port Jervis, a village picturesquely situated among the mountains, at the point of junction of three

States—New York, New Jersey and Pennsylvania, and once enjoying evil repute from the facility with which doubtful characters residing there could quickly change their State and thus baffle the officers of justice. It is now a place of limited summer resort and the end of the first or Eastern Division of the Erie road. [*Falls of the Sawkill*, fine cascades, six miles distant, by carriage or stage-coach.]

Beyond Port Jervis the tourist enjoys fine views of the Delaware and Hudson Canal, in full operation; and then comes the yet wilder scenery of the Upper Delaware, the road running in many places closely along its high rocky banks, and the engineering of the whole line at this section worthy of being remembered beside that of the Rhone Valley road among the heights of Jura, and that of the road through the Apennines between Bologna and Florence. At near *Shohola*, perhaps the finest and wildest portion of the railway scenery is passed; though the views approaching and leaving *Lackawaxen* should by no means be lost. Passing Mast Hope, Narrowsburg, Callicoon (the latter and indeed all the places lately named, great headquarters for trout-fishermen and mountain-sportsmen generally) and Hancock,

At *Deposit* (formerly dinner-station) farewell is bidden to Delaware River. Beyond this point the grade is somewhat heavy and the ascent slow, until the top of the ridge is reached, after which follows correspondingly rapid descent for a certain distance. Not long after commencement of the descent, is crossed the once celebrated

Cascade Bridge, with a single arch over a ravine nearly two hundred feet in depth (now changed to a high embankment); and here begin to be caught wonderful views over the lovely Valley of the Susquehanna and the fine River of that name. Very soon after is crossed the

Starucca Viaduct, a splendid stone structure some 1,200 feet in length and about 120 feet in height— considered one of the noblest railway bridges on the Continent, while the scenery from and around it is wondrously lovely and attractive. Still another high crossing is made over a fine wooden trestle bridge, at *Lanesborough;* and then is reached

Susquehanna, now dinner-station and the end of the second or Delaware division of the road, as well as noted for engine-work and other heavy manufactures. Only a few miles beyond is reached

Great Bend, another important railway station, and the point of intersection with this road, of the Delaware, Lackawanna and Western Road, from the Coal Regions of Pennsylvania. [Near Kirkwood, next station beyond, may be seen an old wooden house possessing a certain interest as the place of birth of the first Morman prophet, Joe Smith]. The next place of importance reached is

BINGHAMTON, handsomely situated at the junction of the Susquehanna and Chenango rivers, and deriving its name from an early settler, Mr. Bingham, ancestor on one side of the present noble English banking family, the Ashburton-Barings. Site of the *New York State Inebriate Asylum;* and a thriving and healthful town. [Connection with the New York Central Railroad, by the Syracuse and Binghamton road.] The next important station is

Owego, a large and handsome village, on creek of the same name, with Glenmary, old residence of N. P. Willis, near it. [Connection, northward, by rail, to

Ithaca, handsome town at the head (or south end), of Cayuga Lake, seat of Cornell University, and with much fine scenery in the neighborhood, among which may be noted no less than fifteen waterfalls, varying from 30 to 160 feet in height, and five of them of 100 feet or more. Very handsome excursions may be made on Cayuga Lake, from Ithaca; or branch rail pursued to Auburn and the New York Central road; or a charming drive taken across country to the head of Seneca Lake, Watkins, and Watkins Glen (see following).]

Pursuing route on Erie road, from Ithaca, some half dozen stations beyond is reached

ELMIRA, another chief town of Western New York, on the Chemung River, with handsome scenery, and much thrift and prosperity. [Connections, northward, directly with Niagara Falls, by the Northern Central road of Pennsylvania; southward, to Harrisburgh, Philadelphia, &c., by the same road; and northward by same road to

Watkins, pleasant village at the head of Seneca Lake, with fine outlook over it, and interesting excursions from it, by water or land; and to

WATKINS GLEN, only for a few years known to the body of travelers, but now with assured prominence as among the true wonders of the American Continent, and already attracting large numbers of visitors from all lands. It has some of the characteristics of both Trenton Falls and the Flume at the Franconia Notch of the White Mountains, with others especially its own. As technically described, the most notable feature is found in a deep ravine or chasm in the hills, through which a stream brawls and struggles in its way to the plain below. In some places the sides of the gorge are not more than twenty feet apart, and rise to a sheer height of two hundred feet. Again they widen, forming a vast amphitheatre four or five hundred feet apart and as many high, and a quarter of a mile in length, with a level floor on which the water spreads out in acres, with a depth of two or three inches. In another place, a steep staircase, almost perpendicular, crosses the ravine in the face of a lofty cascade, having a huge well at its base, of unknown depth, into which the water plunges with great noise and violence. Again, over another fall is formed a beautiful rainbow. Another place is filled with deep pools, and another has a sloping water-way of smoothly worn rock, down which the stream rushes with force literally overwhelming and irresistible.

Says a late writer, of coming out from the Glen:
"Directly below us is the village, with its straight avenues and streets and an abundance of shrubbery and trees. Stretching away for thirty miles in front is the Seneca, one of the most beautiful lakes in the world. Its width at its southern extremity is about one mile, and its length thirty-six. At some points the width is five or six miles. Some of the most noticeable features of this lake are its great depth—in places nearly a thousand feet; the entire absence of islands; the extreme coldness of its waters in summer, and the apparently contradictory fact that it *never freezes*, though located in a high latitude. The drives over the hills in every direction about Watkins are interesting in the extreme, and of endless variety. Geneva, one of the oldest and most aristocratic villages in Western New York, is at the foot of the lake, and can be reached by steamboat three times daily. Ithaca, the seat of Cornell University, is at the head of Cayuga Lake, and is twenty miles east of Watkins, over the hills." Hotels at the Glen and vicinity: the *Glen Park*, *Glen Mountain*, *Lake View*, *Fall Brook*, and *Jefferson*.

Pursuing main route on Erie road, at

Corning, also on the Chemung, occurs a connection with the coal-fields of Pennsylvania, by Corning and Blossburg road. Also, branch of Erie road runs northward direct to Rochester.

ROUTE NO. 2.—NORTHERN.

At *Hornellsville* the Erie Railway branches into two main lines, the one leading west, by

Salamanca [junction with the Atlantic and Great Western road, southwestward to Corry and the Oil Regions of Pennsylvania] and Dayton, to

DUNKIRK, on Lake Erie, terminus of the Erie Railway in that direction, and point of junction with the Lake Shore Railroad for Cleveland and Toledo (Ohio), Chicago, and other points west and northwest.

The second or northern branch of the Erie road, leaving Hornellsville, runs northwestward, by Nunda, *Portage* (with splendid bridge, of great height, and fine Fall of the Genesee, called *Portage Fall*), Warsaw and Attica, to

BUFFALO, on Lake Erie, largest town of Western New York, and one of the most important commercial depots of the Middle States. It only dates from the commencement of the century, owing much of its rapid early progress to the enterprising and unfortunate Benjamin Rathbun, who involved himself fatally in the attempt to make it the Queen of the Lakes. It is the point of entrance to the Erie Canal, from the Lake, and enjoys an immense grain and other shipping trade with the West, by steamers and large schooners. It has now not less than 40 large grain warehouses, with capacity for storing six to eight millions of bushels; has very large iron manufactures; has several public grounds —Terrace Park, Niagara, Delaware, Washington,

Franklin and other squares; has a University, Medical School, Orphan Asylum, Marine Hospital, &c.; and many of the public buildings, including the City Hall, Custom House, Post Office, State Arsenal, Market Houses and some of the Churches (the Roman Catholic Cathedral especially) are worthy the attention of even the temporary sojourner. Afternoon breezes from the Lake, facilities for water-excursions, proximity to the Canadian shore, &c., make Buffalo a charming place of abode during the hot season, though the atmosphere is often too damp for the health of invalids inclined to pulmonary trouble. Prominent Hotels, *Tifft House, Mansion House, Bonney House*, &c.

[Buffalo, by rail to Niagara Falls and Suspension Bridge, for Canada and the East, or for the West, (See close of previous route). Or, direct to Sarnia, Detroit, Chicago, &c., by the Grand Trunk Railway. Or, to Dunkirk and the Lake Shore road thence to the West. Or, by Lake steamer to Cleveland and other points westward.]

ROUTE NO. 3.—NORTHERN.

NEW YORK TO SARATOGA, LAKE GEORGE, LAKE CHAMPLAIN AND MONTREAL, WITH OPTION OF THE WHITE MOUNTAINS.

New York to Albany or Troy, as by Northern Route No. 1. Thence train on the Rensselaer and Saratoga Railroad along the Hudson and Mohawk Rivers, and with a view in passing of the *Falls of Cohoes*, on the latter, and also of the Erie Canal and of Round Lake—to

Ballston Spa, once the rival of Saratoga as a place of medicinal and fashionable resort, and still frequented by a considerable number of health-seekers, though the largest of the hotels, the *Sans Souci*, has long since been converted into a seminary, and the tide of summer travel has turned towards the more celebrated springs. Ballston has original advantages of location over Saratoga, the fine creek or small river, the Kayederosseras, flowing through it, and materially adding to pleasantness as an abode; and while as a watering-place it will never quite decay, it may some day see a return to its old popularity. From Ballston, half an hour, through very flat though well shaded country, to

SARATOGA (better known as "Saratoga Springs")—the most fashionable of the American Spas.

Division A.

AT AND ABOUT SARATOGA.

This most celebrated of summer resorts on the Western Continent, with the possible exception of Niagara—has few natural features to produce such continued celebrity, its situation being comparatively low, its soil sandy, and its climate decidedly hot in midsummer. But long care and much expense have made its grounds shaded and attractive; and the number and varied character of its springs have counterbalanced all opposition and given it a popularity not likely to lessen during the present century. During the past few years, speculation (not to call it by any worse name), has joined with liberal enterprize in providing extraordinary attractions, in the shape of

The Race-Course absorbing attention during a certain number of days of the season, and presenting some of the worst features of the English turf, in the way of high betting; and

The Play-House, in imitation of Baden-Baden and Hombourg, with the addition of being owned and managed by an Honorable M.C. Another and more meritorious feature is

The Leland Opera House, near and attached to the Union Hotel, and affording splendid opportunities for concerts, grand balls and other festivals, more pleasant to the sojourners than (it is to be feared) profitable to those providing the accommodation. Of course the principal source of popularity and profit has been found in

The Springs, of which the whole number must approach twenty, very different in character, while upon two or three of them has been concentrated, until lately, nearly the whole popularity giving patronage to the group. The waters of the *Congress* lead the list, now, instead of monopolizing as they once did: they are bottled extensively and sent everywhere, as well as consumed unlimitedly at the Spring. After them, of late, have come the *Empire,* pressing close upon the Congress as an article of commerce; and no small amount of popularity in the same line is being attained by those of the *High Rock* (held to be specially strong and medicinal), the *Hathorn,* the *Constitution,* &c.,—while the *Iodine,* the *Columbian* and others command extensive home-consumption. The virtual "Pump-Room" of Saratoga, meanwhile, has been and continues in the Congress Spring, most picturesquely located and best kept, and with fine grounds near to add to its attraction.

[Saratoga suffered very severely by fire in 1865 and 1866, two of the oldest and largest of the hotels, the United States and Congress Hall, almost as truly features of the place as the Springs themselves, and endeared by a thousand recollections as well as made classic by Willis' charming sketches, going down in those years. Both of them have since been rebuilt, however, with enlarged accommodation; the additions have been numerous; and though there have been supplementary fires among the hotels, in 1871 and 1874, there is no fear whatever of Saratoga permanently suffering from deficiency of hotel accommodation.

[The hint is worth something, to strangers—that the most delightful time for visiting Saratoga is to be found later than the full season—say in September and early October, when the climate is delicious, and when the loveliest sunsets of the world (finer than the Italian) can be enjoyed from the hills just northward.]

Excursions from Saratoga are not many or remarkably varied. The most popular is found in the afternoon ride to the *Lake*, three miles distant—a handsome forest-girded bit of water, with fine facilities for boating and fishing, and with Moon's and Abell's "Lake Houses" to supply entertainment to visitors. With this ride is often combined a visit to *Barhydt's Mill*, on the road—also made classic by Willis. Another excursion, generally made, is that to the *Battle Field of Stillwater*—scene of Sir John Burgoyne's surrender to Genl. Gates in 1777.

Prominent Hotels at Saratoga, *Grand Union, Congress Hall, United States, Clarendon,* &c.

Division B.

SARATOGA TO AND AT LAKE GEORGE.

The route from Saratoga is by cars of the Saratoga and Washington Railroad, to

Fort Edward, on the Hudson—site of one of the old fortifications of the French and Indian War period, but now a thriving village, with picturesque river-scenery. At Fort Edward branch rail is taken to

Glenn's Falls (often called simply " Glenn's "), a village also picturesquely situated on the Hudson, at a pass of the river through rocks of terrible wildness, with a broken fall, at and around which Cooper laid the scene of a part of the "Last of the Mohicans." Glenn's Falls has also large lime manufactures. Here stage is taken for Lake George, over a mountain road affording scenery of equal beauty and grandeur, forming fit introduction to the Lake. Half way between Glenn's and the Lake is passed

Bloody Pond, scene of the defeat of Col. Williams by the French and Indians under Baron Dieskau, and slaughter of all his force, in 1755, during the old French wars, and of which the name is said to have been derived from the literal filling of the pond with bodies on that occasion. Shortly after leaving Bloody Pond, and on emergence from the forest on high ground, is enjoyed one of the most magnificent views supplied by the Western Continent, in the beautiful "Horicon" (Indian name of Lake George) its islands and mountain borderings.

Caldwell, south end of the Lake, is the spot where the traveller is set down by the coach; and here and near are located some of the most enjoyable of the hotels welcoming visitors

Rowing, Sailing, and Fishing on Lake George are privileges not to be ignored: the more enjoyable for the wonderful clearness of the water, which often allows the bottom to be seen at twenty or thirty feet, and which won for it from the French the name of "Le Lac du St. Sacrament" and induced the carrying of the water to great distances for baptismal purposes. The variety of fish caught—trout, perch, pike, &c., commends it to the special favor of sportsmen. It is while on the water, too, that the beautiful panorama of the Lake, with its islands and encircling mountains, admitted to be among the finest on the globe, can best be enjoyed.

The Old Forts must command a certain degree of attention from the visitor to Lake George, combining, as they do, historical interest with their location. Of Fort William Henry, the small traces of embankment remaining lie immediately beside the Hotel of the same name, from in front of which the best views are commanded and the steamboat embarkations on the Lake are made. Of Fort George, half a mile eastward, considerable portions of the crumbling walls yet present themselves, half buried by earth and overgrown with trees. Leading hotels at Lake George, the *Lake House* and *Fort William Henry*.

[From Lake George may be visited, by stage-wagon or other conveyance, *Schroon Lake* a small wild, picturesque sheet of water, lying north-westward; and thence, the lower part of the

Adirondack Mountains, among the boldest and most interesting chains of the East, and of late years very popular as resorts for pleasure-seekers and health-seekers who have no objection to "camping-out" and "roughing" it a little. Particulars of special routes, best obtained of those who manage the conveyances; as all other information on such partially-opened lines, must be more or less unreliable and risky.]

Leaving Caldwell for the passage northward, a small steamer is taken; and the entire passage to Ticonderoga, about 35 miles, is one of the most charming in any land, affording otherwise unattainable views of the surrounding mountains and the almost countless islands of the little body of water so favored, the actual number of which is said to reach nearly or quite three hundred. Among the most notable of these in this part of the Lake, are *Diamond Island*, Burgoyne's military depot in 1777; *Long Island*, north of Diamond; *Twelve Mile Island*, near Bolton. Not far beyond the latter, *Tongue Mountain* thrusts itself out into the Lake to a great distance (whence the name), forming a part of the *Narrows*, entered just beyond, under the shadow of *Black Mountain*, the highest peak of the lake-shore. North of the Narrows comes *Sabbath Day Point*, a strip of low, cultivated land, so named, as alleged, by Genl. Abercrombie, from a Sunday morning embarkation of troops made there. Not far beyond, passing the bold headland of *Rogers'*

Slide, are passed *Prisoners' Island,* used as a place of military confinement by the English during the old French war; and *Lord Howe's Point,* where that English general landed to make his attack on Ticonderoga. Directly beyond comes an insignificant landing, at which concludes the beautiful sail on Lake George, and the tourist enjoys a three mile ride, often in a rough wagon instead of a stage-coach, over a rough road that still seems to be unobjectionable and in keeping with the journey, to the ruins of Ticonderoga.

Division C.

TICONDEROGA BY LAKE CHAMPLAIN TO MONTREAL.

Crossing from Lake George, by stage-coach or wagon, as above,

Fort Ticonderoga will be found only a ruin, with one gable remaining to show its original height. It was first constructed by the French, about 1756, but derives its principal interest from the peculiar mode of its summons to surrender by the madcap Vermonter, Ethan Allen, in 1775, the formula being: "In the name of the Continental Congress and the Great Jehovah!" It was soon retaken by the British, however, and held during the war. [From Ticonderoga detour may be made to *Crown Point,* another place of revolutionary interest, taken at nearly the same time; and thence may be reached most conveniently by wagon and on foot, *Lake Sanford, Lake Hender-*

son, and beyond the famous *Indian Pass* and the great peaks of the *Adirondack Mountains;* *Tahawus*, or *Mount Marcy, Mount McIntyre,* the *Dial Mountain,* etc.]

At the wharf at Ticonderoga, to continue main route northward, steamer on Lake Champlain is taken; and thenceforth, in fine weather, is found a sail of many hours, not often equaled in enjoyment. Besides the towns and hamlets studding the shores, there are special points of interest on the Lake in the shape of singular rocks and islands, of which the most notable, below, may be mentioned as *Split Rock,* an immense mass of ironstone, half an acre in extent, split away from the main only about twelve feet; the *Four Brothers,* small islands always haunted and half covered with noisy gulls, like Ailsa Craig; *Juniper Island* and *Rock Dundee,* both masses of rocks rising to the height of over 30 feet. It is not in these particulars, however, that lies the chief charm of sailing on noble Champlain (130 miles in length, and width varying from $\frac{1}{4}$ mile to 13: area covered, about 500 sq. miles). That principal charm lies in the presence of a noble range of mountains at either side: at the right, the *Green Mountains* of Vermont, among the highest in Eastern America; on the left, at greater distance, the equally noble range of the *Adirondacks.*

Landings are made, on the right, at

BURLINGTON, Vermont, one of the largest and most important towns in the State, with a University, many fine buildings, manufactures, and a great concentration of railway, steamboat and stage-coach routes. At Burlington are also enjoyed, as from the Lake approaching it, fine views of the two highest peaks of the Green Mountains, *Mt. Mansfield* and *Camel's Hump*. Hotels, the *American*, &c.

[At *Burlington*, rail may be taken, by those who prefer, by *St. Alban's* and *St. John's*, direct to Montreal. See Division D, following.]

Continuing from Burlington by boat, the Lake is crossed, north-westward, to

Plattsburg, thriving town of New York, lying on the west shore, and scene of the land-and-naval battle between the English and Americans, in September, 1814, won for the latter by General Macomb and Commodore McDonough. Hotel: *Fouquet's*.

[From *Plattsburg* may be visited

Keeseville, a thriving town of Essex County; and thence the *Au Sable River*, the *Saranac Lakes*, and the great fishing and pleasure grounds of the

NORTHERN ADIRONDACK MOUNTAINS. For either, and especially for the latter, stage is taken at Keeseville, and special routes traced out through particular information locally derived. For any extended advance into the mountains, however, certain provisions, conveniences and changes of clothing must be provided, after taking the special local advice above noted, and before leaving the towns on the shores of Lake Champlain, for the absolute wilderness lying behind them.]

Continuing from Plattsburg by boat, final landing is made at

Rouse's Point, also on the western shore of the Lake, and unimportant except for this transit and the fact that it lies at the very border of the Dominion of Canada.

From Rouse's Point, by rail, to *St. John's* and to MONTREAL. (For description, &c., see p. 247.)

Division D.

TICONDEROGA TO MONTREAL BY BOAT AND RAIL.

As by previous route (Division C) to

Burlington, Vermont. At Burlington leave Champlain boat and take rail of the Vermont Central road to

St. Alban's, Vermont, one of the handsomest towns in the State, lying near Lake Champlain, with fine scenery, many noble buildings, considerable popularity as a summer-resort, an immense butter-and-cheese market, and a historical celebrity on account of the "raid" made upon it, from Canada, on the 19th of October, 1864, by the Confederate refugees then resident in the Dominion. Principal hotel, the *Welden House.* [Railway connection from St. Alban's, by the Missisquoi road, to *Sheldon,* and the *Missisquoi Springs,* popular hygienic resort.]

From St. Alban's, by rail, by St. John's to MONTREAL. (See p. 247.)

Division E.

SARATOGA TO MONTREAL, BY RAIL.

Leave Saratoga by Saratoga and Washington road, (as by Division B,) to

WHITEHALL, New York, at the southern end of Lake Champlain—town of age, and much importance in connection with the lumber trade and the extensive transportation through the Champlain Canal, commencing at that point, from the Lake to Albany. [Point of departure of steamboats on Lake Champlain, for Northern New York, Vermont or New Hampshire Mountains, or Canada,—for those coming up directly from New York or other more southerly points, by Albany or Troy. See Divisions C and D, pp. 99 and 101.]

Continuing by rail from Whitehall, and entering the State of Vermont, through the great marble-quarry region of that State; by *Castleton*, virtual centre of that trade; to

RUTLAND, thriving and handsome town, with railway connections in all directions, pleasant location, and fine mountain-and-valley scenery, as well as much productive industry. Hotel, the *Bates House*.

From Rutland, by *Middlebury* and minor stations, to BURLINGTON (see that place in Division C, p. 99). Burlington, by *Vergennes* and minor stations, to ST. ALBAN'S (see that place in Division D, p. 101). St. Alban's to *St. John's* and MONTREAL. (See p. 247.)

ROUTE NO. 3.—NORTHERN. 102a

Division F.

FAVORITE TOURIST ROUTE FROM NEW YORK TO MONTREAL.

New York, by Central Rail Road, Day Boat or Night Boat, to *Albany* or *Troy* (see Route 1, Division A, page 62). Albany or Troy to *Saratoga, Lake George*, and take Champlain boat at *Ticonderoga*, as by Route 3, Divisions A, B and C, pp. 91 to 99. Or, Albany or Troy to *Saratoga* (omitting Lake George); thence rail to *Whitehall* and take Champlain steamer there. By boat on Lake Champlain to *Burlington*, and thence rail by St. Alban's and St. John's to MONTREAL; or by boat to Burlington, Plattsburg and *Rouse's Point*, and thence rail by St. John's to Montreal. (See p. 247.)

Division G.

EASTERN-STATES ALL-RAIL ROUTE FROM NEW YORK TO MONTREAL.

New York to *New Haven, Hartford* and SPRINGFIELD, as by Route No. 4, Division A, pp. 103 to 106. Springfield, by Connecticut River and connecting roads, to

Bellows Falls, railway-centre of importance on the Connecticut River, with connections eastward to BOSTON, &c. Thence to

White River Junction, another railway-centre with equally important connections, at the intersection of the Connecticut and White Rivers. Thence to *St. Alban's*, *St. John's* and MONTREAL. (See p. 247.)

Division H.

HINTS FOR RETURNING SOUTHWARD.

As stated in many other places in this volume, it is a matter of policy, always, in returning from one of two points to another, to vary the route from that selected in going, unless special reasons require passing over the same ground. And in no direction does this require more closely to be borne in mind, than, say, between New York and the Canadian cities; the routes being so many and all so interesting, that no choice supplying variety can well be amiss, if time or other circumstance does not prevent. The reminder need scarcely be added, that, all the preceding routes being marked out as *going northward*, for proceeding southward any one of them needs simply to be reversed.

ROUTE NO. 4.—EASTERN.

NEW YORK TO BOSTON, BY NEW HAVEN, HARTFORD, AND SPRINGFIELD (RAIL); BY PROVIDENCE (RAIL); BY NEWPORT, NEW LONDON OR STONINGTON (SOUND-BOAT).

Division A.

BY RAIL, BY SPRINGFIELD.

Leave New York by morning express of New Haven Railroad, by *William's Bridge* (point of divergence of the New York and Harlem road), by several unimportant stations (with occasional and pleasant views of Long Island Sound, at the right), to *Stamford, Darien* and *Norwalk* (Connecticut), (the latter the scene of a serious accident, train running into the River, at the Bridge, many years since); then by other unimportant stations, to

Bridgeport, on Long Island Sound, large and important manufacturing town, especially in the detail of Sewing Machines, of which two of the largest factories in the world, the Wheeler & Wilson, and Howe, are located here. Also, point of intersection of lines of railway leading to the manufacturing interior of Connecticut (Housatonic and Naugatuck); and old residence of the celebrated showman, P. T. Barnum. Bridgeport to

NEW HAVEN, also on Long Island Sound (lines of steamers to and from New York); one of the most important towns of the East, and seat of *Yale College*, as well as noted for the shaded beauty of its streets and the peculiar magnificence of its elm-tree avenues, the latter feature giving it the name of the "Elm City." New Haven is well worthy of a sojourn for examination. The first point of interest is of course to be found in the *College Buildings*, of which there are some fifteen, with a remarkable air of antiquity, for America (the College founded in 1700); the *College Green*, or *Campus*, with *Chapel*, and fine old *Churches;* the *State House*, an imposing edifice, of marble, recently completed; the *Fine Art Building* and *Trumbull Gallery*, in the latter of which are the original fine historical pictures by Colonel Trumbull (Washington, etc.); the recently built *City Hall*, etc. Some interesting Monuments are to be found in the *Grove Street Cemetery;* among others those of Roger Sherman, founder of Rhode Island, Noah Webster, Pierrepont Edwards, the poet Hillhouse, etc.; and in the Campus, tomb of the regicide Whalley. Excursions from New Haven to *East Rock, Savin Rock, Wallingford*, &c. [Connection, by rail, to

MIDDLETOWN, flourishing town, with manufactures, seat of *Wesleyan University, Industrial School, State Insane Asylum, Berkeley Divinity School,* &c. Opposite Middletown, *Portland*, with great brown-stone quarries.]

ROUTE NO. 4.—EASTERN. 105

Prominent hotels at New Haven, the *New Haven House, Tontine, Tremont,* &c.

Resuming rail, on the New Haven, Hartford and Springfield road, and now running northward, away from the Sound—passing *Wallingford, Meriden* (great Brittaniaware and other metallic manufactory) and other stations of less importance, is reached

HARTFORD, on the Connecticut River, a large town with much beauty of location, large manufacturing interests, and lately selected as the sole seat of government of the State. (Reached by steamers from New York). It has an educational institution of eminence, known as *Trinity College;* the *Connecticut Historical Society;* the *Watkinson Libary,* with rare books, pictures and statuary; *Wadsworth Atheneum,* etc.; and among the handsome buildings of the town are the *Deaf and Dumb Asylum, Retreat for the Insane, Hospital,* etc. The *Charter Oak* (place of hiding of the old Connecticut Charter from a tyrannical Governor) long one of the boasts of Hartford, blew down in 1856; but the place where it stood is still shown by a slab. Among present curiosities are the late *Col. Colt's Fire-Arms Manufactory,* the house occupied by the late Mrs. Sigourney, the poetess, etc. There are also many picturesque short excursions from Hartford, the most prominent among them being those to *Talcott Mountain, Wethersfield, Prospect Hill,* &c. Leading hotels, *Allyn House* and *United States.*

Beyond Hartford, pasing *Windsor,* and *Windsor*

Locks (water power and important manufactures), and other minor stations, is reached

SPRINGFIELD, Massachusetts, also lying on the Connecticut River, one of the most important towns of the State, and peculiarly notable for its diversity of railway communication. [Connection, here, eastward to Boston and westward to Albany, by the Boston and Albany road; southward to Hartford, New Haven and New York, by the New Haven, Hartford and Springfield; northward to the White Mountains of New Hampshire, to Vermont and Canada, by the Connecticut River and other intersecting roads]. A prominent source of prosperity as well as object of interest is the *United States Arsenal and Arms Manufactory*, the largest in America, located here, furnishing extensive employment and supplying the celebrated "Springfield Rifle." (Written of by Mr. Longfellow, in one of his finest poems, "The Arsenal at Springfield.") It has also other and important manufactures—especially of carriages; handsome public grounds, in the *Cemetery, Hampden Park*, &c.; and is considered one of the most charming places of residence in the East. Prominent hotels, the *Massasoit, Cooley's*, &c.

From Springfield, by *Palmer*, direct to

WORCESTER, another of the large and important towns of Massachusetts, with extensive manufactures and even more numerous railway connections than Springfield. [Westward, by Boston and Albany road (Western) to Springfield and Albany, and Spring-

ROUTE NO. 4.—EASTERN. 107

field, New Haven and New York. Eastward, by Boston and Worcester, to Boston. Northward, by Worcester and Nashua, to the White Mountains and Canada. Southward, by Norwich and Worcester, to New London, and Shore Line road and line of steamers to New York. South-eastward, by Worcester and Providence, to Providence, Newport, &c.] It has some fine public buildings, among which may be mentioned the *State Lunatic Asylum, Mechanics' Hall,* building of the *American Antiquarian Society,* &c., and divides with Springfield pre-eminence in the manufacture of railway and other carriages. Leading hotel, the *Bay State.*

From Worcester, by *Grafton, Framingham, Natick* (home of U. S. Senator Wilson) *West Newton, Brighton* and other minor stations, direct to

BOSTON. [See ahead—"At and about Boston."]

Division B.

BY RAIL, BY PROVIDENCE (SHORE LINE).

Leave New York by 12.15 P. M. express of the New Haven Railroad. (May leave by night-express, but at sacrifice of scenery). Take tickets by "Shore Line," as distinguished from those by "Springfield;" and be sure that Shore Line carriage is taken. To *New Haven,* as from Springfield route preceding.

From New Haven, due east (New Haven, New London, and Stonington road) along or near the shore of the Sound, with closer and still finer views than those before reaching New Haven—by Guilford, Madison, Clinton &c., to

Crossing of the Connecticut River, at *Lyme*. (At *Saybrook Junction*, near, connection by Valley road, south to *Saybrook*, north to *Middletown*, &c.) By S. Lyme, and E. Lyme, Waterford, &c., to

NEW LONDON, at the mouth of the Thames River —a sea-port of some importance, and formerly depot of one of the great whaling-fleets, before the late decay of that trade. [Line of large and fine steamers from and to New York, every evening: communicating by rail to and from Boston, by Norwich and Worcester.] Harbor considered one of the finest on the Atlantic coast, and defended by splendid fortifications, *Fort Trumbull* being the principal, below the city and at the right, towards mouth of the harbor. New London, an attractive place of resort and residence in many respects, has a peculiar and melancholy interest as having been long the business place of Benedict Arnold, the traitor, whose sign over one of the old shops is still pointed out. The principal public buildings, worth notice, are the *Custom House, Court House, Female Academy*, &c. At the mouth of the harbor the *Pequot House* is a very attractive place of summer sea-side resort.

From New London the Thames is crossed by ferry boat (part of train carried over, with through-passengers, and lunch on boat) to *Groton*, on the opposite bank—for some years the depot of another steamboat line between New York and Boston, now

ROUTE NO. 4.—EASTERN. 109

abandoned. Groton, by rail, still within frequent sight of the Sound, to *Mystic*, somewhat famous for wooden-ship building, and

Stonington, Connecticut, Sound port of some importance, lying at the mouth of river of same name. [Line of large steamers to and from New York, every evening: communicating by rail to and from Boston, by Providence.] Stonington, by Westerly and other stations, including

Wickford [railroad and steamboat communication direct to NEWPORT, in connection with trains]; and

East Greenwich [old steamboat route to NEWPORT in connection with trains]—to

PROVIDENCE, capital of the State of Rhode Island, and one of the principal towns of the Eastern States. It lies on Providence River, extending from Narragansett Bay; has much beauty in location and enormous wealth in buildings and the appointments of residents; manufactures very extensively, in engines, heavy machineries, cottons, prints, jewelries, &c.; and has nearly two hundred and fifty years of antiquity since its foundation by Roger Williams, when driven from the colony of Massachusetts Bay on account of his religious opinions. It is the seat of *Brown University*, a literary institution of the first eminence, with a large and valuable library; and is also noted for the number and excellence of its public schools. The two handsomest public buildings in the town are the *Rhode Island Hospital* and the *Custom House;* though there are very many fine edifices connected with the numerous public charities of the city, among which may be named the *Reform School*, the *Dexter Asylum for the Poor, Butler Hospital for the Insane, Home for Aged Women*, &c. It has also several imposing churches, banks and other edifices; and *Swan Point Cemetery, Narragansett Park*, and other public grounds deserve visit and notice. The *Soldiers' and Sailors' Monument*, recently erected, is also worthy of notice. Leading hotels, the *City Hotel*, and *Aldrich House*.

[Railway communication with Boston, by Boston and Providence road; with Worcester, by Providence and Worcester; with Hartford, by Hartford, Providence & Fishkill; with Newport, by Providence and Newport; with New London, by Stonington and Providence, &c.; with New York, by road just traversed, and by lines of steamers from Fall River and Newport, &c.],

[*Pawtucket*, near Providence, is the seat of heavy manufactures, and of the first cotton-mill ever built in America.]

Providence, by Pawtucket, Attleboro, Mansfield, Foxboro, Readville, &c., to

BOSTON.

Division C.

BY BOAT, BY NEWPORT OR FALL RIVER.

Leave New York, 5 P. M., daily (except late autumn, winter, and early spring, when the hour is 4 P. M.—see bills at hotels) by boats of the Narragansett Steamship Company, by Long Island Sound, for Newport or Fall River as may be preferred. This route, as well as the other Sound routes about to be named, affords not only a delightful sail, in the customary fine weather of summer, but conveys a better idea than can otherwise be attained, of the size and magnificence of the vessels employed in this transit. Leaving the pier and proceeding past the whole line of the city, then past the islands lying in the Sound or East River, and up the Sound itself,—unequalled opportunities are enjoyed for observing the water-front of the city, the extent of the penal and benevolent institutions on *Blackwell's Island, Randall's Island, Ward's Island,* &c., the rocky dangers of *Hell Gate,* the attractive scenery of the river shores (Long Island on the right; New York or Manhattan Island on the left); the extensive fortifications guarding that approach to the city, in *Fort Schuyler,* at Throg's Neck, etc.—daylight lasting, in the warm season, until all these points of interest are passed, and the remainder of the course up the Sound offering few attractions other than those of a marine character.

At an early hour in the morning is reached the end of the route by Sound, and place of debarkation for those who wish to vist the watering-place and afterwards proceed thence to Boston by rail,—in

NEWPORT, one of the largest and most important towns of Rhode Island, and one of the most celebrated and fashionable of American sea-side resorts, for the past quarter of a century or longer. It lies on Narragansett Bay, at near the entrance from Long Island Sound, and boasts a harbor of peculiar beauty as well as one of a depth of water almost unequalled. It has a fine bathing-beach, markedly safe, within short-riding-distance of the principal hotels; and at greater distance are to be found and visited the remarkable groups of rocks known as *Paradise, Purgatory,* the *Hanging Rocks,* etc. The *Glen,* the *Spouting Horn, Lily Pond* and the *Dumpling Rocks,* are also places of much picturesque interest to visitors and residents; while at some ten miles distant, south-eastward, lie *Seconnet Point* and *West Island,* the latter supplying the very best sea-shore-fishing on the American coast. *Fort Adams,* at near the mouth of the harbor, is one of the largest and strongest fortifications in the North; and the ride to it, from the town, is one of the afternoon features of Newport life. Another peculiarity of Newport is the fine sailing in and about the harbor, securing the constant presence of yachts, and many regattas during the season, on a more or less extensive scale. And yet another is to be found in the wide extent of lawned and terraced bluff, overlooking the sea, where are located an immense number of summer-cottages of the wealthy, giving a higher tone to the prevalent hotel-life, even while moderating and to some degree lessening it. One marked object of interest is to be found at Newport—the *Round Tower,* alternately called a Norse remain and a wind-mill, but around which Longfellow, adopting the former belief, wove his marvellously beautiful poem, the "Skeleton in Armor." There are also some patriotic erections and antiquities of interest: among the structures the old *State House*, *Commodore Perry's House*, the *Vernon Mansion*, the *First Baptist Church* (1638), the *Perry Monument*, &c.; and of minor antiquities, *Franklin's Printing Press* (now or late in the office of the *Newport Mercury* newspaper), the ancient *Chair of State* of the Colony, etc. Of modern buildings of merit, the number is considerable. Newport has the additional celebrity of having been the birth-place of Gilbert Stuart, the painter, Malbone, the miniature-painter, and Commodore Perry; and Cooper flung round it a romantic interest as the opening scene of the "Red Rover." Leading Hotels: the *Ocean House*, *Atlantic*, *United States*, and *Perry*.

[Above Newport, within convenient riding or sailing distance, lies the fine eminence of *Mount Hope*, with interesting reminiscences of the Indian King Philip, and splendid views over Narragansett Bay, the city, harbor, &c.]

[Newport to BOSTON, by rail, by Fall River and connection with the Old Colony road, or by Providence.]

If not wishing to stop at Newport, and still proceeding to Boston, on some New York steamer from which debarkation has before been supposed, the route will be pursued by remaining on boat until its next and final landing, at

FALL RIVER, a thriving manufacturing town on Taunton River, eastern branch of Narragansett Bay, within the State of Massachusetts though near the Rhode Island border. Peculiarly noted for works in machinery, in heavy irons, and in cottons and prints. [Communication with Newport and Providence by boat and rail.] *Mount Hope*, before alluded to, is in view from Fall River and may be most conveniently reached from this point; and the bridge connecting Rhode Island (island) and the main land is near, at *Tiverton*.

Fall River to BOSTON, by rail of the Old Colony Road.

Division D.

BY BOAT, BY NEW LONDON, NORWICH & WORCESTER.

Leave New York, 5 P. M., by boats of the Norwich and Worcester Line, on the Sound, the route displaying precisely the same features as that before named, (except that the run by sea is shorter and less exposed in rough weather, and that rail is taken at an earlier hour) to

NEW LONDON [see previous description.]

New London, by rail on the Norwich and Worcester road, to

NORWICH, very old and handsome small town of Connecticut, picturesquely situated at the head of navigation of the river Thames, with its steep streets

ROUTE NO. 4.—EASTERN. 115

literally lying on terraces, but many manufactures, much commercial prosperity, and no small number of old buildings recalling the early historic days of the State.

From Norwich, still by rail of the Norwich and Worcester road—by *Plainfield* [junction, for Providence, Newport, &c.], by Putnam, Webster, WORCESTER, &c., to BOSTON.

Division E.

BY BOAT, BY STONINGTON AND PROVIDENCE.

Leave New York, 5 P. M., by boats of the Stonington Steamboat Company, on the Sound, with same features as those of two previous routes, though less extensive in sea-voyage than that to Newport, and longer than that to New London—to

STONINGTON, Connecticut (before referred to in Shore-Line route by rail), at mouth of Stonington river, near the Sound,

Stonington by *Providence*, by rail, with same features shown in that division of the Shore-Line rail route, to BOSTON.

Division F.

AT AND ABOUT BOSTON, WITH EXCURSIONS.

BOSTON, Capital of the State of Massachusetts, one of the largest, most influential and handsomest of the cities of America, and in many regards the most remarkable of all—lies at the extreme western point of Massachusetts Bay, where that body of water is entered by the Charles River; and most of the old city is erected on a peninsula of several hundred acres, extending up from *Roxbury*, at the south, and curved around by the wide mouth of the Charles River, which thus divides from it *Cambridge* on the west, *Charlestown* on the north, and *Chelsea* and *East Boston* on the east. All these form parts of the present city, however, by means of different bridges spanning the river mouth and edge of the harbor; and the result is that Boston seems from some points of view to be almost as completely a "City of the Sea" as Venice. Northeast of it, at some miles distance, the bold headland of *Nahant* runs southward from the mainland at *Lynn*, behind Chelsea point, adding to the picturesqueness of the whole harbor, as well as aiding the several islands (*Castle Island*, fortified by Fort Independence; *Governor's Island*, Fort Winthrop; *George's Island*, Fort Warren; *Deer Island*, occupied by House of Industry and other public buildings; and others, minor in size and importance) in sheltering it from the rough winds of the east. An additional feature of the old city, or "Boston Proper," is found in three eminences or slight hills on and among which it was originally built, giving it the name of the "Tri-Montane City," and originating the name of "Tremont" so intimately connected with it. On the highest of these stands the *State House*, the whole city appearing to slope up to it, and the view, on approach, being thus rendered peculiarly impressive.

With reference to transit through and about Boston, it may be said that many of the streets, especially in the older portions of the town, are crooked and involved to a proverb, but that the street-car system is very extensive, complete and convenient, and that carriage-hire, though high in comparison to European, is less exorbitant than in New York.

Of Streets, the best worth noting are *Beacon Street*, at the top of the Common, the most fashionable; *Tremont Street*, at the bottom of the Common, blending of fashion and business; *Washington St.*, nearly parallel with the latter, southward, business centre; *State, Congress,* and other streets in the neighborhood of the Old State House, financial, law, etc. Other and newer streets and avenues, lying on the Back Bay, west of the Public Garden, are now, however, fashionable; and here have been erected the Coliseums for the two great Musical Jubilees.

Of Public Grounds, Boston has two, within the city proper, of peculiar prominence: the *Common*, a triangular park of nearly fifty acres, sloping down from the State House, handsomely shaded, with a Pond or Lake, and in an enclosure near the middle, the celebrated *Old Elm* called the "Liberty Tree;" and the *Public Garden*, adjoining the Common on the West, with a handsome Lake, bridges, floral walks, and a fine statue of Washington, by Ball.

Of **Antiquities**, principally connected with the

War of the Revolution, Boston has many of interest: *Faneuil Hall*, Faneuil Hall Square, otherwise known as the "Cradle of Liberty," where early meetings of patriots were held (still used for meeting purposes, and containing some national portraits); the *Old State House*, State Street; *Brattle Street Church*, Brattle Street (with one of the round shot of the Charlestown bombardment still embedded in the front wall;) *Old South Church*, corner of Washington and Milk Streets; *Ordway Hall*, Province House Court, once the residence of the Colonial Governors; *Liberty Tree*, Boston Common; and many others of minor consequence.

Of Public Buildings, deserving attention, are the *State House* (Capitol), Beacon Street, with interesting military and other memorials, legislative chambers, etc., within, and splendid and extensive view from the roof; *Custom House*, foot of State Street; *Exchange*, State Street (Post Office below); *Court House*, Court Square; *City Hall*, School Street (colossal statue of Franklin, in front); *Massachusetts General Hospital*, Allen Street; *City Hospital*, Harrison Avenue; *Quincy Market*, adjoining Faneuil Hall; *Boston Public Library*, Boylston Street; *Masonic Temple*, corner Tremont and Boylston Streets, etc. Other erections of interest, the *Boston Water Works* (Reservoir), Derne Street; the *Bridges*, connecting the various suburbs with the city proper; the *Wharves* (Long, India, Central, Commercial, etc.), several of them of great extent and the system the best on the Continent.

ROUTE NO. 4.--EASTERN. 119

Of Monuments, of course, the first place is taken by the *Bunker Hill Monument*, on Breed's Hill, site of the Revolutionary battle of the first name. It is a plain obelisk of granite, of great height, ascended from within, and from the top commanding a most extensive and magnificent view. Near it stands the *Warren Statue*, in honor of Dr. Joseph Warren, who fell in the battle. In State House, statue of *Washington*, by Chantrey; and in front of same building, bronze statues of *Daniel Webster* and *Horace Mann* (great Massachusetts organizer of education). In front of City Hall, colossal *Franklin*, before noticed. In Public Garden, equestrian *Washington*, by Thos. Ball, also before noticed.

Churches of prominence: *St. Paul's* (Episcopal), Tremont Street; *Christ Church* (date 1722), Salem Street; *Old South* (date 1730), Washington and Milk Streets; *Brattle Street* (Unitarian—date 1773), Brattle Street; *King's Chapel* (Unitarian—date 1750), Tremont and School Streets; *Park Street* (Congregational, with finest spire in the city), Park Street, facing Tremont; *Central* (Congregational: considered the handsomest in the City), Berkeley and Newbury Streets; *Trinity* (Episcopal—date 1735), Summer and Hawley Streets; *Tremont Temple* (general devotional) Tremont Street; *Immaculate Conception* (Roman Catholic), Harrison Avenue, &c., &c.

In Libraries and Literary Institutions Boston is peculiarly rich, the intellectual and educational status of the City being especially enviable. Among the more notable libraries may be mentioned the *Boston Public Library;* the *Athenæum,* (with gallery of paintings and sculpture); the *Mercantile; American Academy of Arts and Sciences; Natural History Society; Massachusetts Historical Society; State, Law, General Theological,* and others.

Commercial Buildings of much merit in architecture abound in Boston; though many of the finest on *Franklin, Devonshire, Summer, Washington, Congress,* and other streets, were destroyed in the great fire of November, 9-10th, 1872—the largest ever occurring in America, after that of Chicago, and involving the loss of $70,000,000. Boston has wonderful powers of recuperation, and great intrinsic resources, however; and already displays all its former magnificence, with many improvements.

Principal Theatres, etc. the *Boston Theatre* (opera-house, at intervals), Washington Street; *Globe Theatre* (late Selwyn's), Washington Street; *Boston Museum,* Tremont Street; *Howard Athenæum,* Howard Street; *Music Hall,* Winter Street, near Tremont (with organ of immense size and power, second in the world), etc. Prominent Hotel Buildings (also Hotels): the *American,* Hanover Street; *Parker,* School Street; *St. James,* Newton Street; *United States,* Beach Street; *Tremont,* Tremont Street; *Revere,* Bowdoin Square, etc.

Excursions from the City, on foot, by horse-car, or carriage, include those to HARVARD UNIVERSITY, Cambridge, with 15 buildings, an Anatomical Museum, an Observatory, and the first educational rank in the Western World; to the *Washington Head Quarters* (now residence of Professor Longfellow, the poet,) also at Cambridge, with Tree, under which Washington took command of the American forces; to *Mount Auburn Cemetery,* four miles from the city, with Tower, commanding excellent view; Chapel, containing stained windows, busts of Adams, Winthrop, Story, &c.; and Spurzheim, Bowditch, and other handsome and attractive monuments in the grounds; to *Forest Hill* and *Mount Hope Cemeteries,* Roxbury; to *Woodlawn Cemetery,* near Chelsea; to *Cochituate Lake,* whence the water-supply for Boston is drawn; to *Wenham Lake,* whence is derived most of the American ice-supply for Europe; to *Fresh Pond,* a place of summer resort near Mount Auburn, etc. Those by boat or carriage will include *Nahant,* bold headland on the east of the harbor, once a fashionable watering-place, and always cool, attractive and pleasant; *Lynn,* near Nahant, famous as the head of the shoe-manufacture of the world; *Chelsea Beach, Swampscott* and *Phillips' Beach,* northward of Nahant; *Nantasket Beach,* south side of the harbor, etc.

From Boston, also, may be conveniently reached [by Boston and Lowell railroad],

LOWELL, large and thriving town on the Merrimac River, at its junction with the Concord. It is the largest of the American manufacturing towns, and considered the Manchester of the Western

World, not less than 50 to 60 large mills being employed in the manufacture of cottons, prints, woollens, etc., and the operative labor reaching to the number of from 14,000 to 15,000, a large majority females, of rare intelligence for their class. The *Pawtucket Falls*, near the city, furnish the water-power for all the *Mills*, many of which, with the Falls themselves and some of the principal buildings and public grounds of the town, are worth examination. Leading Hotels: the *Merrimac, Washington*, and *American.* [Rail connection to Groton for all points westward; to *Nashua*, for points northward; to *Lawrence*, eastward, etc.]

May also be conveniently reached from Boston, south-eastward, [Old Colony road],

PLYMOUTH ("Plymouth Rock"), place of landing of the Pilgrim Fathers, with *Pilgrims' Hall* and many interesting relics of the early settlement; and

NEW BEDFORD, on Vineyard Sound, at the head of what remains of the whaling business, and a seaport of picturesque location and prominence; or [by same and Cape Cod railroad],

Cape Cod, Yarmouth, Hyannis, and all that wild and desolate but interesting section of the Atlantic coast.

May also be conveniently reached from Boston, (by Eastern railway, by Somerville, South Malden, Chelsea, Lynn and Swampscott),

SALEM, very old town and port on the coast, with a certain celebrity on account of the witch-burnings and other events of Colonial times, and very picturesque in location and many of its buildings; but much more notable, now, as at one time the residence of Nathaniel Hawthorne and scene of his "House of the Seven Gables" and other stories. Also (by Fitchburg Railway),

Concord, on the Concord branch of the Merrimac River, noted for beauty of scenery in the neighborhood, and in connection with the literary labors of Henry D. Thoreau, Hawthorne, and others.

Also may be visited by rail from Boston to Wood's Hole, and boat; or from Fall River (New York boat); or by steamer from New Bedford,

Martha's Vineyard, island off the coast, spot selected every year in August for the great annual Camp-Meeting of the Methodist denomination, and now becoming a place of popular resort for bathing and sea-shore residence, with hotels. (May also be reached, direct from New York, by steamer for Portland).

ROUTE NO. 5.—EASTERN.

BOSTON TO PORTLAND, QUEBEC AND MONTREAL, BY BOSTON AND MAINE, EASTERN, AND GRAND TRUNK ROADS.

Division A.

BOSTON TO AND AT PORTLAND, BY BOSTON AND MAINE ROAD.

Leave Boston by rail on the Boston and Maine railroad, by Medford, Melrose, *South Reading Junction* [connection for North Danvers, Georgetown and *Newburyport*], Reading, *Wilmington Junction* [connection for LOWELL], and minor stations, to

LAWRENCE, large manufacturing town of the State of Massachusetts, with heavy specialty of cotton and prints, lying on the Merrimac River, whence, by means of a dam, the important water-power is derived. Some of the mills are of immense size and capacity, employing operators to the number of thousands. Has a *Common*, a *City Hall*, and other buildings worth notice; and an *Operative Library* forming a special feature. [Railway connection with LOWELL, and thence with *Nashua* and the North, with Boston and the South, &c.; also Northwest with Manchester, Concord, &c.]

Lawrence by N. Andover, *Bradford* [connection for Georgetown and *Newburyport*], *Haverhill* (with fine long Bridge over the Merrimac to Bradford, and

ROUTE NO. 5.—EASTERN.

some educational institutions of prominence), Atkinson, Newton, &c., to

EXETER, New Hampshire, lying on Exeter River, and a place of importance in coasting commerce and manufactures; thence by S. Newmarket to

Newmarket Junction [connection west to *Concord* and the Franconia Range of the White Mountains; and east to

PORTSMOUTH, New Hampshire, on the Piscataqua River, second city of the State in importance, with a large and very fine harbor; a *United States Navy Yard;* and a connection, by bridge, with *Kittery*, Maine, also an important naval station. From Portsmouth can be reached *Rye Beach* and *Hampton Beach*, attractive bathing-places on the New Hampshire coast, and the *Isles of Shoals*, off the coast, celebrated fishing and summer resorts.]

Pursuing the main line, Newmarket Junction, by Newmarket, Durham, &c. (within sight of the broad Piscataqua) to

Dover, New Hampshire, thriving town on the Piscataqua. [Connection, west, for Alton Bay, Lake Winnepesaukie, and the White Mountains.]

Dover, by *Salmon Falls* [connection for Great Falls, Rochester, and to *Alton Bay*, &c.]; by *South Berwick Junction* [connection eastward for *Kittery* and *Portsmouth*]; by Wells, Kennebunk, Biddeford, *Saco* (large manufacturing village on the Saco River, with extensive water-power and very handsome Laurel Hill Cemetery), West Scarboro, Cape Elizabeth, and minor stations, to

PORTLAND, commercial metropolis of the State of Maine, and one of the most important cities of the East, lying on a peninsula at the Southwest of Casco Bay, with a very handsome and convenient location and one of the deepest and best harbors on the Atlantic coast. The harbor has many fine islands, and is defended by *Fort Preble* and other extensive fortications. A great fire, in 1866, destroyed a large portion of the city, but the marks are now only visible in the increased beauty of the well-laid-out and handsomely-shaded city. From the *Observatory*, overlooking the harbor, fine views can be caught over the sea and coast, and over the distant country, West to the White Mountains. The most extensive thoroughfare is *Congress street*, which runs the whole distance of the peninsula. Among the most notable buildings are the *City Hall, Court House, Marine Hospital*, and some of the churches, manufacturing and commercial structures. The *Atheneum* and *Mercantile Library* have fine libraries; and the *Natural History Society* possesses an excellent cabinet of varied character. Excursions from Portland include the *Islands in the Bay; Cape Elizabeth*, a favorite bathing and fishing resort on south side of tne Bay; *Sebago Pond;* and many of minor interest. Prominent Hotels at Portland: the *Falmouth, Preble, &c.*

[The *Allan Lines of steamships* between Liverpool and Glasgow, and Halifax, Quebec and Montreal, make Portland an important depot at all seasons and the port and end of sea-route in the winter season.]

[Railway connection from Portland southward, by route just traversed; to Montreal and Quebec, by Grand Trunk (see route following); to *Augusta, Bangor*, Moosehead Lake, &c., by the Maine Central; to Lake Winnepesaukie and the White Mountains, by the North New Hampshire, &c.]

Division B.

BOSTON TO PORTLAND, BY EASTERN RAILROAD.

Leave Boston by rail on the Eastern Railroad, by

LYNN, important manufacturing town, on the upper side of Boston Harbor, with specialty of the most extensive shoe-manufacturing in the world; by

SALEM, old town and port on the coast, with an important history in colonial times, and interesting reminiscences of Hawthorne (see p. 122); by

Beverly, celebrated as the home of the peculiar New England dish, "baked-beans" (connections eastward to Gloucester and Cape Ann); by *Ipswich;* by

NEWBURYPORT, town and coasting-seaport of prominence, lying at the mouth of the Merrimac River, with a fine harbor and much beauty in location and surroundings, and by many considered one of the handsomest towns in Massachusetts. Hotel, the *Merrimac House*. [Connection west for Bradford, *Lowell*, &c.]

Newburyport to

Salisbury, small town of age and past importance, and with a mingled celebrity as the place where many considerable events in colonial history occurred, of which, and past residents, many interesting monuments remain in the neighborhood—as also as the birthplace of the mother of Daniel Webster, as that of Caleb Cushing, &c. [Connection westward is made from Salisbury to *Amesbury*, pilgrimage of no secondary importance as the home of one of the first of American poets, JOHN G. WHITTIER.]

Salisbury to

PORTSMOUTH, leading seaport and naval dépôt, belonging to the State of New Hampshire, and the only marine port of the State; lying at the mouth of the Piscataqua River, with fine harbor, United States Navy Yard, costly dry-docks, and all appurtenances of such a station; also with some interesting churches, many fine buildings (some very old—among others the Langdon residence), tomb of Sir William Pepperell, well shaded streets, and much celebrity as a place of summer resort, of itself and as a place of departure for *Rye Beach*, *Hampton Beach*, the *Isles of Shoals*, and other hot-weather habitats. (See p. 125.) Hotels, the *Philbrick, Rockingham, City*, &c.

Across the Piscataqua lies the town of

Kittery, Maine, virtually a part of Portsmouth,

ROUTE NO. 5—EASTERN. 128a

though in another State, and forming also a part of the naval station.

Portsmouth to
Conway Junction (connection westward for Conway and the White Mountains). To
South Berwick Junction. [Connection with the Boston and Maine road, from the southward—identical with this route thence by *Kennebunk*, *Biddeford* and *Saco* to PORTLAND.] (See p. 126.)

Division C.

PORTLAND TO QUEBEC OR MONTREAL.

Leave Portland by rail on the Grand Trunk Railway, by minor stations to *Yarmouth Junction* [connection for *Augusta*, capital of the State of Maine, lying on the Kennebec River; for *Bangor*, important town on the Penobscot River; and for towns and sections farther east]; to *Danville Junction* [connection for Bangor, for *Skowhegan* and *Moosehead Lake*]; by minor stations to GORHAM, at the northern edge of the White Mountains [important intersections, by stage-coaches, to and from the mountain towns and resorts; and views of the mountains, in fine weather, peculiarly striking, from all this section of the road]; to *Island Pond* [connection, southwestward, with the Connecticut and Passumpsic River Railway, from Vermont and Franconia Notch sections]; to *Stanstead* [carriage communication with Lake Memphremagog]; to *Sherbrook* [another connection with the Connecticut and Passumpsic River line]; to *Richmond* [point of divergence of the branches of the Grank Trunk road, to Montreal and Quebec].

Pursuing the route to Montreal: Richmond by St. Hyacinthe, St. Brune, St. Hilaire, and other unimportant stations, to *St. Lambert*, on the St. Lawrence River, the Victoria Bridge and *Montreal.*

Pursuing the route to Quebec: Richmond by Danville, *Arthabasca* [connection by Bulstrode, to *Doucet's Landing*, on St. Lawrence River, at lower end of Lake St. Peter; thence by ferry to *Three Rivers*, Canada]; by Becancour, Black River, and minor stations, to *Chaudiere Junction* [connection for *Riviere du Loup* and Lower St. Lawrence]; to *Point Levi*, on the St. Lawrence, whence ferry to *Quebec.*

[For notes of Montreal and Quebec, see Canadian routes.]

ROUTE NO. 6.—NORTHERN AND EASTERN.

BOSTON TO LAKE WINNIPESAUKIE, THE WHITE MOUNTAINS AND PORTLAND (OPTION OF CANADIAN CITIES)—BY BOSTON AND MAINE RAILROAD, &c.

Leave Boston by Boston and Maine railroad, as by route to Portland, &c. As by that route, to

Dover, New Hampshire. Thence Dover and Winnipesaukie road, by Gonic, *Rochester* [junction with road from Salmon Falls by Great Falls, and its extension northward to *Unionville*] Farmington, Davis', New Durham and Alton, to

Alton Bay, at the extreme southern point of *Lake Winnipesaukie*—pleasant residence, with fine views of the Lake and mountains northward, but deriving its principal importance from the railway and steamer transit through it. From Alton Bay a visit should be paid, if time allows, before proceeding northward, by "Lady of the Lake" or other staunch little steamers on the Lake, to

WOLFBORO', on the eastern side of the Lake, a charming summer resort, with fine views, excellent sailing and fishing, and much attraction and popularity as a residence. Hotel: the *Pavilion*. [Stage-coach may be taken at Wolfboro', for proceeding northward to Conway, without visiting Centre Harbor; but this course is scarcely advisable on a first visit.] Wolfboro', again by steamboat, through charming lake-scenery, to

CENTRE HARBOR, larger village on the northern shore of the Lake, the location of which is considered unequalled by many tourists, as the Lake itself, with its exquisite combination of island groups and wooded shore, with bold mountains forming a background in all northerly directions, is one of the very finest in America and with few superiors elsewhere. Leading Hotel: the *Senter House*, Among the finest points of mountain view, from Centre Harbor and elsewhere on the Lake, may be named *Mounts Salmonbrook*, *Whiteface*, *Ossipee*, *Major*, *Chicorua*, *Red Mountain* (ascent by carriage and on horseback), *Kearsarge* and *Monadnock*. Many and charming excursions are made from the village, on the lakes, to the mountains and elsewhere; and among the most notable is that to *Squam Lake*, lying a few miles west of Winnipesaukie very romantic in scenery, and supplying rare trout and other fishing.

At Centre Harbor stage-coach is taken, for remainder of the route northward to the White Mountains. This affords one of the most magnificent rides attainable in the world, especially if fine weather allows outside seats on the coach to be used. The road leads up the Saco River, along the charming *Conway Valley*, with views of the Lake district lingering behind, and others of the great mountain section continually changing ahead, and with *Mount Washington*, the monarch of the eastern range, often in sight. This ride terminates at NORTH CONWAY, a picturesque village lying in the valley, from which the views of the White Range are something, in comparison, like those of Mt. Blanc from Chamounix, while the number of easy excursions to celebrated points is almost unequalled. It is here that many of the artists' summer sketches, especially of *Kearsarge* and *Chicorua* and the higher peaks of the White Mountains, all in full view, are made; while the *Ledges* (grand perpendicular cliffs, nearly one thousand feet in height) *Artists' Brook* the *Cathedral*, *Diana's Bath*, &c., are within convenient reach. Prominent Hotels: the *Kearsarge*, *Washington*, *McMillan*, *Cliff*, etc.

North Conway, by stage-coach or carriage, through *Pinkham Notch*, surrounded by the lesser giants of the White Range, to the

GLEN HOUSE, with much fine scenery in the neighborhood, but especially notable as being the nearest of any of the mountain resorts to the great peaks of the White Range, and giving the rarest views of them—as well as the point from which the ascent of *Mount Washington* is made, by rail. Among the points of interest to be visited from the Glen, are *Thompson's* and *Glen Ellis Falls*, the former on the Peabody River, some two miles from the hotel, and the latter on the Ellis, about four miles; the *Crystal Cascade*, near Glen Ellis; *Garnet* and

Emerald Pools, with peculiar colors indicated by their names, &c. But the speciality of the Glen House, as before noted, is the

Ascent of Mount Washington, by railway. The features of this ascent need no description, especially to those who have made Alpine crossings by rail. It is considered eminently safe, has little fatigue involved, and certainly supplies all the elements of the picturesque and the exciting. Stout clothing is advisable, if not always necessary. This ascent being made in the morning, the top of the giant will be reached at the most favorable hour, and the *wonderful view from the summit enjoyed,* if the capricious weather allows that great privilege. This view is quite equal to that from the Rhigi or Pilatus, over Switzerland, though perhaps lacking the variety in scenery. To the west, in bright weather, are seen the higher peaks of the Green Mountains of Vermont; southwest, some of the White and many of the Franconia Range—especially Lafayette; north and north-east, the other great peaks of the White Range, and more distant the mountains of Canada; east the sea, beyond Portland; southeast and south those surrounding Lake Winnipesaukie, and that Lake itself; while various rivers, small lakes, towns and hamlets combine to make up a picture of marvellous extent and beauty. Dinner is provided at the *Tip-Top House,* on the summit, where during the last seasons scientists have resided all winter, to make observations.

Horses (kept in waiting) and guides should be taken at the summit, and the descent made in the other direction, crossing *Mts. Franklin, Monroe* and *Pleasant;* and the three wondrous gulfs, the *Gulf of Mexico, Tuckerman's Ravine,* and *Oakes' Gulf* (some or all of them containing deep snow in midsummer) will be pointed out by the guides. At the end of nine miles' descent will be reached the

CRAWFORD HOUSE, lying in what is now called the Willey Notch, and nearly at the foot of *Mt. Crawford,* while *Mt. Webster* and other giants of the range show grandly northward. The most marked feature in the neighborhood of the Crawford, is the

Willey House, standing at a short distance up the Notch, where in 1826 a landslide from the mountain above destroyed the family of the same name, and their residence—of which catastrophe many relics are yet pointed out and a few of them still offered for sale. From the Crawford may also be made the

Ascent of Mt. Willard, practicable either by carriage or on foot, and affording a most magnificent series of views from near the summit; as also visit to the *Devil's Den,* a cave of peculiar wildness and some danger of access. Also may be visited, from the Crawford, *Gibbs' Falls,* a cascade of much beauty, reached by short walk from the house.

From the Crawford House, by stage-coach or carriage, by the *White Mountain House, Falls of the Ammonoosuc*, and *Bethlehem*, to the

PROFILE HOUSE, in the Franconia Notch.

[For notes on the Profile House and neighborhood, see termination of route: "New York to the White Mountains, by New London, &c."—Route No. 7.]

[The tourist who has made his arrival at the Franconia Notch by the just completed route from Boston, and who yet wishes to return southward without proceeding to either Quebec or Montreal, should pursue one of the following named routes in return, for the sake of variety in direction and scenery. 1st. From Littleton (stage-coach from the Profile House), by rail by Wells River, Plymouth, Weir's Landing, Concord, Worcester and New London, and steamboat of Norwich and Worcester line from New London to New York. (See route No. 7: "New York to the White Mountains," reversing.) Or, 2d. From Littleton to Wells River, and continue by rail by White River Junction, Bellows Falls, Springfield, Hartford and New Haven to New York. Or, 3d. From Littleton to Wells River, White River Junction, Bellows Falls, Rutland, Troy or Albany; and down the Hudson River by boat or rail to New York. Or, 4th. From Littleton to Wells River, White River Junction, Burlington, boat on Lake Champlain to Ticonderoga (for Lake George) or Whitehall, Saratoga, Albany or Troy, and boat or rail to New York.]

ROUTE NO. 6.—NORTHERN AND EASTERN.

[To go northward from Littleton to Montreal or Quebec. For MONTREAL, to *White River Junction*, thence to *Burlington, St. Alban's*, and *St. John's* to the Victoria Bridge and Montreal. For QUEBEC, to *Wells River, Newport* (Lake Memphremagog), *Lenoxville, Richmond* and *Arthabasca,* to Point Levi and ferry to Quebec.]

ROUTE NO. 7.—NORTHERN AND EASTERN.

NEW YORK TO THE WHITE MOUNTAINS AND CANADA, BY NEW LONDON, NORWICH AND WORCESTER, LAKE WINNIPESAUKIE, ETC.; OR BY NEW LONDON AND NORTHERN ROAD.

Division A.

BY NEW LONDON, NORWICH AND WORCESTER, MERRIMAC AND WINNIPESAUKIE ROUTE.

Leave New York at 5 P. M., on Sound, by Norwich and Worcester boat, as by corresponding line for Boston. (See Boston route: "By boat by New London, &c.") As by that route, to *New London, Norwich*, and to

WORCESTER, point of separation of the trains eastward for Boston and northward for the Mountains. Worcester to

Groton Junction [connections eastward for *Concord* and BOSTON; also eastward for *Lowell* and *Lawrence;* also westward for the *Hoosic Tunnel* (immense work of engineering, on the Mt. Cenis plan, not yet completed), for ALBANY, *Troy*, &c.] Very soon after leaving Groton Junction comes into view the *Merrimac River*, with the striking and picturesque scenery of the

Valley of the Merrimac, considered among the

ROUTE NO. 7.—NORTHERN AND EASTERN. 137

finest rivers in New England, and thenceforward accompanying the traveler almost to the foot of the mountains. Next important point is

MANCHESTER, New Hampshire, large and thriving manufacturing village, on the Merrimac, the mills and some other factories worthy of attention from those whose leisure permits stoppage, but showing even more than ordinary interest in manufacturing detail, even from the train. Hotel: the *Manchester House*. Manchester, still along the Merrimac, to

CONCORD, capital of the State of New Hampshire, lying on the same river, and presenting many points of attraction for visit or residence. It has handsome public grounds; notable public buildings, in the *State House* (recently rebuilt), the *State Lunatic Asylum, State Prison,* and some of the municipal and other erections; and *Main street,* the principal thoroughfare, is remarkably long, fine and well kept. It has great granite quarries in the neighborhood, a considerable amount of manufactures and much general prosperity. Leading Hotel: the *Eagle House.* [Connection by rail, eastward to *Dover, Portsmouth,* &c.; westward to the Connecticut Valley routes northward and southward, &c.] Concord (with distant but very fine views of the Winnipesaukie and White Mountains commencing, and thence continuing, with infinite variations, to the end of the route), by Sanbornton and other stations to

Weir's Landing, at the western edge of *Lake*

Winnipesaukie, with very fine views over the Lake
and its many islands. [Connection, by boat on the
Lake, for *Centre Harbor* or Wolfboro', and thence by
stage-coach for *Conway* and the White Range.]
Weir's Landing, by Meredith, &c., to

Plymouth, at the foot of the mountains, with
splendid views southward and many attractions as a
place of sojourn. Hotel: the *Pemigawasset*. (Leisurely pause, for dinner).

[At Plymouth stage-coach or private carriage
may be taken, for the splendid drive of twenty-five
to thirty miles, up through the *Valley of the Pemigawasset*, to the *Profile House*—during which a series of views will be enjoyed, approaching the mountains, not often equalled in any land.]

From Plymouth, by rail, literally among the mountains, and among glorious scenery, to

Wells River [connection westward for *Montpelier*
(capital of the State of Vermont) and Northern
Vermont; southward for *White River Junction*.
Route may also be pursued northward, either before
or after visiting the Franconia Notch, to *Newport*
and the beautiful LAKE MEMPHREMAGOG, lying on
the border between Vermont and Canada, and offering fine views, picturesque scenery, excellent fishing,
and many other attractions. Or, the same route
may be pursued, to Newport, thence on by way of
Richmond, &c., to QUEBEC, or bending westward
from Richmond, to MONTREAL.]

Wells River, through even grander scenery than
that from **Plymouth**, to

Littleton, small village at the entrance of the Franconia Notch, whence stage-coach is taken, for the ride through the Notch, with many of the best features of American mountain scenery, to the

PROFILE HOUSE. [For notes on the Profile House and neighborhood, see immediately following.]

Division B.

BY NEW LONDON AND THE NEW LONDON NORTHERN ROUTE.

New York by Norwich and Worcester boat on the Sound, 5 P. M., as by route just concluded, to

New London. (Later rest is secured, by this route, than by that by Worcester and Winnipesaukie, from the non-necessity of taking the train until 5 A. M.) From New London by rail, by *Norwich*, through a very pleasant and prosperous part of the State of Connecticut, and past villages embodying large manufacturing interests; by *Willimantic* (manufacturing village, with railway connections westward to the Hartford, Providence and Fishkill road); by Tolland, Stafford, Monson, &c., to *Palmer* [connections eastward to *Worcester* and BOSTON, westward to *Springfield*, for either Hartford, *New Haven* and NEW YORK, or *Pittsfield*, ALBANY and *Troy*]. Palmer to *Amherst*, where the peculiarly splendid scenery of the line, embodying the bold characteristics of the Green Mountain region of Vermont, may be said properly to begin, continuing thence all the way to White River Junction. Amherst to

Grout's Corners, important station. [Connections, eastward to *Fitchburg, Groton* and BOSTON; westward to *Greenfield, North Adams*, &c., and to ALBANY and Troy.] Grout's Corners, by South Vernon, to

BRATTLEBORO, Vermont, thriving town on the Connecticut River, with some manufactures, a specialty of being markedly healthy as a residence, and a *State Lunatic Asylum* bearing a very high reputation. Brattleboro to

Bellows Falls, also on the Connecticut River, deriving its singular name from an ancient peculiarity of the river in the neighborhood. [Connections northwest to *Rutland, Burlington*, Lake Champlain, &c.; and southeast to *Keene, Groton*, BOSTON, &c.] Bellows Falls by Claremont and Windsor, to

White River Junction, at the intersection of the White River with the Connecticut, important place of transfer in cross-travel. [Connections, west to *Rutland, Whitehall*, Saratoga, &c.; northwest to *Montpelier, Burlington, Rouse's Point* and CANADA; east to *Concord, Salem*, BOSTON, &c.] White River Junction to

Wells River. [Northern connections to Newport, *Lake Memphremagog, Quebec* or *Montreal*, as in last previous route.]

Wells River to *Littleton;* thence by stage-coach as before noted, to the

PROFILE HOUSE.

Division C.

AT AND ABOUT THE PROFILE HOUSE (FRANCONIA NOTCH).

Probably no section of mountain scenery in America, of like extent, presents so many points of interest and beauty as appear in the Franconia Notch, though in the detail of absolute grandeur it can by no means claim the same distinction. Taking the Profile House as the central point, the principal objects may be found grouped around it within very brief distance, as follows:

Echo Lake, lying within a few hundreds of yards, embosomed in fine woods, under the brow of *Eagle Cliff*, affording fine views of *Mt. Lafayette*, charming boating, and a repetition of *echoes* (from the Cliff), scarcely second to those of the Eagle's Nest at Killarney. The

Cannon Mountain, at the base of which the Profile House stands, and ascended from it, with moderate difficulty, a magnificent view being the reward. On the top of the mountain, at near the brow overhanging the valley, some rocks, singularly disposed, suggest the shape of a *Cannon*, mounted on its carriage, whence the name; and the extreme brow of the mountain itself forms, in a peculiar combination of great rocks, the

Old Man of the Mountain, colossal face, sixty feet in height from chin to brow, hanging over the immense gulf, and perfect in every detail of a majestic human face, as seen from the road at some distance below the Profile (which of course takes its name from that view). Below this, which is undoubtedly the most striking single curiosity of all the range, lies the little *Profile Lake,* sometimes called the "Old Man's Bath," or "Washbowl," or "Mirror," affording a wonderful reflection of the stony face in calm weather, and said to be full of fine trout. A mile below the Profile is to be reached (ride or walk), the *Basin,* pool of remarkable shape and character, and *Old Man's Foot,* lying in it in colossal stone. Thence, five miles further, the *Flume House,* summer resort, now disused; and near it

The Flume, only second to the Old Man of the Mountain as a great natural curiosity, being an immense fissure or split in the solid rock of the mountain, varying from 10 to 20 feet in width, and the walls from 20 up to 100 feet in height, with a small rapid stream brawling over rough stones below, and a boarded walk up the gorge. At one point, a huge oval stone, of many tons in weight, hangs by the two points midway up the chasm; and at another a dangerous bridge has been thrown over, at the top, by the falling of a tree. At no great distance from the Flume lies

The Pool, a literal hole in the rock, of great depth and singularity of appearance, reached by a difficult climb down the bank, and formerly the abode of a strange madman named Merrill, who paddled visitors round it in a crazy boat, declared it the "centre of the earth," and exhibited a letter to him from Queen Victoria, dated at the Kitchen of Buckingham Palace!

From the front of the Flume House and neighborhood is to be seen a natural wonder of great prominence, the

Dead Washington, being the profile face and form of that hero, in a recumbent position and as if shrouded, lying at a length of miles, the shape supplied by the shapes and position of several mountains of the Haystack group. May also be seen, between the Profile and the Flume, at some distance from the road, *Walker's Falls*, a fine cascade; and two miles below the Flume, *Georgiana Falls*, the largest in the range.

Of Ascents from the Profile, besides that of the Cannon, the principal are those of

Mount Lafayette, the highest peak of the Franconia Range, and commanding a fine view, with only a limited amount of toil (horseback or foot)—and *Bald Mountain*, a lower elevation, but still with fine view (carriage).

[From the Profile House to *Crawford House*, (carriage) for the White Range and ascent of Mount Washington from that direction, with descent by rail to the Glen House; or to *Littleton*, Wells River and White River Junction, for pursuance of the route to Canada.]

ROUTE 8.—NEAR WESTERN.

NEW YORK, BY RAIL, BY THE NEW JERSEY CITIES, TO AND AT PHILADELPHIA.

Division A.

NEW YORK TO PHILADELPHIA, BY THE PENNSYLVANIA RAILROAD.

Leave New York by the Pennsylvania Railroad, by ferry from foot of Cortlandt street, or foot of Desbrosses street; cross the Hudson river, to

JERSEY CITY, a large and thriving town, lying in the State of New Jersey, but really a suburb and connection of New York, with which most of its more important business interests are identified. It is growing and improving rapidly, is laying out public grounds, has extensive Water-Works, and enjoys the specialty of the *Cunard Docks* near the ferry, from which sail all the steamers of that popular line. Hotels, *Taylor's, American, Fisk's,* &c. From Jersey City, by rail, across flat and uninteresting country, to

NEWARK, on the Passaic River, now largest city in the State, and one of the handsomest, as well as most important in point of manufactures, especially of leather, carriages and fancy work. [Reached by steamboat and other water-conveyance from New

York. Also reached from New York by train on the Newark and New York road, from foot of Liberty street; and (northern portion) by the Morris and Essex road, from foot Barclay street.] It is regularly laid out; has two handsome parks, many charming drives in the neighborhood; a great number and variety of the residences of the wealthy on *Broad* and other principal streets; some public buildings worthy of attention (including the *Post Office, City Hall, County Court House* and several of the many churches); and is famed for the exceptional beauty of its female population, as seen on promenade or elsewhere. Hotel: the *Newark House.* From Newark visit may be paid to *Orange*, very beautiful village, lying near, at the north; to the *Orange Mountains;* to the popular place of resort, *Llewellyn Park*, &c. Or, they may be reached directly from New York by the Morris and Essex road, foot of Barclay street.] Newark to

ELIZABETH, smaller town somewhat resembling Newark in appearance and general characteristics, though less notable in manufactures and possibly excelling the other in the finished beauty of some of its suburban grounds and wealthy residences. Has the specialty of being passed through, daily, by more railway trains than almost any other town in America, two great lines intersecting in it, and an immense coal-trade from Eastern Pennsylvania passing through it to its adjoining town and the principal entrepot and shipping-port of that article,

Elizabethport. Rivals Newark in female beauty, in fashion and the wealth of residents. [Also reached from New York by the New Jersey Central road, foot of Liberty street.] Elizabeth to

Rahway, handsome village, also much affected as a residence of citizens, and with specialty of considerable manufactures, for the Southern and other markets. Rahway to

NEW BRUNSWICK, one of the oldest towns in the State, though inferior in size to several others. It is pleasantly situated on the Raritan River, has a considerable amount of manufactures, and is the point of entrance into the Raritan River and Bay of the same name (Lower New York Bay), of the *Delaware and Raritan Canal,* from the Delaware River at Bordentown. Its principal celebrity, however, lies in its being the seat of *Rutgers College,* and the *Theological Seminary* of the Reformed Dutch Church, both old and influential institutions, holding excellent rank. Among the buildings best worth notice, are those of the *College,* on an elevated square, within view from the railway; the *Theological Hall;* the *County Buildings,* in the public square; and several churches of prominence. Many fine drives are to be enjoyed by those making stay, into the handsome and well-cultivated country in the neighborhood, to *Bound Brook,* &c. Leading Hotels, the *Railroad, Bulls Head,* &c.

Beyond New Brunswick, the railway is accompanied for much of the distance by the Delaware

ROUTE NO. 8.—NEAR WESTERN. 147

and Raritan Canal. At *Monmouth Junction* intersection is made for *Freehold*, the *Battle Ground of Monmouth*, and south-eastern portions of the State. Next stopping place of importance,

PRINCETON—Station, the town lying away at the right, though in sight, and steam connection in waiting. Princeton is another of the old and important towns of the State, with a peculiar status in Revolutionary history as having been the scene of one of Washington's most memorable conflicts, of which the field extends from the town itself to what is called the "Battle Ground," more than a mile distant. Its more marked celebrity, however, lies in its being the seat of the *College of New Jersey* (called alternately, "Princeton College," and often, from one of the oldest buildings, "Nassau Hall.") It is also the seat of the *Theological Seminary* of the Presbyterian denomination, in connection with the College, which has long enjoyed a very high reputation, and which is now presided over by the celebrated Scotch divine, Dr. McCosh, late of Queen's College, Belfast. The grounds of the College (like many of those of the town) are very handsome. Peale's "Washington," in the College library, is a picture of merit and historical interest. To the College has also lately been added an *Astronomical Observatory*, with fine instruments.

Beyond Princeton is soon reached

TRENTON, capital of the State of New Jersey, lying on the left or east bank of the Delaware river, and famous as the scene of Washington's "Crossing the Delaware," Dec., 1776. It is a thriving manufacturing town, especially preëminent in iron works; and has very costly constructions connected with the passage through the town of the Delaware and Raritan Canal. [Railroad connection, north, for *Belvidere, Easton,* and the Upper Delaware and Pennsylvania Coal-Regions; and south to *Bordentown,* and by that route to PHILADELPHIA.] The principal erections of prominence are the *State House,* modern and very handsome (with valuable Revolutionary memorials in the Library); the *State Lunatic Asylum, Arsenal, Penitentiary,* and some of the *County buildings.* The views over the Delaware and the Pennsylvania shore opposite, from some portions of the town, are very fine and memorable. Prominent hotels, the *American* and *Trenton.*

[Optional route may be taken, at Trenton, by rail, down the Delaware River to *Bordentown* and *Camden,* thence to PHILADELPHIA by ferry. See Division B. of this route.]

At Trenton the Delaware River is crossed, by bridge, to the State of Pennsylvania, by

Bristol, handsome and thriving village of that State, and by *Frankford* (with a United States Arsenal) to *Germantown* and *West Philadelphia,* point of debarkation for

PHILADELPHIA.

Division B.

NEW YORK TO PHILADELPHIA, BY CAMDEN AND AMBOY ROUTE.

Leave New York by Pennsylvania Railroad, from foot of Cortlandt street, or foot Desbrosses street, as by Division A, of this route ; by *Jersey City, Newark*, and *Elizabeth*, to *Rahway*. (See Division A.) Thence diverging to

Woodbridge, handsome village on the creek of the same name, emptying into Staten Island Sound; thence to

Perth Amboy, old but decayed seaport, once expected to become the rival of New York, especially in the India and tea trade, and with the noted Thomas H. Smith tea warehouses still standing. From Perth Amboy by ferry (or bridge), to

South Amboy, former place of debarkation from the New York steamers of the Camden and Amboy boat line. [From South Amboy, all-rail route to *Keyport, Middletown* and LONG BRANCH, of the Central Railroad of New Jersey.] From South Amboy continue by rail to

Jamesburg, thriving small town, with State Reform School for Boys. [Connection southward to *Freehold,* thence to Long Branch and the south-east; and northward to Pennsylvania Railroad at *Monmouth Junction,* for Newark, Trenton, &c.] Thence to

Cranberry, Hightstown [connection to *Pemberton* and southwest] and

BORDENTOWN, handsome large village on the Delaware, and point of entrance into that river of the Delaware and Raritan Canal; famous as having long been the residence (at Point Breeze—grounds to the right) of Joseph Bonaparte, ex-king of Spain. [Connection by boat down the Delaware to PHILADELPHIA; by rail to *Trenton*, &c.] Bordentown to

BURLINGTON, also lying on the Delaware, and considered one of the handsomest towns in the State. It is the seat of *Burlington College* (Episcopal), and of several notable male and female schools. [Connection by boat to PHILADELPHIA and *Bordentown*; by rail to *Mount Holly* and other towns in the interior of the State.] Burlington by *Beverley* and other minor places, to

Camden, on the Delaware, opposite Philadelphia. Thriving town, with much agricultural and some manufacturing industry, and residence of many Philadelphians. [Connection by West Jersey Railroad southward to *Bridgeton*; south-eastward to *Millville* and CAPE MAY, favorite sea-coast resort at the Capes of the Delaware; eastward by the Camden and Atlantic to *Atlantic City*, another favorite watering place on the New Jersey coast of the Atlantic; and by Pemb. and Hightstown road to the New Jersey Southern, *Long Branch* and New York]. Ferry across the Delaware to
PHILADELPHIA.

ROUTE NO. 8.—NEAR WESTERN. 150a

Division C.

NEW YORK TO PHILADELPHIA, BY THE "NEW LINE"—(N. J. CENTRAL, BOUND BROOK, AND NORTH PENN.)

Leave New York by the New Jersey Central Railroad, by boat from foot of Liberty street, to Long Dock, Communipaw. By cars of the New Jersey Central Road (see Route 13, pp. 206 and 207), to *Elizabeth*, Westfield, *Plainfield* (with Washington's Rock near), and intermediate stations, to

Bound Brook, a village of some prominence on the Raritan River, a few miles above New Brunswick, to which there is stage communication from it, and also to Basking Ridge, beyond. Within two miles is "Chimney Rock," a somewhat celebrated landmark of the neighborhood; and near Bound Brook was fought a battle between the British and Americans, with defeat of the latter, in 1777; as also the American Army encamped a few miles to the northwest, in the winter of 1778-9.

At Bound Brook the line is continued, taking the rail of the Delaware and Bound Brook road (though with no change of cars—the whole line being run under one management); within a short distance of *Princeton* (see Route 8, p. 147), to which present stage-connection, with branch-rail to follow; by *Hopewell* (branch rail to Trenton), to

Yardleyville, on the Delaware, where that river is crossed, on a new and magnificent iron bridge—the crossing affording fine view of the river and surroundings. (From Yardleyville to TRENTON, connection by the Belvidere Delaware Railroad.) From Yardleyville, through Bucks County, Pa., by *Newtown*, to junction with the Main Line of the North Pennsylvania Railroad, at

Jenkintown. From Jenkintown, by the North Penn. road, direct to PHILADELPHIA.

[The North Pennsylvania Railroad, with which connection is here formed, as above noted, at Jenkintown, supplies one of the great trunk lines of Pennsylvania, forming a favorite and most available route to the North, Niagara Falls, the Lakes, etc. By this line, for the North, from PHILADELPHIA, by Abington, Lansdale (connection to *Doylestown* and *Norristown*), to

Bethlehem, important town on the Susquehanna River (connection to *Easton*, etc., and the East). Thence by Lehigh Valley Railroad, through one of the most picturesque portions of Pennsylvania, along the Valley of the Lehigh, by ALLENTOWN (connection to New York and the East, by the "Allentown Line"—see Route 13); by *Mauch Chunk;* the *Switch Back; Glen Onoko,* etc., to

WILKESBARRE, important town and one of the great centres of the coal-region, lying on the Susquehanna River. (Harvey's Lake and the beautiful valley of Wyoming may be reached in a few miles drive). From Wilkesbarre, by the same road, to Waverley or ELMIRA, on the Erie road; and by the Lake Districts (Geneva, Cayuga, Seneca, etc.), to Niagara, the great Lakes, Canada, etc.]

ROUTE NO. 8.—NEAR WESTERN. 151

Division D.

AT AND ABOUT PHILADELPHIA, WITH EXCURSIONS.

PHILADELPHIA, most important city of Pennsylvania, second in the Union in point of population, largest of all in the extent of ground comprised within city limits, and dividing with Boston the claim of being the most influential after the commercial metropolis—lies on the Delaware River, at about one hundred miles from its mouth at Delaware Bay, and above and very near the debouchure into that river of the Schuylkill, the latter stream running through the city at its western extremity and adding materially to the beauty and healthfulness of location. It is well known to have been founded by William Penn, the Quaker, and to be the headquarters of his denomination (whence its *soubriquet*, the "Quaker City"); and it enjoys, in addition, the distinction of being the most regularly built city on the continent if not in the world, the mass of its streets lying at right angles and giving it an appearance of primness alternately counted a charm and a blemish. From this latter feature, combined with all the streets running parallel with the Delaware being numbered, from one upward—and the space between each of these streets, on the intersecting ones, numbered as one hundred, in supplying street-numbers—less difficulty is involved, in the stranger finding his way through and about it, than through any other city in the world, of corresponding size. Still additionally it should be noted that the street-car system is wonderfully complete and perfect, routes crossing each other at short distances, and a system of "transfers" from one route to another making transit much easier and cheaper than it could otherwise be found. Carriage-hire, cheaper than in New York, though high; not differing materially from the same detail at Boston.

Philadelphia has many notable Streets, of which the characteristics are worth study, for their individual and collective character. First among these is *Chestnut Street*, at once business and fashionable, on which are located some of the best hotels, and which has by far the handsomest display of shop-fronts on the continent. Next to this, perhaps, is *Market Street*, wide thoroughfare, dividing the cross-streets into "North" and "South," and displaying much railway traffic and other heavy trade. *Arch* and *Walnut* are also both business streets of importance. The Exchange stands in *Dock Street*, between Walnut and Spruce; and much of the commercial and financial force of the city is to be found in that neighborhood, and near the Delaware, between *Shippen Street*, on the South, and *Vine Street*, on the North, and *Front Street* to *Sixth Street*, in the cross direction. *Fourteenth Street* is ordinarily called *Broad Street*, and has much fashion and many prominent buildings. *Ridge* and

Girard Avenues hold position as places of fashionable residence, and drives leading to Girard College, Fairmount Park, etc.

Of Public Buildings there are many of importance and interest. The first place is held, historically, by *Independence Hall*, Chestnut street, notable as having been the place of signing of the Declaration of Independence from Great Britain, Fourth of July, 1776. Some historical pictures of value, statues, and many relics are preserved there; and among others the "Liberty Bell," rung at the time of the Declaration, and bearing the strangely appropriate inscription: "Proclaim liberty throughout the land to all the inhabitants thereof." (Admission to the Hall, every day, 9 to 2). The building and wings are now used as public offices. A recently erected statue of Washington fronts the main entrance. Next of the public buildings in importance, is *Girard College*, on Ridge Avenue, some two miles from the city centre—the several buildings modern and of fine architecture, and the grounds handsome, but its principal celebrity (it has very little as an educational institution) lying in the strange will and bequest of Stephen Girard, the merchant, which founded it, and which among other odd features, allows no clergyman to enter it even on a visit. Next in importance is the *United States Mint*, Chestnut street, with very perfect and interesting processes and a splendid collection of coins (admission daily, 9 to 12). Besides these, there are the *Custom House* (formerly the United States Bank), Chestnut street; the *Exchange*, Dock street; the *University of Pennsylvania*, Ninth street near Chestnut; *Jefferson Medical College*, Tenth street near Chestnut; the *Pennsylvania Hospital*, Pine street; *Pennsylvania Insane Asylum*, West Philadelphia (with West's great picture of "Christ Healing the Sick"); *U. S. Marine Hospital*, near the Navy Yard; the *Franklin Atheneum*, and other library and literary buildings; *Pennsylvania Academy of Fine Arts* (with many good pictures: open daily), Chestnut street; *Eastern Penitentiary*, Coates street, near Girard College; *Union League Club House*, Broad street; *Masonic Temple*, Broad street; *Ledger Building*, Sixth and Chestnut; and many Banks, Insurance Buildings, Railway Offices and Dwellings, of much costly beauty. The office-erections of the *Pennsylvania* and *Reading Railroads*, on Fourth street, are especially notable, as well as the freight and market buildings of those roads on Market street. Among the noblest of the other buildings named, are *Lippincott's* great Book-House, Market street; the *Mutual Life Insurance Building*, Chestnut street; *Farmers' Market*, Market street; *Girard Bank*, Third street; *Fidelity Deposit* building, *Provident Life* building, *Pennsylvania Life* building, *Bank of the Republic*, *Old Masonic Temple*, &c., all on Chestnut street; *Western Saving Fund*, Tenth and Walnut, &c.

In Antiquities Philadelphia possesses, besides *In-*

dependence Hall (already mentioned), *Carpenter's Hall*, Chestnut street, used for the first assembling of the Colonial Congress; *Hultzheimer's*, where Jefferson wrote the Declaration, cor. Market and Seventh streets; the *Grave of Franklin*, cor. Arch and Fifth streets; *Indian Queen Hotel*, once residence of Jefferson, cor. Market and Front streets; *Penn Cottage*, Letitia street, near Second; *Penn Treaty Monument*, Beach street, Kensington; *Old Swedes' Church*, Swanson street; *London Coffee House*, Front and Market streets; *Birth-place of the Flag*, 239 Arch street; the *Old Penn House*, near Fairmount; *Old Belmont Mansion*, near Fairmount; part of *Penn's Elm Tree*, in collection of Historical Library Association; and others of minor importance.

Of Public Grounds Philadelphia has more than the average in both variety and beauty. FAIRMOUNT PARK, on the Schuylkill (in connection with the long-celebrated *Fairmount Water-Works*), is one of the largest parks in the world (containing over three thousand acres), with the Schuylkill, a noble and navigable river, running through it, and the upper portion containing the Wissahickon, a smaller river tributary to the Schuylkill, admitted on all hands to be singularly lovely in wood and water effects. Though this Park has been but a few years in course of construction, it has already assumed magnificent proportions, even as compared with the great parks of the Old World; and it was within this Park, in the broad grounds lying eastward of George's Hill, one of the highest eminences of the whole, that the Centennial Exhibition, in honor of the one hundred years of American Independence was held, from the 10th of May to the 10th of November, 1876, in a range of the largest buildings yet erected by any of the nations for similar purposes. And here, in the Main Exhibition Building (still preserved, with Horticultural Hall, the Art Gallery, St. George's Hall, &c.),—the Permanent Exhibition commenced with May 10th, 1877, after the worthy pattern of that at the Sydenham Crystal Palace. Many of the *Bridges* are notable for beauty as well as strength, and must form a feature in the future celebrity of the Park. The Suspension Bridge, at the Water-Works, was built by Col. Ellett, the constructor of the Niagara Suspension Bridge, and afforded a model for the latter. The new Grand avenue bridge drive over the Schuylkill, between the East and West Parks, though a level erection, is very graceful, and the widest in the world. Near it, the New York Railroad Bridge contrasts well with its rival, though entirely different in character, combining round end-arches with one wide flat trussed centre; and the minor erections of the same character display taste blended with solidity. Of art in its more ordinary sense, the two most prominent objects, thus far, are the elegant monument to Frederick Graff, first engineer of the Water-Works, near the works themselves, and a bronze sitting statue of President Lincoln, within the lower entrance, near the Wire Bridge. There are also some fine fountains.

The grounds purchased for the Park contained many old houses, some of them of much interest; and the best of these have been judiciously preserved. Among the most notable is the house once belonging to John Penn, grandson of William, and owned by descendants until the present purchase. On a part of the same property stand the Lansdowne Pines—two trees of great size, age and grandeur of appearance. Even more interesting than the Penn house is the Belmont Mansion, also preserved—dating back to 1745—the home of Richard Peters, an eminent jurist, Member of Congress, and Secretary of the Board of War during the Revolution, who entertained under its roof, Washington, Lafayette, Jefferson, Robert Morris, Rittenhouse, and many others of the Revolutionary worthies, while Talleyrand, Louis Philippe and Tom Moore are known to have visited it. The view from the front of this fine old house (now a restaurant) is almost matchless in varied beauty, over the Schuylkill, the city, &c.; though that from George's Hill, the highest point of the grounds, is necessarily much more extensive, reaching to and beyond the Delaware at League Island. The upper portion of the Park, as already noted, includes not only the fine scenery of that part of the Schuylkill, but also that of the Wissahickon; and partially within it lies the scene of the unfortunate battle of Germantown, which lost Philadelphia to the Americans in 1777. Of no secondary importance, in connection with the Park and the Permanent Exhibition, are the very interesting *Zoological Gardens*, at the east end, near the Schuylkill, with Lion House, Aviary, Bear-Pits, Monkey House, &c.

Fairmount Park, the Permanent Exhibition, or the Fairmount Water-Works, may be reached from the centre of the city by an immense number of street car lines, and other conveyances, easily discovered by the visitor, from the placards announcing the special point of their destination. By the Pennsylvania Railroad, from New York and the East, or from the West (principal depot at Thirty-first and Market Sts., with supplemental station in front of the Centennial Grounds),—or by the New York and Philadelphia New Line (depot at Third and Berks Sts., with horse-car connection),—access to all the grounds of interest is very direct and easy; and quite the same may be said of the facilities for reaching them by the New Jersey Southern Railroad from New York and the New Jersey coast, the connections from that road, at the Market St. ferry, being direct by the Market Street line of cars, now operated by steam, and supplying "rapid transit" in the place of the slow and tedious.

The Fairmount *Water-Works* themselves demand attention, as among the best of their class ; the views over the Schuylkill from the raised promenade

ROUTE NO. 8.—NEAR WESTERN. 159

are notably fine; and the *Suspension Bridge*, already mentioned, should not be overlooked in observation of its rivals. (Other bridges of interest are the *Iron Bridge*, over the Schuylkill at Chestnut street; the *Market Street* Bridge, of wood, lately rebuilt, &c.) (There are also other Water-Works: the *Delaware*, on the river, foot of Wood street, and the *Western*, with a beautiful tower, opposite Fairmount.) Of the other public grounds of the city, the most interesting are *Independence Square*, rear of Independence Hall; *Washington Square*, near it; *Logan Square* (largest of the old), Eighteenth street; *Franklin Square*, Race and Sixth streets; *Penn Square*, Broad and Market streets; *Jefferson* and *Rittenhouse Squares;* and *Hunting Park* (old race-course) on the York road.

Among the most notable of Philadelphia Churches, are the *Cathedral of St. Peter and St. Paul* (Catholic), Logan Square, with a noble dome, an admired altar-piece, and some good paintings; *St. Mark's* (Epis.), Locust street, with tower and spire of peculiar beauty; *St. Paul's* (Epis.), Third street; *Christ Church* (old), Second street, with tall steeple, fine chime of bells, and communion service of the time of Queen Anne; *Church of the Incarnation*, Broad street; *Baptist*, Broad street; *Calvary* (Pres.), Locust street; *St. Stephen's* (Epis.), Fourth street; *St. Peter's* (old), Pine street; *St. Andrew's*, Eighth street; &c., and (as curiosities, though eschewing any attempt at architecture) many of the *Friends'* or *Quaker Meeting Houses*, of which the city has a remarkable number and variety.

Of Libraries, there are a large number, though the aggregate of volumes embraced in all does not reach far beyond a quarter million. Among them are the *Franklin* (sometimes called the "Philadelphia"), South Fifth near Chestnut street; the *Atheneum*, Sixth street; the *Mercantile*; the *Apprentices', Friends', Law Association*, &c.; besides those connected with those prominent institutions, the *Historical Society*, Sixth and Adelphi streets (antiquities and curiosities); *Academy of Natural Sciences*, Broad street; the *Franklin Institute*, Seventh street, &c. The principal Art Gallery is the *Pennsylvania Academy of Fine Arts*, Chestnut street, containing among other prominent pictures, West's "Death on the Pale Horse," Allston's "Raising of Lazarus," and others of merit by Stuart, Sully, Leslie and others. The principal Market, and one of the best-arranged and most luxuriously-supplied in America, is located on Market street, in the lower part of the city, and will well repay a visit, for observance of the varied productions of the surrounding country.

Principal Places of Amusement: the *American Academy of Music*, Broad street, the handsomest and one of the largest musical houses in the United States; *Arch Street Theatre*, street of the same name; *Chestnut Street*, street of that name; *Walnut Street*, street of same name; *Fox's*, Chestnut street;

Simmons and Slocum's Opera House (Ethiopian), Arch street; *Eleventh Street Opera House* (Ethiopian), Eleventh street; *American Museum*, Ninth, and Arch streets; *Musical Fund Hall*, Locust street, &c. Leading Hotels: the *Continental*, Chestnut street; *La Pierre House*, Broad street; *Colonnade*, Chestnut street; *Girard House*, Chestnut street; *American*, Chestnut street; *St. Cloud*, Arch street; *Washington*, Chestnut street; *Merchants'*, Fourth street; *Trans-Continental* and others, at the Exposition Grounds, &c.

For the additional convenience of the many tourists who have not familiarized themselves with the "Quaker City," the following resumés and extensions are given, of location of principal places of interest, places of amusement, and railroad depots, with brief directions for reaching them.

Principal Places of Interest, and Routes.

Fairmount Park and Centennial Grounds.—[Nearly all leading lines of street-cars, and other conveyances. See local directions.]

Independence Hall—Place of signing the "Declaration of Independence," Chestnut street, south side, between Fifth and Sixth. Near lower hotels, and reached from upper by cars on Chestnut street. Admission free at ordinary times, 9 A.M. to 2 P.M., and was naturally a place of great evening resort during the Centennial. Entrance to steeple granted on application to the Superintendent in the Hall.

Carpenter's Hall.—Place of original meeting of Continental Congress. Chestnut street, south side (rear), between Fourth and Fifth. Near Independence Hall, and reached in same manner.

Grave of Franklin.—Plain horizontal slab, covering Benjamin Franklin and his wife, in graveyard of Christ Church. South-east corner Fifth and Arch streets. Very near both of the former; and not far from leading hotels.

Penn's Cottage.—Once the residence of William Penn. Letitia street, between Front and Second, near Market. Close to the Delaware River.

Penn Treaty Monument.—Site of the great elm tree under which William Penn made his treaty with the Indians. Small obelisk, with inscription. Beach street, above Hanover, Kensington. Reached by street-cars marked "Richmond."

Indian Queen Hotel.—Once residence of Jefferson. Corner Market and Front streets.

London Coffee-House.—Existing as a coffee-house, by that name, before the Revolution. South-west corner Front and Market streets, near the Delaware.

Old Swedes' Church.—Built 1700. Swanson street, below Christian street. Reached by Second street cars.

Birth-place of the American Flag.—Place where the first stars and stripes were made. Now 239 Arch street, near the Delaware.

Christ Church.—With oldest peal of bells in America. Second street, north of Market street.

Girard College.—Ridge avenue, above Nineteenth street. Reached by Ridge avenue or Nineteenth street cars. Admission by ticket, procurable at the Ledger office, Sixth and Chestnut streets.

University of Pennsylvania.—Ninth street, above Chestnut. New building, Thirty-sixth street and Darby road. Reached by Market street cars to West Philadelphia; thence Darby road cars.

Philadelphia Library, and
Loganian Library, Fifth street, below Chestnut.
Atheneum, and
Historical Society of Pennsylvania, Sixth and Adelphi streets, below Walnut.

Philadelphia Dispensary.—Oldest institution of the kind in America; established 1786. No. 127 South Fifth street.

American Philosophical Society.—Fifth street, below Chestnut.

Academy of Natural Sciences.—Broad street, below Chestnut. Open Tuesday and Friday afternoons, but opened every afternoon during the Centennial. Admission 10 cents.

Franklin Institute.—Seventh street, above Chestnut.
Mercantile Library.—Tenth street, above Chestnut.
Apprentices' Library.—South-west corner Fifth and Arch streets.

ROUTE NO. 8.—NEAR WESTERN.

Pennsylvania Hospital.—Eighth and Spruce streets.

Penn. Hospital for the Insane.—Haverford road, West Philadelphia. Reached by Market street cars. Admission by ticket, at the Ledger office.

School of Design for Women.—North-west Penn Square, near Broad street and Chestnut.

Deaf and Dumb Institution.—Broad and Pine streets. Exhibitions Thursday afternoons. Admission by ticket, at the Ledger office.

Blind Asylum.—Twentieth and Race streets. Wednesday afternoon concerts. Admission 10 cents.

Blockley Almshouse.—Considered a model institution of its kind. West Philadelphia. Reached by Walnut street cars to Thirty-fourth street. Tickets at No. 42 North Seventh street.

House of Refuge.—Twenty-second street, near Poplar street. Admission every afternoon except Saturday and Sunday. Reached by Union line of Fairmount cars. Tickets at Ledger office.

Episcopal Hospital.—No. 2649 North Front street, on the Delaware.

U. S. Naval Asylum.—Gray's Ferry road, below South. Reached by cars on Pine street, or South street.

Navy Yard.—On line of the Delaware, east of Front street, and south of Prime street. Reached by Second street cars (as to old Swedes' Church).

Moyamensing (County) Prison.—Eleventh street and Passayunk road. Tickets at Ledger office.

Eastern Penitentiary.—Coates street, above Twenty-seventh. Reached by cars out, on Coates street, or Union line of Fairmount cars. Tickets at Ledger office.

Frankford Arsenal.—Frankford. Reached by Richmond line of horse-cars.

Richmond Coal-Wharves.—Greatest single deposit of coal in the world, of the Reading Railroad Company, from the Schuylkill coal regions. On the Delaware, North Philadelphia, opposite Treaty Island. Reached by street cars marked "Richmond."

U. S. Mint.—Chestnut street, above Thirteenth. Admission from 9 to 12 A. M., daily, except Saturday and Sunday.

Custom House.—Chestnut street, above Fourth.

Post-Office.—Chestnut street, below Fifth.

Commercial Exchange.—Second street, below Chestnut.

Mechanics' Exchange.—Third and Walnut streets.

Union League Club-House.—Broad and Sansom streets. Introduction by member of the Club required.

Masonic Hall.—Broad street, below Arch (old, 717 Chestnut, above Seventh).

Smith's Island, and

Windmill Island.—Small islands in the Delaware, opposite the city, and places of public resort. Ferry to Smith's, foot of Market street.

Hultzheimer's New House.—House where Jefferson wrote the Declaration. South-west corner Seventh and Market streets.

Laurel Hill Cemetery.—Ridge avenue. Reached by Ridge avenue cars.

Mt. Vernon Cemetery.—Nearly opposite Laurel Hill, and reached in same manner.

Monument Cemetery.—Broad street, opposite Berks.

Woodland Cemetery.—Darby road, West Philadelphia. Reached by Market street or Walnut street cars to Darby road; thence Darby road cars.

PLACES OF AMUSEMENT:

Academy of Music.—Broad and Locust streets.
Arch Street Theatre—Arch street, west of Sixth.
Chestnut Street Theatre.—Chestnut street, above Twelfth.
Walnut Street Theatre.—Walnut street, below Ninth.
Museum.—Ninth and Arch streets.
Simmons and Slocum's Opera House.—Arch street, above Tenth.
Eleventh Street Opera House.—Eleventh street, above Chestnut.
Musical Fund Hall.—Locust street, below Ninth.
Horticultural Hall.—Broad street, below Locust.
Concert Hall.—Chestnut street, above Twelfth.

RAILROAD DEPOTS:

Pennsylvania Railroad.—(For New York and the East, for the West, or for that connection to Baltimore, Washington and the South). Thirty-first and Market streets, reached by Market street cars; Kensington, reached by Third street cars; and ferry foot of Market street.

ROUTE NO. 8.—NEAR WESTERN.

Reading Railroad.—(For the Schuylkill, coal-regions, or the North). Thirteenth and Callowhill streets. Germantown and Norristown branch, Ninth and Green streets.

Philadelphia, Wilmington and Baltimore Railroad.—(For Chester, Wilmington, Baltimore, Washington and the South). Broad and Prime streets.

North Pennsylvania Railroad.—(For the North and for New York). Third and Berks streets.

Camden and Atlantic Railroad.—(For Southern New Jersey and the Coast). Ferry foot of Vine street.

West-Chester and Philadelphia Railroad.—(For local interior). Thirty-first and Chestnut streets.

Suburban and other Excursions of interest from Philadelphia, include the

United States Navy Yard, on Front street and the Delaware River, entrance from foot of Federal street; with immense Sectional Dock, stocks and materials for war-vessels, munitions of war, &c. [Walk, or street-car.] Arrangements have been made for the substitution of *League Island,* lower down the Delaware, as a new and larger navy yard; and the old is now virtually abandoned. Of scarcely less interest are the

U. S. Arsenals, of which one of the most important is to be reached at *Frankford,* north-east of the city, with interesting collection of arms and the largest powder magazine in the country; and the other near *Gray's Ferry,* south of the city. Also,

Laurel Hill Cemetery, on Ridge avenue, near the Schuylkill, and considered one of the handsomest of the cemeteries of the great cities, on account of height of location, fine river-view, tasteful monuments and adornments. The group of " Old Mortality," by Thom, at the entrance, and the Chapel, deserve attention, as do many of the monuments to well-known men, among others those of Dr. Kane, Gen'l Mercer, Gen'l Patterson, Dr. Bird (the novelist), Joseph C. Neal, Charles Thompson, Hassler, &c. [Reached by street-car, drive, or boat up the Schuylkill from Fairmount.] Second in importance are the *Woodlands Cemetery*, on the Darby road, west of the Schuylkill; *Monument Cemetery*, Broad street; *Glenwood Cemetery*, Ridge road; *Mount Vernon Cemetery*, Ridge avenue; *Ronaldson's Cemetery*, Shippen street; *Friends' Burial Ground*, Arch and Fourth streets, &c. [All, beyond short walk from leading hotels, reached by street-car.]

Other Excursions, to

The Wissahickon, creek or small river of marked shaded beauty, emptying into the Schuylkill. [Drive, on Ridge avenue, past Laurel Hill, or trip by boat on the Schuylkill from Fairmount and Park. To the *Old Bartram Mansion*, with Revolutionary reminiscences and a Botanic Garden, on the west bank of the Schuylkill. [Street cars on Darby road.] To *Penn's Rock*, on the Haddington road (stone said to have been raised by William Penn).

To *Germantown*, site of the battle of that name, fought by Washington in 1777; with interesting reminiscences, in Chew's House, the Headquarters, Buttonball Tree Tavern, &c. To *Manayunk*, on the Schuylkill, with water-power and heavy manufactures. [Street cars on Ridge-road, or boat on the

Schuylkill.] [Street car and short steam connection, every quarter-hour.] To *Greenwich Point* and *Gloucester Point*, on the Delaware, favorite near places of summer resort, a few miles below the city. [Ferry from South street.] To *Red Bank* and *Fort Mifflin*, two miles below the places last named, with Revolutionary reminiscences, Count Donop's Grave, a Battle Monument, &c.; and also to *League Island*, lying near, and the site of the new Navy Yard. [Boats, very frequent.] To *Smith's Island* and *Windmill Island*, lying in the Delaware, midway between the City and Camden, and passed through by the ferry-boats. Resort for relaxation and "clam-chowders." To *Camden*, New Jersey [several ferries: see route from New York, Division B.] To *Bridgeton*, New Jersey, great fruit-packing centre. [Ferry to Camden, and West Jersey Railroad.] To *Vineland*, New Jersey, great grape and fruit-growing centre. [Ferry to Camden, and Camden and Atlantic road to Atsion—thence Vineland Railway.] To *Bordentown* and *Burlington*. [Boat on the Delaware, or rail.]

Still other Excursions will be those to

NORRISTOWN, on the Schuylkill, county seat of Montgomery County, with pleasant location, two fine Bridges, and handsome Court-House. [Railway on Reading road, or long drive of much beauty]. To

VALLEY FORGE, place of the American winter-quarters in 1777–8, on the Schuylkill, with Washington's Headquarters still remaining, as well as the Old Hospital, earth-works, and many other reminders of that trying period—and the King of Prussia Tavern and Paoli, both celebrated in the struggle, at short distance. [Railway on Reading road.] To

READING, important town of the interior, with immense coal and other industries on the road, at and in the neighborhood. [Railway on Reading road.]. To

EASTON, DELAWARE WATER-GAP, &c. [See Longer Excursions from New York.] [Rail on Northern Pennsylvania, and Delaware, Lackawanna and Western roads.] To

HARRISBURG, Capital of the State of Pennsylvania, by *Lancaster*, &c. [Rail on the Pennsylvania Road: see Route 12.] To

PITTSBURGH, great iron manufacturing centre of the State, often called the "American Birmingham," and notable for the resemblance of its smoky atmosphere to that of English manufacturing towns. In connection, to *Wheeling*. [Rail on Pennsylvania road. See Route 12, pp. 200, &c.] To

Altoona and the *Allegheny Mountains*, for fine scenery of the road, considered among the noblest in America Also, to *Cresson* and *Johnstown*, beyond. [Rail on Pennsylvania road, as for Pittsburgh, &c.] To

ATLANTIC CITY, favorite place of summer resort, with fine bathing, on the New Jersey coast, near Egg Harbor and the Inlet of the same name.

Prominent Hotels, the *Atlantic House*, and *Surf House*. [Reached by ferry to Camden, thence rail on the Camden and Atlantic road direct.] To

CAPE MAY (Cape Island), still more prominent and popular as a place of seaside summer resort, and especially chosen by Philadelphians. It lies at the extreme southern point of New Jersey, at the northern entrance of Delaware Bay, has an extensive beach with fine sea-view and bathing, and ranks beside Newport and Long Branch. Prominent Hotels: the *Stockton House, Congress Hall, United States, West Jersey, Columbia, Delaware, Atlantic*, &c. [Reached by ferry to Camden, thence by rail on the West Jersey, and Millville and Cape May roads.] To

LONG BRANCH. [See Longer Excursions from New York.] [Reached by ferry to Camden, thence rail on Pemb. and Hightstown and New Jersey Southern roads. Also, with connection, Long Branch to NEW YORK.

ROUTE NO. 9.—WESTERN AND SOUTHERN.

PHILADELPHIA, BY WILMINGTON (DEL.) TO AND AT WASHINGTON AND RICHMOND.

Division A.

PHILADELPHIA TO BALTIMORE BY WILMINGTON.

Leave Philadelphia by rail on the Philadelphia, Wilmington and Baltimore road, from Broad Street and Washington Avenue, or from West Philadelphia. First point of interest passed is the *Lazaretto*, on the bank of the Delaware, some ten miles below the city and at some distance left from the road—an immense building, with cupola, long used for the detention of cases of infectious disease. In a short distance is reached

CHESTER, the oldest town in the State, and at one time, under William Penn, the seat of government of the province. It has as curiosities, the spot where Penn landed on his first coming from England, a very old *Court House*, &c. Very little beyond, the crossing is made from the State of Pennsylvania into that of Delaware; and still a little beyond is passed the *Brandywine Creek*, scene of the battle of the same name (at Chadd's Ford), defeat of the Americans and wounding of Lafayette, in 1777–8.

After leaving Chester, is reached

Lamokin Junction, [with the Philadelphia and

Baltimore Central Railroad, for *Port Deposit, Havre de Grace* (with very fine Bridge over the Susquehanna), Baltimore, &c.] Lamokin Junction to

WILMINGTON, Delaware, one of the most important towns of that small State, and in the midst of an agricultural section of special fertility, the great peach-growing district being within easy reach of any one making brief stoppage. It occupies the site of the old Swedish Fort Christina; has extensive shipyards, flour and powder-mills, foundries, &c.; and is also distinguished as the seat of *St. Mary's College* (Catholic), and other educational institutions of merit. Among its most prominent curiosities are the ship-yards and powder-mills, before named; the *Old Swedes' Church*, nearly 200 years old, with ancient grave-yard and singular epitaphs; the College, &c. [Railway connection south to *Elkton, Townsend,* DOVER (capital of the State), *Lewes, Salisbury, Crisfield* (for boat to *Norfolk*) &c,; westward to *Hanover,* HARRISBURG, &c.] From Wilmington, passing *New Castle Junction* [connection for *New Castle,* &c.], and minor stations, is reached

Havre de Grace, Maryland, at the debouchure of the Susquehanna River into Chesapeake Bay, and also at the southern terminus of the Tidewater Canal. Here the Susquehanna is crossed by a handsome and costly Railroad Bridge, not long finished; and in crossing, splendid views are caught (below) of Chesapeake Bay and the shore-scenery on both sides.

[Railway connections from Havre de Grace, northwestward, to HARRISBURG and the West and Northwest.] From Havre de Grace, over flat and low country, with passage of the long

Bridges over Bush and Gunpowder Rivers (the former 5-8 of a mile in length, and the latter 1 mile), both of which were destroyed during the secession-war, and rebuilt,—to BALTIMORE.

Division B.

AT AND ABOUT BALTIMORE, WITH EXCURSIONS.

BALTIMORE, on the Patapsco River, branch of Chesapeake Bay, most important town in the State of Maryland, seaport of eminence, considered one of the handsomest cities in the Union, and dividing with two or three others the claim of producing the most beautiful women, while to Europeans it possesses the peculiar interest of having supplied wives to a remarkable number of the English aristocracy (Wellesley family, and others), and also a wife (Miss Patterson) to Jerome Bonaparte. It has a striking situation, on rising ground sloping up from the harbor, in that respect rivalling Boston; and the numerous spires and monuments fitly crown a picture otherwise of great beauty. Baltimore has an inner and outer harbor, above and below *Fell's Point*, into the latter of which the largest ships enter without difficulty; and the city proper is divided, nearly North and South, by a narrow stream with many bridges, called *Jones' Run*. A strong and handsome fortification, *Fort McHenry*, defends the harbor, and figured conspicuously in both the war of 1812 and that of the secession. Among the chief boasts of the city, and the first objects of interest to the traveller, are

The Monuments, so notable that they have given to Baltimore the soubriquet of the "Monumental City." The first in importance is the *Washington*, in an elevated position on Mt. Vernon Place, at Charles and Monument streets—a base and shaft reaching 200 feet in height, with a statue surmounting all, of "Washington Resigning his Commission." (Accessible, and fine view from balcony at top.) Next in interest is the *Battle*, at Calvert and Fayette streets—a Roman column, with emblematical sculptures, in honor of those who fell in defence of the city, in September 1814. The third, or *Armistead*, in honor of the defender of Fort McHenry in 1814, is merely a tablet, on North Calvert street, and only of interest in the patriotic connection.

Of streets, the most important is *Baltimore street*, running east and west the whole length of the city, and really its Broadway or Regent street. *Holliday, Calvert, Fayette, Lexington, Eutaw, Madison, Park, Saratoga, North Charles, Mt. Vernon Place, Charles avenue*, and other streets on the west side of Jones' Falls, are among the notable; and as centres of business, *Lombard, Caroline, Bank, Gay, High, Market, Broadway,* and other streets on the east side, with those surrounding the City Dock (basin) and principal wharves, lying in that vicinity. Of Public Buildings, among the most notable are the *Exchange*, Gay street, with noble dome; (*Custom House* and *Post Office* occupying part of the same building); the *Maryland Institute*, Baltimore street, devoted to industrial exhibitions, fairs, &c., and a Market; the *City Hall*, Holliday street; *County Court House*, Monument square; *U. S. Court House*, North and Fayette streets; *Penitentiary and Prisons*, Madison street; *Corn Exchange*, South street; the *Shot Tower*, Front and Fayette streets; Of Churches, in Baltimore as in Philadelphia, the most imposing is the Catholic, the *Cathedral*, at Cathedral and Mulberry streets, being the finest ecclesiastical edifice in the city, with impressive towers and dome; one of the largest organs in the country; and two pictures of great value within, a "Descent from the Cross" and "St. Louis Burying His Dead," respectively the gifts of the French Kings Louis XVI. and Charles X. After this, in architectural interest, come the *Unitarian*, North Charles and Franklin streets; the *Presbyterian*, Madison and Park streets; *Grace* (Epis.), Monument and Park streets; *St. Paul's*, Charles street, and many others, the city being by no means deficient in this detail.

Of Literary Institutions and their edifices, may be named the *University of Maryland*, with celebrated Medical Department, Green and Lombard streets;

ROUTE NO. 9.—WESTERN AND SOUTHERN. 167

the *Peabody Institute* (founded by the late George Peabody), Charles and Monument streets; *St. Mary's College* (Catholic), Franklin and Greene streets; *Maryland Historical Society, Baltimore Library, Mercantile Library,* &c., rooms in the *Atheneum,* Saratoga and St. Paul streets; *College of Loyola* (Catholic), Madison and Calvert streets; *College of Pharmacy,* North Calvert street; &c. Principal Theatres: the *Holliday Street,* street of same name; the *Front Street,* or *American,* Front street; *Baltimore Museum,* Broad and Calvert streets; *Grand Opera House* (new); *Concordia* (German), South Eutaw street. Prominent Hotels: the *Mt. Vernon, Carrollton, Barnum's, Eutaw, Gilmour's, Fountain,* and *Maltby's.*

Cemeteries of prominence: *Green Mount,* Belvidere street and York avenue, with fine gateways and many handsome walks and monuments; *Loudoun Park,* also with fine gateway, Frederick road; *Baltimore Cemetery,* North Gay street; *Mount Olivet,* Frederick road; *Mount Carmel, Western,* and other minor. Other Parks and Public Grounds: *Druid Hill Park,* very large and handsome grounds, recently laid out, in the Northern suburbs [street-car from city centres]; *Patterson Park,* East Baltimore street, with remains of earthworks of war of 1812; *City Spring Grounds,* North Calvert street; *Union Square,* West Lombard street; *Federal Hill,* with Signal

House and one of the very best views of the city and harbor; *Franklin Square*, Fayette street; *Jackson Square*, Hampstead street; etc.

Favorite Excursions, among others, to

Fort McHenry and *North Point*, entrance of the harbor (before spoken of); to *Franklin*, the Convent, &c., by the Frederick road [favorite drive]; to *Govanstown*, by the York road [drive]; to *Catonsville* and *Ellicott's Mills* [horse-car]; to *Towsontown* (military barracks, &c.) [horse-car]; to *Bel-Air*, *Franklinton*, &c.] [stage-coach]. *Down the Chesapeake Bay* [boat, very frequent from harborwharves, during the warm season]. Longer Excursions, among others, to

ANNAPOLIS, Capital of the State of Maryland, and seat of the celebrated national *Naval Academy*. It lies on the little River Severn, near Chesapeake Bay; has a history of interest, dating back to 1649; was the spot where Genl. Washington resigned his commission at the close of the War of Independence; and has, in addition to the other attractions named, an educational institution of prominence, *St. John's College*, a *State House*, and much fine river and coast scenery in the neighborhood. [Reached from Baltimore by the Baltimore and Washington road to *Annapolis Junction*, thence branch road direct.] Also, by daily boat on Chesapeake Bay, to

NORFOLK, Virginia, on the Elizabeth River, at the extreme southern point of Chesapeake Bay, and the second town in Virginia in point of population

ROUTE NO. 9.—WESTERN AND SOUTHERN.

It has a fine harbor, with great depth of water; and is one of the greatest markets of wild-fowl (especially the celebrated "canvas-back" ducks of the Chesapeake), oysters, fruits and other supplies, to be found south of Philadelphia. Across the river from it are the *Portsmouth Naval Depot*, formerly the most extensive in the Union, but materially damaged by fire at the commencement of the secession war (1861), with the burning of the Pennsylvania, Merrimac and other war vessels,—and the *Gosport Navy Yard*, with Dry Docks of great size and cost. Norfolk and Portsmouth harbor proper are defended by *Fort Calhoun* and the works on *Craney Island;* while the entrance from the sea is commanded by *Fortress Monroe*, the largest fortification in the United States, erected at *Old Point Comfort* (also place of favorite summer resort), on the opposite or north side of the wide mouth of the *James River* (Hampton Roads), directly north and some fourteen miles distant. In the latter neighborhood may also be visited, *Elizabeth City* and *Hampton*, more or less interestingly connected alike with the early history of Virginia and the secession troubles of 1861-5. May also be visited, from Norfolk or Old Point Comfort [boat], the site and *Ruins of Jamestown*, place of first settlement in Virginia, and scene of the romantic episode of Captain John Smith and Pocahontas. [From Baltimore to Richmond, every day during summer, by boat of the Baltimore Steam-Packet Company, in connection with the Atlantic Coast Line,—with fine views throughout.] [Norfolk to RICHMOND, by boat up the James River; or may be visited from Richmond, by same conveyance.] Also, by Baltimore and Ohio Railroad (or by same road from Washington), through the Monocacy Valley, along the Upper Potomac and the Chesapeake and Ohio Canal, to

Point of Rocks (railway connection to *Frederick*, Md.); to *Hagerstown Junction* (railway connection to *Hagerstown*); and to

HARPER'S FERRY, on the Upper Potomac, at the intersection with that stream of the Shenandoah, with mountain and river scenery of the first magnificence, and the additional interest of having been the site of an important U. S. Armory and Arsenal (destroyed by fire in April, 1861), and the spot where John Brown, of Ossawatomie, made his celebrated raid and virtually commenced the conflict of the secession, in October, 1859. *Maryland, Bolivar* and *Loudoun Heights*, and their fortifications, demand notice, as do a thousand natural beauties and warlike reminiscences certain to be suggested on the spot.

From Harper's Ferry, route on the Baltimore and Ohio road may be pursued to *Sir John's Run*, with stage connection to *Berkeley Springs;* to *Cumberland*, and across one of the finest passes of the Allegheny Mountains to PITTSBURG and the West. Or, from Harper's Ferry rail may be taken down the Shenandoah Valley, through the Valley of Virginia, to *Charlestown, Winchester, Strasburg, Harrisonburg* and *Staunton*, with connections and detours of great interest. (See Route 9½).

Division C.

BALTIMORE TO WASHINGTON, BY BALTIMORE AND OHIO RAILROAD.

[From New York and Philadelphia to Baltimore, see Routes 8 and 9, pp. 144 and 162.]

Leave Baltimore by the Washington Branch of the B. and O. Road, from Camden Station, by Carroll and Camden Junction, to

RELAY HOUSE and *Relay Station.* (First-class hotel and refreshment station, both owned and operated by the B. and O. Railroad Company, and somewhat noted for their excellence). Relay House and the vicinity were necessarily quite celebrated during the Secession War, the movements of troops over the lines of rail between the different sections, and especially between Baltimore and Annapolis, and Baltimore and Washington, throwing the central point into great prominence, and making the control of it no secondary consideration in the warlike arrangements of the period. At Relay House also diverges the alternate line, with branch to *Frederick,* joining the main line at Point of Rocks.

Relay House by Elkridge, Hanover, Dorsey's and Jessup's to

Annapolis Junction. [Connection to ANNAPOLIS, site of the Naval Academy, and the State capital of Maryland: see "Excursions from Baltimore," preceding]; thence by Savage, Laurel, Contees, Beltsville, Paint Branch, &c., to

Bladensburgh. [Junction of branch to *Shepherd,* on Potomac River, opposite Alexandria, and to Alexandria, where connection is made with steamboats for Fredericsburg, Richmond, &c., by Acquia Creek and the Richmond and Potomac R. R. Also, from Shepherd or from Alexandria, by the Washington City, Virginia Midland and Great Southern Railroad, passing *Manassas Junction* and the scene of the important battle of Manassas, 1861, *via Gordonsville,* to RICHMOND, and any Southern connection that may be desired.]

Bladensburgh, small town on the Eastern Branch of the Potomac, with a mineral-spring and some celebrity as a healthful summer resort for Washington residents and others near; but much more as the scene of the disgraceful defeat of the American by the British forces, in August, 1814, immediately previous to the temporary occupation of the Capital—and also as the spot long famous as a duelling-ground for Congressional and other disputants. Very soon after leaving Bladensburg, is caught, what should by no means be lost, the

First View of the Washington Capitol, scarcely second to the corresponding distant view of the dome of St. Peter's, in approaching Rome—the dome of the Capitol, since re-erection, being among the largest and finest in the world, and the first sight peculiarly impressive. But a little time and distance, following, before entering the somewhat straggling city, and disembarking at the foot of Capitol Hill—WASHINGTON.

Division D.

BALTIMORE TO WASHINGTON, BY THE BALTIMORE AND POTOMAC RAILROAD.

[From New York and Philadelphia to Baltimore, see Routes 8 and 9, pp. 144 and 162.]

Leave Baltimore, from Union Depot, by Lafayette, Winans', Stony Run, Severn, *Odenton* [connection to Annapolis, by Annapolis and Elk Ridge R. R.], Patuxent, *Bowie*, [connection with branch to *Pope's Creek*, on the Potomac, whence may be conveniently reached, Port Tobacco and other places of that section—a part of it somewhat notable for events connected with the escape of John Wilkes Booth from Washington, after the killing of President Lincoln,] Seabrook, Wilson's, Benning's, then Washington.

Entering Washington by this route, one of the first objects of interest is the Navy Yard, with which a station of the road is connected. [See, for Navy Yard, p. 181.]

[From Washington, the Baltimore and Potomac Railroad continues, crossing by fine new Bridge over the Potomac (affording view of the White House, the Treasury Buildings, and many other objects of interest), to *Alexandria*, affording connection with the Alexandria and Fredericsburg R.R. for Quantico, Fredericsburg, Richmond and the South.]

172 *ROUTE NO. 9.—WESTERN AND SOUTHERN.*

Division E.

AT AND ABOUT WASHINGTON, WITH EXCURSIONS.

WASHINGTON, capital city of the United States of America, and on many accounts specially interesting, as bearing the name of the Great Soldier and Patriot, as having been selected by him as the seat of Government, as having been the scene of all the central legislation of the country and many of its other historical events, and as possessing a location with many marked advantages and certain equally marked disadvantages almost counterbalancing the favorable,—lies in the District of Columbia, on the north bank of the Potomac River, at some 70 miles from the embouchure of that river into Chesapeake Bay, and about 30 miles directly westward from the nearest shore of that Bay, at a little southward of Annapolis. In its selection, undoubtedly the first object held in view was to secure the nearest possible approach to centrality between the North and the South, that between the East and the West, now grown so important, not being at all calculated. It supplies a geographical meridian of importance: Lat. 38° 53' 39" N.; Long. 77° 2' 48" from Greenwich; and lies in a direct line about 120 miles south-west from Philadelphia, and about 200 in a corresponding direction from New York. It dates, as the Capital, from the removal from Philadelphia, about 1800, though the corner stone of the Capitol was laid in 1793. The city, as a municipality, dates from nearly the same time—is large in extent, and by no means compact in its character; that fact having given rise, many years ago, to the irreverent soubriquet: the "City of Magnificent Distances."

Among the undeniable advantages of Washington, before referred to, are its picturesque location, with elevations and fine views at two points,—those of the Capitol, at the south-eastern end of (main) Pennsylvania Avenue, and the President's House and principal Government Buildings, at the north-western end; its ease of access from the sea, and accessibility by railway from various important points; its moderate climate in winter, principal season of legislative assemblage; and its proximate centrality, as between North and South. Among the disadvantages may be named the doubtful healthiness of some portions (including the Executive Mansion) in summer; and its entire want of centrality towards the limited East and the widely-extended West—the latter feature having given rise to much dissatisfaction, of late years, and some efforts at effecting the removal of the seat of government to some one of the Western cities—St. Louis being oftenest named. The governmental conveniences now existing on this spot, however, and the late completion of the enlarged Capitol, render it entirely improbable that any such removal will take place within the present century, and leave Washington to be visited and considered as the **permanent capital of the United States.**

Of course first among its attractions, to the tourist, at whatever season, will be found

THE CAPITOL, standing on Capitol Hill, fronting east and west, and occupying the same site as the original, founded by Washington and burned by the British in 1814, when the Congressional Library, many valuable pictures, the President's House and other buildings, shared the same fate. The present structure, undeniably one of the noblest government buildings in the world, and with many grand and beautiful details in architecture, is an enlargement of that which replaced the burned building, and has consequently the blemish of showing some incongruity in materials and "afterthought" in design. It is immense in extent, however, the entire length being some 750 feet, with a wing depth of 300 and a body depth of 200; and the whole space of ground covered is said to be three and a half acres. Handsome grounds surround the Capitol, with fine shade trees and some good landscape gardening; and from these grounds, below either front, and from the two fronts themselves, remarkably fine views may be obtained.

The *East Front*, (main) has an immense colonnade and portico, with Persico's statues of Columbus, of Washington, allegorical figures of Peace and War, Greenough's "Civilization," etc., on the portico and in the grounds adjoining; and it is here that the inauguration ceremonies of each incoming President take place, the auditory filling the portico and the grounds below. The *West Front*, less elaborate, has the view down Pennsylvania Avenue and over the city. The next most prominent feature, and perhaps the most notable of all, is

The Dome, before spoken of as among the noblest in the world. It surmounts the center of the pile, rising to a height of nearly 400 feet, crowned with a colossal statue of Freedom, by Crawford; and is ascended from within, by a spiral stairway, for the extensive and magnificent view of Washington, the Potomac, the near portions of the District, of Virginia, Maryland, etc. In the *Rotunda*, immediately under the dome, are to be seen the eight large historical pictures, " Discovery of the Mississippi," "Baptism of Pocahontas," "Declaration of Independence," "Surrender of Burgoyne," "Surrender of Cornwallis," "Washington Resigning his Commission," and "Landing of Columbus." The Rotunda has also a "Massacre of the Innocents," portraits of Lincoln and others, some interesting historical bas-reliefs, etc. The Canopy, surmounting, is elaborately painted in fresco, by Brumidi, and contains an immense number of allegorical and historical figures. Naturally the next objects of interest will be the

Senate and Representative Chambers, the former situated in the north wing (or " extension "—new part of the building) and the latter in the south wing. They are both large, with good accommodation for spectators (in the Strangers' Galleries), elaborately finished, lighted from above by hidden gas-burners through ground glass, and extremely well ventilated, but with their impressiveness materially marred by the low, flat ceilings. Both are reached by elaborate and costly stairways, really among the most notable features in the building.; and it may be said of both that, with whatever faults of construction, they are among the best of their class, in the world. Next in interest is to be visited the

Supreme Court Room, a large semi-circular apartment in the north wing, with busts of former Chief-Justices Jay, Rutledge, Ellsworth and Marshall; and beneath it the Old Supreme Court Room, now the *Law Library*, with a fine collection of books in the higher branches of jurisprudence, and some peculiarities in the architecture of the room, commanding surprised attention. The

Library of Congress, with some 90,000 to 100,000 volumes (now accumulating very rapidly, as copies of all works published in America must be deposited there, to secure copy-rights—as in the British Museum), and an immense number of valuable documents and manuscripts,—is in the western portion of the main building, and shows fire-proof bookcases and all appliances to guard against the recurrence of fire, which has twice destroyed previous collections (1814—war; and 1851, accidental.) But perhaps quite as interesting as any of the apartments named, is the

Old Hall of Representatives, in the south wing of the center building, semi-circular, with panelled ceiling and cupola, row of splendid columns in Virginia green-stone; and containing, among other objects of interest and value, Vanderlyn's "Washington," a full-length of Lafayette, Franzoni's statue of History, statues and busts of Washington, Kosciusko, Lincoln, Johnson, &c. Here, also, have spoken nearly all the great legislators of America in the past, making the place historically memorable. Opening from this into the corridor, may be seen the

Bronze Columbus Door, modelled by Rogers and cast at Munich (where the model remains), representing various scenes in the life and death of the discoverer, and considered among the best of contemporary works.

Many other apartments of interest may be visited in the Capitol, among them the President's and Vice-President's Rooms, the Speaker's, Senators', Reception, &c., and some of the Committee Rooms, in the latter of which will be found displayed quite as much luxury (not always in the best taste) as can be found in any other portion of the structure.

[Admission to the Capitol, and access to most of its rooms, every week-day, 10 to 3. Congress generally in session from early December to 4th March, in the years with odd numbers; in those with even numbers, (as 1876) the sessions often continuing far into the summer, and even later. Admission to the Congressional Sessions, without card, and only limited by the capacity of the large galleries. In connection it may be well to say that the same hours (10 to 3) and the same freedom from routine or special application, apply to most of the Department buildings at Washington.]

Next in importance to the traveler, of the buildings of Washington, is the

PRESIDENT'S HOUSE (familiarly known as the "White House," especially in political parlance), situated on the high ground at the opposite or north-western extremity of (main) *Pennsylvania Avenue* (principal drive and fashionable promenade of the city). It is of white stone, as its name indicates, has a colonnaded front, but little architectural merit, stands near the Potomac, and commands a fine view of that river and the opposite shore. It contains some handsome and well-appointed rooms, the *East Room* being the most notable ; but the location is not considered healthy in summer, and the Presidential family does not often steadily occupy it throughout that season. [Calls, without ceremonial or previous introduction, are generally received by the President every week-day, 10 to 1, except those devoted to Cabinet meetings or other special appointments. No court-dress necessary or proper. Levees, during the Congressional Season, fortnightly; and weekly receptions, generally on Saturday mornings, by the Lady of the White House, with the President present.]

THE PATENT OFFICE, after those named, is undoubtedly the most interesting place of visit in Washington, for its massive architecture and on account of its extraordinary collection of mechanical and labor-saving implements, in which it has no equal in any country. It is located on F street (many of the Washington streets being thus designated by letters) between Seventh and Ninth streets. The *Model Room*, occupying one entire floor, is divided into four halls, of which the East Hall is occupied by practical models; the West Hall by rejected ones; the South Hall (with handsome frescoed ceilings) by personal effects of Washington, other Revolutionary relics, (sword of Washington and cane of Franklin, among others) medals and Treaties with, and presents from foreign powers, Powers' Statue of Washington, &c., forming a unique, most valuable and interesting collection. Near the Patent Office is to be visited the

General Post Office, an imposing Corinthian structure, with the internal arrangements commanding a certain degree of attention, and some valuable records of Franklin. Also, the City Post Office, in same building. The

State, War and Navy Departments have buildings near each other and near the President's House, on Pennsylvania Avenue. Little of interest is to be found in either, except the Library of the State Department, and the Collection of Relics of the War and Navy. Of much more importance to the visitor is the

Treasury Department Building, on Fifth street, immense in size and of some architectural merit;

while the details of *Paper Money Printing* [admission by order from the Secretary of the Treasury—easily obtained], carried on in the upper and lower portions of the structure, are worthy of close attention from their extent and completeness. The

Smithsonian Institute (founded by the late James Smithson, Esq., of England), stands in extensive and highly ornamented grounds, called the Mall, west of the Capitol, and south-east of the President's House. It is of large extent, built of red sandstone, Norman in architecture, and has nine towers, of irregular heights. It contains an immense library-room, picture-gallery, lecture-room, laboratory, etc., and is already doing a noble work in the advancement of science. At no considerable distance from this, stands the

Washington Monument, intended to be one of the largest in the world, but thus far simply one of the largest failures, the funds to complete it from its present height of 170 feet to the contemplated 600, not being forthcoming. It is at present no monument, but a curiosity. The

National Observatory stands on Western Pennsylvania Avenue, half way between the President's House and Georgetown. It has a large transit and some other fine instruments, astronomical library, clock, etc.

The Public Grounds of Washington are principally comprised in the *Mall*, on the banks of the Potomac, at and near the Smithsonian Institute;

the *Capitol-Grounds*, before spoken of; and *Lafayette Square*, near the President's House (with Clark Mills' equestrian statue of Jackson). Principal Churches: the *Epiphany*, (Epis.) G. Street, near Thirteenth; *Trinity* (Epis.) Third street; *St. John's* (Epis.) Lafayette Square; *Presbyterian*, Four-and-a-half Street; *St. Aloysius* (Cath.) near the Capitol; *Foundry* church, (Meth. Epis.) Fourteenth street. Principal Theatres: the *New National* and *Wall's Opera House*. (*Ford's Theatre*, once a favorite, and the scene of the assassination of President Lincoln, April, 1865, is to be seen as a curiosity, but has never since been opened as a place of amusement). Public Hall: *Lincoln Hall*. Prominent Hotels: the *Arlington; St. Cloud; Howard; St. James'; Willard's*.

Suburban and other excursions from Washington, will include those to the *Soldiers' Home* (Military Asylum), three miles north of the city, and favorite resort of Presidential families in summer; the *Arsenal*, Greenleaf's Point, junction of Eastern Branch and Potomac, with interesting collection of ordnance. To the

Navy Yard, with ship-houses, an armory, etc., on the Eastern Branch, short walk south-east of the Capitol. To the

Congregational Cemetery, lying on the Eastern Branch, north-east of the Capitol, with many scores of monuments to Members of Congress who have died at Washington, and specially notable monuments of interest, to William Wirt, George Clinton, Elbridge Gerry, and others; also *Glenwood*, rival cemetery of much beauty, lying north of the Capitol. To the

Long Bridge, crossing the Potomac to the Virginia shore, from near the Mall, to Alexander's Island, and computed to have carried over half a million of troops during the war of the secession. To

GEORGETOWN, a handsome suburb, lying at the West, beyond Rock Creek, with fine view from the *Heights*, and much interest in the *Aqueduct*, carrying the Chesapeake and Ohio Canal over the Potomac; also, *Georgetown College* (Jesuit), at the west end of the town, with library, museum, observatory, etc.; the *Convent of the Visitation*, Fayette street; Asylum for Children ; *Oak Hill Cemetery* (with handsome Chapel, fine monument to M. Bodisco, etc.) To

Arlington House, former mansion of George Washington Parke Custis, stepson of Washington, and later of General Robert E. Lee, of the Confederate service, but the property since occupied as a Freedman's Village, and most of the rare Washington and other relics carried away, though the place must always retain a certain historical interest. To

Little and *Great Falls*, of the Potomac, above Georgetown, with handsome scenery, and specially fine fishing. [All the last named places are most conveniently reached by carriage.] To

ROUTE NO. 9.—WESTERN AND SOUTHERN. 183

ALEXANDRIA, old town of Virginia, on the Western side of the Potomac, seven miles below Washington—once of heavy commercial importance, but now decayed. It has interesting historical reminiscences, in the fact that Gen. Braddock's unfortunate expedition to Fort Duquesne, which brought Col. Washington to notice, was fitted out here; also in his pew in Christ Church, still preserved, and other relics of the Father of his Country. It has a later and melancholy interest as the spot (at the Marshall House) where Col. Ellsworth, the Zouave, and his slayer, Jackson, were both shot, in May, 1861. It has also a Museum, Court House, Theological Seminary, etc. [Reached from Washington by special boat here and to Mount Vernon; or by regular daily boat on way to Acquia Creek, Fortress Monroe, and Richmond. Also, by rail or road. Railway connection, north to WASHINGTON; south to *Acquia Creek,* RICHMOND, etc.; northwest to *Leesburg,* HARPER'S FERRY, *Chambersburg,* etc.; west and southwest (through a succession of the early battle-fields of the secession war), to *Fairfax Court House, Manassas Junction* (battle-field of *Bull Run* in immediate neighborhood) connection northwestward to *Strasburg, Winchester,* etc.), *Warrenton Junction* (for Warrenton), *Culpepper, Orange Court House, Gordonsville,* CHARLOTTESVILLE (seat of the *University of Virginia,* and with "Monticello," home of Thomas Jefferson, lying near), *Summit,* and other stations, to

Staunton, principal depot of the Chesapeake and Ohio road (connection northward to Harrisonburg and to Harper's Ferry); to *Goshen* (near connections to Rockbridge Alum, Bath Alum, Jordan Alum and other Springs; and by stage to Rockbridge Baths, Lexington, the Natural Bridge, &c.); to *Covington;* through the Alleghenies to *White Sulphur Springs,* (see, for all these connections, Route $9\frac{1}{2}$); to HUNTINGTON, on the Ohio River, terminus of the Chesapeake and Ohio road, &c.]

Of course the most interesting of all excursions from Washington will be that to

MOUNT VERNON, old residence and burial place of Washington, lying on the west bank of the Potomac, eight miles below Alexandria. It is, to Americans, unquestionably the most sacred of places on the continent, and only less interesting to those from other lands. Though somewhat decayed, the *House* (now the property of the Nation, through the labors of Edward Everett and the ladies of the "Ladies' Mount Vernon Association"), commands a beautiful view of the river, is in fair preservation, and contains many valuable relics, among others, pictures and furniture of Washington, the Key of the Bastille, presented to him by Lafayette, etc. *The Tomb*, of brick, stands near the house, under heavy shade, with an open grated doorway through which the sarcophagi of Washington and his wife are seen; with other tombs of the family visible without; the archway of the tomb bearing the simple inscription; "*Within this enclosure rest* the remains of General George Washington." Not far distant is the original Tomb, now crumbling to dust. [Reached from Washington by boat; or by boat to Alexandria, and drive, or by drive. If by boat, with view of and stop at old *Fort Washington*, once a fortification of some consequence, on the eastern side of the Potomac, between Alexandria and Mount Vernon.]

Other Excursions from Washington, those to *Bull Run*, scene of the first important battle of the secession [reached from *Alexandria*, by Manassas Junction], and other fields of the late conflict. Also, nearly the same, in different directions, with obvious variation of railway routes, as those from Baltimore —see close of Division B, this route.

Division F.

WASHINGTON, TO AND AT RICHMOND, VA.

Leave Washington by morning boat on the Potomac river, to *Alexandria*, Va., on the right, [See previous Division]; thence by *Fort Washington*, on the left [See same], and *Mount Vernon*, on the right [See same]; or, by rail from Washington to

Acquia Creek, small village deriving its only importance from this transit, at the junction of the Creek of that name with the Potomac. Thence rail, on the Richmond, Fredericsburg and Potomac road, to

FREDERICSBURG, on the right bank of Rappahannock River—old town of importance in early Virginia history, and especially notable from the fact that GEORGE WASHINGTON was born in the immediate neighborhood. This event, so important to the Western World, and indeed to all mankind, took place upon what has long been known as the Wakefield Estate, at an inconsiderable distance from the town, within the limits of Westmoreland county; and though the birth-place has long been destroyed, the spot is commemorated by a stone slab erected there by George W. P. Custis, step-son of Washington, in 1815, and bearing the brief inscription: "*Here, the 11th of February, (O. S.) 1732, George Washington was Born.*" The mother of Washington resided, late in life, at Fredericsburg, and died and was buried there; her monument, in the outskirts of the town, inaugurated by President Jackson in 1833, still shamefully remaining unfinished. The house is still pointed out, at the corner of Lewis and Charles streets, where she saw her distinguished son for the last time. Fredericsburg has also a later celebrity, as the scene, and in the neighborhood, of a considerable amount of the fighting of the secession war, in 1862, '63, and later; and the country in the vicinity has by no means recovered from the devastation of those conflicts. Fredericsburg, by *Milford, Chester, Sexton's Junction* [connection westward, by Chesapeake and Ohio Railroad, to *Gordonsville, Staunton,* and *White Sulphur Springs,*] to

RICHMOND, on the James River, capital of the

State of Virginia, and ever memorable as the later seat of the Confederate Government, and the object of an investiture and siege by the United States forces, that seemed literally hopeless and interminable. It lies on the left or north bank of the James, at the Lower Falls, or end of that series of rapids extending six miles above and supplying the city with the needed water-power for its many flour-mills, tobacco and other manufactories. The most conspicuous object in the city, from the height of its position as well as from other causes, is

The Capitol, located on Shockoe Hill, a considerable elevation, and thus looking down upon the major portion of the city. It is Greek in the character of its architecture, with porticos, and a tall, narrow dome, and is generally impressive in effect, though the details are by no means faultless. It stands in a public square elevated as above named, and commands a fine view, especially from the portico or dome, over the James River, its islands, and a wide stretch of country. Internally, there is not much of interest in the legislative halls; the principal attraction centering in the splendid marble statue of Washington, by Houdon, considered the best extant, standing in the central hall, under the dome—and in the historical reminiscences, now so varied, inevitably clustering round the principal place of direction of the short-lived Confederacy.

Other Principal Buildings, worth visit: *Richmond* and *St. Vincent Colleges;* the *City Hall, Custom*

House and *Penitentiary;* and, as special objects of interest connected with the war, *Castle Thunder* and the *Libby Prison.* Also may be visited with profit, some of the many *Flouring Mills,* in which some of the best wheat in the world is prepared. Leading Churches: *St. John's* and the *Monumental,* with many others only less interesting. Other objects of interest:.the old *Lines of Fortification* defending the city during the siege; the *Rapids* (or Falls of the James); the entrance of the James River and Kanawha Canal, etc. Leading Hotel: the *Ballard.*

[Principal railway connections from Richmond: northward, by routes just traversed, to WASHINGTON, etc.; eastward to the *White House* and Chesapeake Bay; southward, by Petersburg and Weldon road, to *Weldon* and *Wilmington* (N. C.); westward, by Sexton's Junction and *Gordonsville,* to *Charlottesville, Staunton, Covington, White Sulphur Springs,* &c.; south-westward, by Richmond and Danville road, to *Greensboro* (N. C.); and *Columbia* and CHARLESTON (S. C.); also south-westward, by South Side and Tennessee roads (by Burkeville Junction) to *Lynchburg,* and across the Alleghenies to *Knoxville* (Tenn.), and other places in extreme south and west. (See routes following.)]

ROUTE No. 9½—SPECIAL VIRGINIAN TOUR.*

BALTIMORE OR WASHINGTON TO PRINCIPAL VIRGINIA SPRINGS, NATURAL CURIOSITIES AND MOUNTAINS, AND TO LYNCHBURG AND RICHMOND.

Division A.

BY HARPER'S FERRY TO BERKELEY SPRINGS.

Leave Baltimore or Washington by Baltimore and Ohio railroad, along the Upper Potomac and the Chesapeake and Ohio Canal, with burned bridges and other traces of the late secession war, through Monocacy Valley to

Point of Rocks, commencement of the rough division made by the Potomac River between the States of Maryland and Virginia (railway connection northward to *Frederick*); to *Hagerstown Junction* (railway connection northward to *Hagerstown*); to

---

* Tickets, information, and all facilities for this tour, are supplied by Messrs. COOK, SON & JENKINS, 261 Broadway, New York, one of the members of which firm has deserved the thanks of travelers by his efforts for better opening Virginia to tourists, and calling closer and wider attention to the noble scenery of the section.

HARPER'S FERRY, at the intersection of the Upper Potomac with the Shenandoah, and considered one of the most picturesque passes in America, as well as a point of much importance in late history. (See Route 9, Division B, p. 170.) Among its objects of special interest are the ruins of the U. S. Arsenal; Maryland, Loudoun, and other heights, through which the Potomac makes its grand passage; the very fine iron bridge over the river, &c. At this point the railroad, which has before followed the Maryland shore, crosses to that of Virginia, and continues for some distance within sight of the Potomac. The next station of importance is that of

Martinsburg, famous during the war for conflicting loyalty and rebelliousness, and the home of the ultra-Southern heroine, Belle Boyd: now a thriving town, with railway-shops, the county Fair-Grounds, and a rough but picturesque location. By minor stations to

Sir John's Run, on the Potomac, spot of one of the encampments of General Braddock, on the way to his disastrous defeat at Fort Duquesne, and named for Sir John Sinclair, commander of his vanguard. Also noted for the experiments of Rumsey, who here constructed one of the earliest steamboats.

[Beyond Sir John's Run, for *Cumberland*, PITTSBURG and the West, continue by the Baltimore and Ohio road, crossing the Alleghenies, through scenery of marked magnificence. See "Route $9\frac{3}{4}$."]

At Sir John's Run, for the purposes of this tour,

stage is taken, through very fine mountain scenery, for a short ride to

BERKELEY SPRINGS, one of the oldest and most noted of the Virginia watering-places, at which Gen. Washington, Thomas Jefferson and other great men of the past had summer residences, and sought health and relaxation. The Springs lie in a pleasant valley, hemmed in by mountains, and are alleged to possess a specially breezy atmosphere, at all seasons; and the waters, merely tepid, have a high repute for bathing. The place has a certain additional celebrity, as the residence of "Porte Crayon" (Gen. D. H. Strother), the well-known illustrator of Virginia scenery. Principal Hotel: the *Pavilion*, with fine grounds and Baths of great completeness.

Return from Berkeley Springs to Sir John's Run and to Harper's Ferry, for pursuance of this tour; changing cars at Harper's Ferry to Winchester and Potomac road.

Division B.

HARPER'S FERRY TO AND AT WEYER'S CAVE.

Leave Harper's Ferry by the Winchester and Potomac road, down the Shenandoah Valley, with shallow river on the left, and many marks of the destruction wrought in the Valley, by fire and otherwise, during the secession war. Through a very fine agricultural country, opening what is more generally called the "Valley of Virginia." Half an hour from Harper's Ferry brings

Charlestown, a village of little prominence, but always notable, henceforth, as the place where John Brown, of Osawattomie, was tried and executed, for his armed invasion of the State, at Harper's Ferry. The spot where Brown was hung is visible in a high field, at the left of the road, shortly after passing through the main village. Continuing through a very rich agricultural country, something less than one hour brings

Winchester, thriving town of the Valley, with the Ice Mountain, where blocks of ice are said to be found all the year round; the Capon Springs, the Hanging Rocks, and other natural curiosities, within easy reach—and having now a peculiar historic and romantic interest, as the spot of an important conflict and the place of termination of T. Buchanan Read's celebrated poem, "Sheridan's Ride." During all this ride down the Valley of Virginia, grand mountain scenery accompanies, at a distance, the Blue Ridge at the East and the North Mountain range at the West, seeming to shut the whole Valley away from the world. Also, many ravines and high bridges add picturesqueness to the journey. At

Strasburg Junction connection is made with the Washington City, Virginia Midland and Great Southern railroad, from and to Manassas Junction, WASHINGTON, *Alexandria*, &c. Passing *Woodstock*, *Mount Jackson*, and other stations, and *Newmarket* (stage connection for *Gordonsville*), is reached.

SPECIAL VIRGINIAN TOUR. 189d

Harrisonburg, former end of rail in this direction, now stopping-place of a certain interest. Hotel, *Effinger's*. Rail may be continued to *Staunton* ; or, at Harrisburg or Weyer's Cave Station, a few miles beyond, stage-coach or private carriage may be taken for the ride, through a moderately broken country, to

WEYER'S CAVE, one of the most remarkable and beautiful subterranean passages in the world, and considered more varied in its spectacles than the Mammoth Cave of Kentucky, though much smaller. It lies on one of the branches of the Shenandoah, a few miles west of the Blue Ridge, and has been principally made known to the world (though known since 1804), by "Porte Crayon," in his "Virginia Illustrated." For any adequate impression of this cave, its many chambers, great extent, wonderful variety, and the singular character of its stalactites and stalagmites, dependance must be entirely placed upon personal observation, the guide (always in readiness), and the local hand-book cheaply supplied. The visitor should be advised, however, (1) that he is undoubtedly visiting one of the most notable subterranean marvels in any land ; (2) that a considerable amount of fatigue is involved in any thorough exploration ; but that (3) no danger whatever is incurred, if the guide's directions are obeyed ; though (4) fine clothing is apt to become a trifle smirched, and ladies' long dresses are out of place ; and (5) night is considered a better time for the visit than day, as the eyes are not subjected to such changes between the world outside the cave and the torchlight realm within it. Hotel (and place for procuring guide), Mohler's *Weyer's Cave Hotel.* In the vicinity of Weyer's Cave are *Madison's Cave* (described by Thos. Jefferson in "Notes on Virginia"), *Fountain Cave,* and others minor but interesting to those making longer sojourns.

From Weyer's Cave, return by stage-coach or carriage to connection with the rail between Harrisonburg and Staunton, at Weyer's Cave Station, thence by rail to *Staunton;* or, to *Mount Sidney,* and continue by carriage (turnpike, and fine drive), to STAUNTON.

Division C.

AT STAUNTON, AND TO THE WHITE SULPHUR SPRINGS.

STAUNTON, thriving town of considerable age, county town of Augusta County, noted for its Collegiate Schools, and seat of two State institutions of consequence—the *Hospital for the Insane,* and the *Asylum for the Deaf and Dumb* and the *Blind,*—has lately sprung into increased prominence as the head-quarters of the just-completed Chesapeake and Ohio railroad, extending from Chesapeake Bay to the Ohio River. It has also additional importance as a place of rendezvous for tourists to the various springs and natural curiosities adjacent. Principal hotel: the *American*. [Railway connections, east to *Charlottesville*, RICHMOND, *Norfolk*, &c.; west by route about to be traversed; south by stage (rail in contemplation) to *Bonsack's*, and the Virginia and Tennessee road, for the south-west.]

From Staunton, for pursuance of this route—by the Chesapeake and Ohio Railroad, by

Goshen, village with important connections to many of the more important Springs, the Natural Bridge, &c., (hereafter to be noted); at this point the scenery along the road commencing and continuing to be singularly wild and grand, ranking among the best of its class in America—all the distance through and from the North Mountain chain, to and through the Alleghenies. Among the most prominent points to be noted, are the rocky pass of Panther Gap, the huge bulk of Griffith's Knob, and the picturesque mouth of the Cow Pasture River. At

Millboro is the point of leaving the rail by coach for the *Warm Springs*, and the Warm Spring Mountain, long celebrated for grandeur of view. Pursuing route by the rail, however, is passed the grand scenery of Clifton Forge, with the wild entrance of Jackson's River; and not far beyond is reached

Covington, mere railway hamlet; beyond which point the scenery is even wilder than before, with the great Clay Cut, the tremendous embankment of Jerry's Run, and two immense Tunnels—the second and longest through one of the mountains of the main Allegheny ridge ; shortly after which are reached

White Sulphur Springs (station, and place of popular resort).

[Beyond the White Sulphur Springs, for those going west, rail is continued, by *Gauley Bridge*, *Charleston*, *Barboursville*, &c., to HUNTINGTON and the Ohio River.] The

WHITE SULPHUR SPRINGS (hotel and grounds) lie very near the station. The grounds are very extensive, and well laid out ; and the hotel building, taking name from the Springs, is large and commodious, though old (having entertained the flower of Southern aristocracy through the summers of more than half a century), while nearly one hundred cottages, in "Rows," circling the grounds, afford favorite accommodation. The waters of the Springs are strongly sulphuric, as the name indicates, and are held to be a specific in many diseases ; though no doubt the principal attraction of the place is, after all, compounded of fashion and the fine surrounding scenery.

SPECIAL VIRGINIAN TOUR.

Division D.

TO LEXINGTON, THE NATURAL BRIDGE, LYNCHBURG AND RICHMOND.

Return, from the White Sulphur Springs, by Chesapeake and Ohio road, by Covington, &c., to

GOSHEN, before named in proceeding westward—important as being the center or point of departure for many places of popular resort. [Among others reached from Goshen by coach, are the *Cold White Sulphur Springs*, 2 miles; the *Rockbridge Alum Springs*, 8 miles; and the *Jordan Alum Springs*, 8 miles; besides others embraced in the tour following.]

Leave Goshen, by stage coach, through the very wild and picturesque Goshen Pass, along the North Fork of the James River, to

Rockbridge Baths, popular place of summer resort, beside the North Fork of the James, and with iodine and magnesia waters, said to be of the first excellence. Hotel: the *Rockbridge Baths*.

From Rockbridge Baths, continue by stage-coach to

LEXINGTON, important town and tourist center, seat of the *Virginia Military Institute*, and of *Washington and Lee University*, and with the tombs of Generals Robert E. Lee and Stonewall Jackson commanding attention. Has also, at the University, an Astronomical Observatory of note, founded by McCormick, inventor of the Reaper, a native of this county (Rockbridge). Leading Hotel: the *National*.

[From Lexington, by stage or private carriage, excursion may be made to the *Peaks of Otter*, mountains of peculiar beauty, southward; or stage may be taken to *Bonsack's*, and connection made with the Virginia and Tennessee road.]

From Lexington, by stage or carriage, to the

NATURAL BRIDGE, first curiosity of Virginia, and one of the grandest in the world. It crosses, in a natural arch of some ninety feet, and with a height of over two hundred feet, the deep chasm of Cedar Creek, flowing into the James; and neither pen nor pencil can do justice to the absolute grandeur of the structure, as witnessed from below and above. Best points of view, and peculiar oddities of resemblance to faces and animals under the arch, pointed out by guides. The tourist may or may not recognize the Eagle with outstretched wings, the Lion's Head, the Goddess of Liberty, and other striking similitudes to men and animals, in the moss and discoloration of the under-surface; but it is sure that he will realize the grandeur of the structure, which is so wide, above, and so solid, that one of the great public roads of the county passes over it, and thousands ride across in stage-coach or wagon without being aware of the terrible gulf beneath, except their attention is called to it. Much interest is always excited by the initials cut at different heights under the arch, by adventurous climbers;

and many fancy, perhaps with reason, that those of George Washington (known to have been a visitor and admirer of the Natural Bridge) may be discovered in a certain locality. From above, at both sides, very fine views over the creek and the adjacent country may be obtained; though prudence should be observed in going near to either edge. There is also a view, at some distance from the road, of the Bridge itself, which should not be lost. Hotel: the *Natural Bridge*. Some notable Caves lie in the neighborhood, partaking of the character of Weyer's and others.

From Natural Bridge, by carriage, to *Gilmour's Mill;* and thence daily (evening) packet-boat on the James River and Kanawha Canal, through fine scenery, to

Lynchburg, on the James River—flourishing town, and great depot of the tobacco trade, as well as railway center of importance. [Connections, westward by the Virginia and Tennessee road; northward to *Charlottesville* and *Gordonsville*, for Eastern Virginia, WASHINGTON, &c.; southward to *Danville*, for North Carolina, &c.; eastward by route about to be traversed.] Leading Hotels: the *Norvell* and *Piedmont*.

From Lynchburg, by the South Side railroad, by *Burkeville Junction*, to RICHMOND. (See Route 9, p. 186 and following.)

Richmond to WASHINGTON by reverse of route 9, Division E, p. 185; or by Chesapeake and Ohio road to *Gordonsville* (Junction), and thence by Washington City, Virginia Midland and Great Southern road,—for return northward; or eastward, or southward, by other lines of connection from that city. (See Route 9, p. 188.)

ROUTE No. 9¼.—WESTERN AND SOUTH-WESTERN.
WASHINGTON OR BALTIMORE, BY BALTIMORE AND OHIO ROAD, TO CUMBERLAND, GRAFTON, AND WHEELING; AND TO CHICAGO, ST. LOUIS, ETC.

Division A.
WASHINGTON OR BALTIMORE TO GRAFTON.

Washington or Baltimore, by B. and O. Road, to Sir John's Run, as by previous route ("Special Virginia Tour," No. 9½), with unequalled opportunities, on all the earlier portions of this route, through and by the Maryland towns, for visiting some of the most noted battle-fields of the secession war, to wit: GETTYSBURG from *Frederick*, ANTIETAM from *Hagerstown* or *Point of Rocks*, &c.

Passing *Point of Rocks*, *Harper's Ferry*, &c., as by that route, and with or without detour at Sir John's Run, to Berkeley Springs, as also by that route,— .

From *Sir John's Run*, continuing west, the railroad crosses the Great Cacapon by a fine bridge 300 feet long, and the Potomac (south branch) by one 400 ft. long; and then, passing by a Viaduct 700 ft. long, crosses to the N. side of the Potomac into Maryland again; and next reaches

Cumberland, the second city of the State of Maryland, situated at the eastern foot of the range of the Alleghenies. It is the center of a most important coal and iron district; has some handsome public buildings, and hotel; is the seat of large iron works, the railroad repairing-shops, and one of the largest steel rolling-mills in the country. Cumberland is the Eastern terminus of the Great National Road through Wheeling, &c., to the Mississippi; also the Western termination of the Chesapeake and Ohio Canal; both of which modes of transit, of the greatest importance in their day, have been to a great extent superseded by railroads.

[Railway connections from Cumberland to Cornellsville and Pittsburgh; also to the Oil Regions of Pennsylvania. Short ride via Bridgeport, to the celebrated *Bedford Springs.*]

Leaving Cumberland, westward, is entered the grand scenery of the Ascent of the Alleghenies, for some 45 miles, among the best on the continent, to the summit, at *Altamont*. Important points are passed, on this ascent, at *Keyser*, 21 miles from Cumberland, and at *Piedmont* (the "mountain foot"), 28 miles from Cumberland. [Important connections, at Piedmont, with the Cumberland and Pennsylvania Railroad, through the coal and iron regions, among the most important in those productions in America.]

At Piedmont commences the famous "17-mile grade," reaching the summit of the Alleghenies at *Altamont*, 2,720 feet above tide-water at Baltimore. Near Altamont, some three miles distant, at Deer Park, is the favorite hotel and summer-resort, the *Deer Park House*. The descending grade of the Alleghenies is commenced at *Cranberry Summit*, 23 miles from Altamont; and very soon after, the magnificent scenery of the *Cheat River Valley* and the river of the same name comes into view. The scenery of this valley is considered almost unrivalled. The valley is crossed by a noble viaduct; and the ascent of the "Cheat River Grade" exposes the splendid scenery of the Laurel Hill range. Among the best and boldest engineering work in America is to be found on this road, during the passage to *Cassidy's Summit*. Again descending, *King Wood Tunnel* is passed through, 4,100 feet in length. Shortly after is reached

Newburgh, (W. Va.), 267 miles from Baltimore. Beyond, the rapid descent of the Three Forks leads to
Grafton, 1,000 feet above tide-water at Baltimore, where diverge the two great sub-divisions of the Baltimore and Ohio: 1st, the Central Ohio Division, to *Newark, Columbus, Sandusky*, &c., thence to *Chicago;* and, 2d, the Main Line to *Parkersburg*, with connections to Cincinnati, St. Louis, the West and Southwest.

Division B.

GRAFTON BY WHEELING TO CHICAGO.

Prominent places passed on this route are :
Fairmount, (W. Va.), county seat of Marion Co.; Mannington, among the beautiful scenery of the Buffalo Valley; *Moundsville*, near which arise the wondrous Indian Mounds of such size and prominence, puzzling all the historians and men of science; Benwood (with connection to Wheeling); *Bellair* (entrance into the State of Ohio); Cambridge; *Zanesville*, important town and county seat of Muskingum Co.; *Newark*, county seat of Licking; COLUMBUS, capital of Ohio (see p. 202); [detour from Newark]; *Mansfield*, county seat of Richland; *Shelby* [connection, by the Cleveland, Columbus, Cincinnati & Indianapolis R. R., with the Atlantic & Gt. Western and Erie roads, direct to New York and the East] ; *Sandusky*, important town of Lake Erie; thence by *Tiffin* (railway junction of importance), Defiance, &c., to CHICAGO.

Division C.

GRAFTON BY PARKERSBURG TO ST. LOUIS.

Passing through a mountainous and wooded country, producing coal and petroleum in great abundance, is reached

Parkersburg, (W. Va.), county seat of Wood Co., on the Ohio, at the mouth of the Little Kanawha—prosperous town, and center of petroleum and other industries. The Ohio river is here crossed by one of the most magnificent bridges in the world, with a height above tide-water of some 80 feet, spans of 350 feet, and a total length of one mile, 550 yards. Two miles below may be seen *Blennerhassett's Island*, so intimately connected with the fortunes of Aaron Burr and his alleged victim, Herman Blennerhasset. At *Belpre* are to be found the great stock-yards of the company. The next place of importance is *Athens*, (O.), county seat of county of same name, and seat of the State University and one of the State Lunatic Asylums. Many of the noted Indian Mounds in the neighborhood. [Railway connection to COLUMBUS, by Hocking Valley road.] Then follow *Hamden*, [branch road to *Portsmouth*, county seat of Scioto, and center of coal and iron industries];

Chilicothe, founded in 1796, and capital of Ohio until 1810—now county seat of Ross, and with many handsome public and other buildings [branch rail to Hillsboro]; *Loveland* [connection with the Little Miami road]; to CINCINNATI, (see p. 204).

From Cincinnati, by *Lawrenceburgh* [connection to *Indianapolis*]; *North Vernon* [branch to *Louisville*, Ohio, and steamers on that river]; *Flora* [connections north to Beardstown, south to Shawneetown, &c.]; *Odin* [connection south to *Cairo*, NEW ORLEANS, &c.] This route terminates with the crossing of the Mississippi river, by one of the most stupendous and magnificent iron bridges in the world, to ST. LOUIS.

ROUTE No. 10.—SOUTH-WESTERN (SEMI-SKELETON.)

RICHMOND BY RALEIGH, WILMINGTON, COLUMBIA, CHARLESTON, ATLANTA, MONTGOMERY AND MOBILE, TO NEW ORLEANS.

Richmond by rail on Petersburg and Weldon road, to PETERSBURG (with fortifications remaining, and other traces of the late struggle). [Connection south-eastward to *Suffolk* and NORFOLK.] Thence by *Hickford Junction* [connection south to *Weldon, Goldsboro* and *Wilmington*], where Raleigh and Gaston road is taken,—and by *Ridgeway Junction;* to

RALEIGH, capital of the State of North Carolina, on the Neuse River, and named after Sir Walter Raleigh. It has an imposing *State House*, handsome *Union Square, State Lunatic Asylum* and many other objects of interest. From Raleigh; by the North Carolina and Wilmington roads, to

WILMINGTON, on the Cape Fear River, largest and chief commercial city of the State, with steamers to New York; extensive exports of naval stores; some good public buildings; *Forts Fisher* and *Caswell* (bombarded during the war), etc. Wilmington, by Columbia and Augusta road to *Florence;* thence by North-eastern road to

CHARLESTON, principal city of South Carolina,

and one of the leading sea-ports of the South [may be reached by steamer direct from New York], as well as especially celebrated as having been the spot at which the first fighting of the secession occurred, and for a long time the stronghold of the Confederates and object of Federal siege. It lies at the confluence of the Ashley and Cooper rivers, has a fine harbor, and very strong fortifications, in *Forts Moultrie, Castle Pinckney,* etc., and also the ruins of the celebrated *Fort Sumter.* It has many good public buildings, though many were destroyed during the war, from which the city is only slowly recovering. Among the most interesting buildings are the *Old State House* (now Court House), *New Custom House, City Hall, Orphan Asylum, St. Michael's Church* (with fine old tower), *Charleston College,* etc. Principal Public Ground: the *Battery,* at the harbor-side. Principal Cemetery: *Magnolia Cemetery,* considered the finest in the South. Leading Hotels: the *Charleston, Mills House* and *Pavilion.* [Near connection south-westward, by Charleston and Savannah road, to

SAVANNAH, principal town of the State of Georgia, on south bank of the Savannah River, with remarkably wide streets, fine shade, many notable public buildings, revolutionary and secession reminiscences, and considered one of the healthiest of the Southern cities. Principal Hotels: the *Screven, Pulaski,* and *Marshall.* Connection from Savannah south-westward to *Tallahassee* and other towns of Florida.]

From Charleston, by South Carolina road, by *Branchville* and *Kingsville*, to

COLUMBIA, capital of South Carolina, beautifully situated on the Congaree river, with what is considered the handsomest *State-Capitol* in the Union, the *South Carolina College*, and many other attractions, though burned during the war, and only partially recovered. Leading Hotel : *Nickerson's*. From Columbia, by Columbia and Augusta road, to

AUGUSTA, important town of Georgia, and second in the State ; on the Savannah River, with *Powder and Cotton Factories*, a large *U. S. Arsenal* in the neighborhood, handsome *City Hall*, and many attractions as a residence. Leading Hotels : the *Augusta* and *Planters'*. From Augusta, westward, by the Georgia road, to

ATLANTA, capital of the State of Georgia, lying at the intersection of the Georgia road west, the Atlantic road southward from *Chattanooga* and NASHVILLE, the Macon road south to *Macon*, &c.; and with a certain other interest in its siege during the war, and as the point of departure of Sherman, on his "March to the Sea." Hotel : the *Kimball*. From Atlanta, by Atlanta and West Point and Montgomery and West Point roads, by *West Point*, to

MONTGOMERY, capital of Alabama, and for a time the seat of the Confederate Government, before removal to Richmond. It lies on the Alabama river, has a commanding site, a *Capitol* worthy of attention, and many other good buildings, though having several times suffered severely by fire. Prominent Hotels: the *Central* and *Exchange*. From Montgomery south-westward, by Mobile and Montgomery road, by *Pollard* (Junction: railway connection to *Pensacola*, handsome town on Pensacola Bay, near the Gulf of Mexico, with fine harbor, U. S. Naval Station, etc.—leading Hotels: *Bedell, Winter* and *St. Mary's Hall*); to

MOBILE, on the Bay of the same name, branch of the Gulf of Mexico. It is the most important seaport of Alabama, and, in spite of bad navigation, the second of the great cotton ports of the Gulf. It has few public buildings of interest, but fine water-views, extensive fortifications, and a romantic historic interest as the scene of Farragut's fearful "passage of the Forts," and lashing himself in the shrouds of his vessel in the midst of their fire. [Communication by steamers and sailing-vessels, to NEW ORLEANS, *Galveston*, and many other ports on the Gulf.] Leading Hotel: the *Battle House*. From Mobile, by Mobile and Texas road, to

NEW ORLEANS, largest city of the State of Louisiana, and first cotton port of the South, as well as entrepot for products coming down the Mississippi River, of which it lies at near the debouchure into the Gulf of Mexico. New Orleans, familiarly called the "Crescent City," from its shape on the river, used also to be called the "Paris of America," and has not quite lost all the characteristics of gaiety bestowing the name. It lies on land lower than the river, rendering necessary a great embankment, called the *Levee*, which also supplies both wharves and promenades, along which may be seen the most marked features of the city. Among the later notable events connected, were another "passing of the Forts," below (*Forts Jackson and St. Philip*), by Admiral Farragut, and the occupation of the city by the somewhat-unpopular commandant, Gen. B. F. Butler. Among the most important buildings are the *Custom House*, Canal Street, one of the largest in America; the *U. S. Branch Mint*; the *City Hall; Odd Fellows' Hall*; *Masonic Hall*; *Merchants' Exchange; U. S. Marine Hospital*, etc. It has many fine churches, with the Roman Catholic *Cathedral of St. Louis* the most prominent; and of its public grounds the most notable are the *New City Park, Lafayette Square, Jackson Square*, etc. Most attractive Cemeteries: *Cypress Grove, Greenwood,* and *Monument* (soldier's). There are two Monuments of interest: the *Clay*, on Canal Street, and the *Jackson* (unfinished) on the Battle-field, below the city. One of the most interesting features of New Orleans is to be found in the *Markets*, which should be visited early in the morning, not only to observe the immense variety of articles on sale, but the negro, half-Spanish and half-French characters of dealers and customers. Principal Theatres: the *Opera House, St. Charles, Varieties* and *Academy of Music*. Prominent Hotels: the *St. Charles, St. Louis, St. James,* and *City*. Excursions may be made to the *Battle-*

field, scene of Gen. Jackson's victory over Sir Edmund Pakenham, Jan. 8th, 1815, four or five miles below the city ; to the *U. S. Barracks*, a little above ; to *Lake Ponchartrain*, above the city (famous for fishing and shooting, in the season); to the *Delta* and the *Mouths of the Mississippi*, some twenty-five miles below.

[New Orleans has regular communication, by steamer, to NEW YORK ; to *Havana* (Cuba) ; to *Galveston* (Texas) ; and nearly all important Gulf ports. Also by steamer up the Mississippi, to *Memphis, Cairo, St. Louis,* and all important towns on that river. Also by rail, by *Jackson* (Miss.) to *Memphis ;* and thence to all towns and cities in the North, North-east or North-west.

ROUTE NO. 11.—SOUTH-WESTERN (SKELETON.)
WASHINGTON OR RICHMOND, BY LYNCHBURG, KNOXVILLE AND CHATTANOOGA, TO MOBILE AND NEW ORLEANS.

Washington by rail, by *Alexandria*; and by Orange, Alexandria and Manassas road (by *Manassas Junction*) to *Charlottesville* (Junction—connection westward to *Staunton*, etc.); thence direct to Lynchburg. Or, Richmond by South Side road to *Burkeville* (Junction—intersection with Richmond and Danville road, southward); thence direct by *Appomattox*, and other stations, to

LYNCHBURG, on the James River, and the James River and Kanawha Canal—important tobacco-depot and flourishing town. [Most convenient railway point, from which to reach, by canal-packet or carriage, those great natural curiosities, the *Natural Bridge* and the (Mountain) *Peaks of Otter*.] From Lynchburg, by Virginia and Tennessee road, by *Bonsack's* [stage connection to *Natural Bridge, Lexington*, &c.]; *Big Tunnel* [passage of the Alleghany Mountains; horse-car connection to *Alleghany Springs*]; *Bristol*, and other stations, to

Knoxville, important town of the State of Tennessee, on the Holston River, with the *University of*

East Tennessee, many railway connections, and much popularity as a place of residence. Knoxville to

CHATTANOOGA, on the Tennessee river, near the boundaries of Alabama and Georgia, and one of the most important railway centres of the south-west; but additionally celebrated, since the war, for the battles of *Chickamauga* and *Lookout Mountain,* fought in the immediate neighborhood. In the vicinity of the Lookout (easily visited from Chattanooga,) is to be found scenery of equal grandeur and loveliness. Hotel: the *Crutchfield House.* Chattanooga, by the Alabama and Chattanooga road, by *Tuscaloosa* and other important stations, to

Meridian, railway town of the State of Mississippi, [with connections east to *Montgomery,* west to *Jackson* (capital of the State), north to *Memphis,* etc.]. From Meridian, by the Mobile and Ohio road, direct to MOBILE and New Orleans, as in Route No. 10.

ROUTE No. 11½—SOUTHERN (SEMI-SKELETON.)

BALTIMORE (BY WASHINGTON AND RICHMOND) TO
WELDON, WILMINGTON, CHARLESTON,
SAVANNAH, THE FLORIDA
RESORTS, ETC.

Leave Baltimore, by Baltimore and Ohio, or Baltimore and Potomac route (see Route No. 9, p. 171, &c.), to WASHINGTON (see p. 172). From Washington, by Baltimore and Potomac Railroad, and connections, by *Fredericksburg* (see p. 185), RICHMOND (see p. 186), *Petersburg* (see p. 189*l*), to

Weldon, town of some importance, of North Carolina. At Weldon, connection by the Seaboard and Roanoke Railroad, to NORFOLK and the steamboat line on the Chesapeake Bay to *Baltimore* for WASHINGTON and the North. Also, at Weldon, connection by the Wilmington and Weldon Railroad, to

Wilmington, chief commercial city of the State of North Carolina, and great naval store depot, on Cape Fear River (see Route No. 10). From Wilmington by Florence to COLUMBIA, capital of South Carolina, by the Wilmington, Columbia and Augusta Railway (see p. 191); and by brief connecting road, to AUGUSTA, Georgia (see p. 191.) From Augusta, brief ride to *Aiken*, celebrated health-resort of South Carolina, enjoying remarkable freedom from cold winds of the Atlantic slope. From Augusta by the Central Georgia Railroad, to SAVANNAH (see p. 190). Or, with return from Augusta or Columbia to *Florence*, rail on North-eastern Railroad to CHARLESTON (see p. 189*l*), and by the Savannah and Charleston Railroad to *Savannah* (see p. 190).

From Charleston, for Florida, by boat, every Friday and Saturday evening, touching at *Savannah*. Thence to *Fernandina, Jacksonville, St. John's River* ports, and to *Palatka*. Or from Savannah by boat, as in connection.

From Savannah (all rail), rail on the Atlantic and Gulf, and Jacksonville, Pensacola and Mobile roads, to JACKSONVILLE. Branch rail, Jacksonville to *Fernandina*.

For *Tallahassee, St. Marks,* and *Apalachicola*, rail on Atlantic and Gulf road from Savannah; or on Jacksonville, Pensacola and Mobile road, from Jacksonville.

For *Pensacola* (and for MOBILE), rail as for Tallahassee, &c.

For *Cedar Keys*, rail on Florida road, from Fernandina, or from Jacksonville.

For ST. AUGUSTINE, daily morning boat up the St. John's River from Jacksonville, landing at *Tocoi*—thence St. John's Railroad, about one hour. The same steamer, from Jacksonville, for *Mandarin, Hibernia, Magnolia, Green Cove Springs, Picolata,* and *Palatka*; with smaller boats making trips further up the river to Dunn's Lake, Lake George, &c.

ROUTE NO. 12.—WESTERN.

NEW YORK TO PHILADELPHIA, HARRISBURG, PITTSBURG, CINCINNATI, ST. LOUIS, CHICAGO, ETC., BY PENNSYLVANIA RAILROAD AND CONNECTIONS.

Division A.

NEW YORK TO PHILADELPHIA, OR MANTUA JUNCTION.

Leave New York (as by Route No. 8) by the Pennsylvania road, by *Jersey City, Newark, Elizabeth, Rahway, New Brunswick, Trenton,* etc., to PHILADELPHIA, if for stop at that city; if for through passage to the West, without stop at Philadelphia, New York by the same towns to MANTUA JUNCTION, where close through-connection is made.

Division B.

PHILADELPHIA, OR MANTUA JUNCTION, TO AND AT HARRISBURG.

Leave Philadelphia (West Philadelphia), or Mantua Junction, if without stop at Philadelphia, by rail, by the Pennsylvania Railroad; by *Downington* [connection northward for *Waynesburg*]; by *Coatesville* [connection northward for *Reading*, southward for *Wilmington*], etc.; to

LANCASTER, pleasantly situated on the Conestoga Creek, in a fine agricultural section; seat of *Franklin and Marshall College;* with *Court House* and other creditable buildings, and interesting series of *Canal Locks* in the neighborhood, at mouth of the creek. Was for some years, at beginning of the century, the seat of government of Pennsylvania. Leading Hotels : the *City*, and *Michael's*. Lancaster, by *Branch Intersection* [connection northward to *Reading*, southward for *Columbia, York*, etc.], *Mt. Joy* and *Middletown*, to

HARRISBURG, capital of the State of Pennsylvania, on the east bank of the Susquehanna river (originally "Harris' Ferry" over that river). The most notable building is the *Capitol*, on high ground, with fine view from the dome, with State Library, Legislative Chambers, etc. Also should be visited, the *Court House;* the *Old Harris Mansion*; and some of the extensive Iron and Steel Works in the vicinity; as well the Susquehanna river and some of the bridges spanning it—one of them very old, and showing a remarkably high arch. Principal street; *Front Street*. Principal Public Ground; *Harris Park*. Prominent Hotels; the *Lochiel, Jones House*, and *Bolton's*. [Important railway connections from Harrisburg : by Lebanon Valley road, east to *Lebanon* and *Reading;* by Northern Central road, southeast to BALTIMORE, etc.; by the same road northward to *Elmira* and the Erie Railway and its connections : by Cumberland Valley road, southwestward for *Carlisle, Chambersburg*, etc.; by Philadelphia and Erie road, northwestward for *Williamsport, Corry, Erie* and Oil Regions.]

Division C.

HARRISBURG TO AND AT PITTSBURG, WHEELING, ETC.

From Harrisburg, continuing by Pennsylvania Central road ; by *Lewistown* [connection northward for *Milroy*, northeastward for *Sunbury*, etc.] ; by *Tyrone* [connection northeastward to *Lock Haven* and the Philadelphia and Erie road, northwest to *Clearfield*, etc.] ; by *Huntington*, etc., to

ALTOONA, at the commencement of the ascent of the Allegheny Mountains ; great locomotive-shop of the Pennsylvania Central Company ; and surrounded by magnificent mountain-scenery, making a sojourn very pleasant in summer. Hotel : the *Logan House.* [Spur southward to *Martinsburg*, and stage thence to *Bedford Springs.*] From Altoona should be made, by daylight, to enjoy the fine scenery, the

Railway ascent of the Alleghenies, with features quite as grand as most of the Alpine rail-routes, and double power necessary in drawing up the trains. An immense *Tunnel*, nearly three-quarters of a mile in length, is passed through before reaching the summit, at

CRESSON (Cresson Springs), a popular summer-resort, on account of its elevation and healthful air. Hotel : the *Mountain House*. [Spur northward to *Ebensburg.*] From Cresson the *descent of the Alleghenies* is made, *without the use of steam*, the speed being regulated by brake-power; to *Conemaugh Station;* and to *Johnstown*, with the extensive Cambria Iron Works in the neighborhood, and heavy manufactures. Hotel : the *Scott House*. From Johnstown, by *Blairsville* [connection northward for *Indiana*, northwestward to *Freeport* and points on Allegheny Valley road] ; by *Greensburg*, etc., to

PITTSBURG, at the confluence of the Allegheny and Monongahela rivers (forming the commencement of the Ohio) ; and on the spot once occupied by old Fort Duquesne ; with Braddock's Field, of the French war, in the near vicinity. Very extensive manufactures are carried on, in Pittsburg, in *Allegheny City* (across the Allegheny, and connected by fine bridges), in *Birmingham* (similarly situated across the Monongahela, with bridges), *Lawrenceville*, and other suburbs—in iron, glass, steel, brass, wooden-ware, and many other industries. It is also a great coal and oil centre, and has the smokiest atmosphere in America.

In addition to the *Manufactories* and the extensive *Railway Buildings*, other objects of interest will be found in the *Levee* (wharves) on the Monongahela; the Ohio and Mississippi boats loading there, with many peculiarities for the stranger ; the *Inclined Railway* up Mount Washington, across the Monongahela, whence a fine view of the city may be commanded, etc. Among prominent public and other buildings will be noticed the *Roman Catholic Cathedral*; *Presbyterian* and *Baptist Churches* ; *Court House* ; *Custom House* ; (with Post Office); new *City Hall* ; *Mercantile Library Hall*, etc. ; and in Allegheny City, the *Theological*

Seminaries, Western Penitentiary, etc., and more elegant residences of the citizens. There are no less than four Cemeteries : the *Allegheny ; St. Mary's ; Hilldale ;* and *Mt. Union.* Leading Hotels : the *Monongahela, Union, St. Charles,* and *Merchants'.*

(Railway connections from Pittsburg are very general. Northward, by the Allegheny Valley road, to *Venango, Oil City,* and the Oil Regions generally ; eastward by route just traversed ; westward, to places named, by the Pittsburg, Cincinnati and St. Louis and Pittsburg, Fort Wayne and Chicago roads ; northwestward to *Cleveland,* by Cleveland and Pittsburg road ; and to *Erie* by the Erie and Pittsburg road ; southeastward to *Cumberland, Harper's Ferry,* etc., by the Pittsburg and Baltimore and Washington road. There is also steamboat communication, down the Ohio river to *Wheeling* and thence to *Cincinnati,* during the open season.]

From Pittsburg, by Cleveland and Pittsburg road, a visit may be paid to

WHEELING, West Virginia, a large and important town, lying at a debouchure of Wheeling Creek into the Ohio River—with manufactures of the same character as those of Pittsburg, only second to them in extent. Apart from its *Manufactures,* the two greatest points of interest are the *Wire Suspension Bridge* of the National Road, with 1,000 feet of span ; and the new and splendid *Railway Bridge.* Oil and coal trade also immense, as at Pittsburg. [Railway connection southeastward by the Baltimore and Ohio road to *Harper's Ferry, Baltimore* and *Washington* eastward to *Pittsburg* and northwestward to *Cleveland* and Lake Erie, by the Cleveland and Pittsburg road. Or, by Baltimore and Ohio road, from Wheeling by *Belle Air;* and ZANESVILLE, thriving and handsome town on the Muskingum River, with immense water-power and fine railroad-bridge —[connection southwestward, by Cincinnati and Muskingum Valley road, to *Cincinnati*) : to *Newark, Columbus,* etc. Steamboat communication to *Pittsburg,* and down the Ohio to CINCINNATI during the open season. Hempfield railway will connect directly to Pittsburg when completed.]

Division D.
PITTSBURG TO AND AT COLUMBUS, OHIO.

From Pittsburg, by rail, on the Pittsburg, Cincinnati and St. Louis road (or from Wheeling by rail to same point) ; by

STEUBENVILLE, pleasant village on the Ohio river, county seat of Jefferson County, with many manufactures and fine scenery in the neighborhood ; by *Mingo Junction* [connection northwestward to *Cleveland,* eastward to *Rochester,* etc.] ; by *Dennison,* COSHOCTON, and *Dresden Junction* [connection south to ZANESVILLE, etc.] ; to .

NEWARK, handsome and thriving town on the Licking river, with extensive railway connections : roads to *Sandusky* and Lake Erie, to *Zanesville* and the south, intersecting. From Newark to

COLUMBUS, on the Scioto River, capital of the

State of Ohio, and one of the most important towns of the State. It is beautifully laid out and very handsomely shaded ; *Broadway*, its main street, being considered unsurpassed. The *Capitol*, on the elegant public ground, *Capitol Square*, has fine chambers, good sculptures and pictures ; and there are, of other public buildings of interest, the *City Hall ;* U. S. *Arsenal*, with fine high grounds ; *State Penitentiary ; Central Ohio Lunatic Asylum* (building, in place of that burned in 1868) ; *Blind* and *Deaf* and *Dumb Asylums ; Starling Medical College; St. Mary's Female Seminary*, etc. Also worthy of attention are the *Holly Water Works*, with steam raising-power. Other Public Grounds than the one already named, and the fine ones surrounding most of the public buildings : the *City* and *Goodale Parks*, and those of the *Franklin Agricultural Society*. Most popular Cemetery : *Green Lawn*. Theatre : the *Opera House*. Hotel : the *Neil House*. [Railway connections extensive : eastward by the route just traversed ; northward by the Cleveland, Columbus, Cincinnati, and Indianapolis road, to *Toledo, Cleveland*, etc. ; south-westward to *Cincinnati* (as see route following) ; south-eastward to *Athens* and the Baltimore and Ohio road, etc.]

Division E.

COLUMBUS TO AND AT CINCINNATI.

From Columbus, by the Little Miami road ; by *London ;* by *Xenia*, very handsome town, with water-power and manufactures on the Little Miami river [connection westward for DAYTON and *Richmond*]; by *Morrow*, [connection east with the Cincinnati and Muskingum Valley road] ; by *Loveland*, [connection east by the Marietta and Cincinnati road, for Marietta, and the Baltimore and Ohio road] ; to

CINCINNATI, on the Ohio river, called the "Queen City," principally built upon two terraces sloping back from the river ; while opposite it, and divided from it by the Ohio river, are the large towns of *Newport* and *Covington*, in the State of Kentucky ; with *Newport Barracks*, important U. S. military station, on the river bank, near the former. Cincinnati has also heavy commerce and important manufactures.

Among the public buildings of prominence are the *Custom House* (with Post Office attached), on Fourth Street ; the *City Hall* (with neat grounds), Plum Street ; the *Court House*, Main Street ; *Cincinnati College*, Walnut Street ; *St. Xavier's College* (Catholic), Sycamore Street ; *Convent of Notre Dame*, Sixth Street ; *House of Refuge*, north of the city ; *City Workhouse*, near the latter ; *Cincinnati Hospital*, Twelfth Street ; etc. Principal Churches : *St. John's* (Epis.) ; *St. Paul's* (Meth. Epis.) ; *First Baptist* ; *St. Peter's Cathedral* (Catholic) ; *First Presbyterian*, etc., though with many others creditable. Places of Amusement : the *National* and *Wood's Theatres* ; *Pike's Music Hall* ; *Melodeon* ; *Gymnasium* ; *Queen City Skating Rink*, etc. Prominent Hotels : the *Burnet, Spencer, Gibson, St. James, Carlisle*, etc.

Public Grounds : *Eden Park*, east of the city, elevated and with *fine view* ; *Fountain Square*, with magnificent bronze fountain lately presented by Mr. Henry Probasco ; *City, Lincoln, Washington*, and *Hopkins Parks*. Cemeteries : *Spring Grove*, one of the handsomest in the West, northwest of the city, with splendid avenues of approach, and a fine soldiers' monument ; *St. Bernard, Wesleyan*, and others minor. Other Objects of Interest : the great *Suspension Bridge* over the Ohio, with longest span in the world ; the *Licking Bridge*, also a suspension, and only less remarkable in length ; the *Railroad Bridge* (new) ; remains of entrenchments thrown up during the Confederate "siege" ; the *Levee*, along the river, with steamboat-landings and a very fine idea of the industry of the city ; steamboat-building-yards ; and many of the very extensive Manufactories, with diversified products.

[Railway connections: eastward, by route just traversed—also, by Marietta and Cincinnati, and Chesapeake and Ohio roads to *Richmond*, etc. : northeastward, by the Little Miami and other roads, to *Cleveland, Sandusky*, etc.; northward, by Cincinnati, Hamilton and Dayton road, to *Toledo;* northwestward, by same road and connections, to CHICAGO ; westward, by Ohio and Mississippi road, by *Vincennes* to ST. LOUIS and the Mississippi river.

Also, steamboat transit on the Ohio river, to all points on that stream, to *Cairo* and the Mississippi.]

Division F.

PITTSBURG TO AND AT ST. LOUIS.

Pittsburg to Columbus and Cincinnati, as by route preceding.

Leave Cincinnati by the Indianapolis, Cincinnati and Lafayette road, by *Delhi, North Bend, Valley Junction* [connection with White Water Valley Railroad], *Lawrenceburg*, [connection with Ohio and Mississippi road, for VINCENNES, etc.,] *Morris, Greensburg, Shelbyville,* [connection with Jeffersonville road, south for LOUISVILLE, etc.,] to

INDIANAPOLIS, capital and largest town of the State of Indiana, lying on the White river, in a very fertile plain, with heavy manufactures, and supplying one of the most noted railroad centres of the West. It is also celebrated for its school system; has an imposing but old *State House*, on Washington Street; *State Lunatic Asylum, Institute for the Blind, United States Arsenal, Northwestern Christian University,* a very large *Union Depot,* an *Academy of Music,* etc. Prominent Hotels : *Bates House* and *Mason House.* [Railway connections, as before indicated, universal.]

From Indianapolis, by the St. Louis, Vandalia and Terre Haute road, by Greencastle, to

TERRE HAUTE, very handsome town on Harrison Prairie and the Wabash river, and also on the Wabash and Erie Canal, and with extensive railway connections. It is elegantly shaded, has many noble residences, *St. Mary's Seminary* (Catholic), the *State Normal School*, and a handsome Opera House. It is also largely engaged in manufactures, forging, etc. Hotel: the *Terre Haute House* (with a wonderful *echo* near it, excelling any other known in the world in the number of repetitions.)

Terre Haute by *Marshall* and *Greenup*, to EFFINGHAM [connections north to *Chicago*, south to *Cairo*, etc., by branch of the Illinois Central road]; to

VANDALIA, on the Kaskaskia river, thriving town and once capital of the State of Indiana. [Connections north to *Bloomington* and CHICAGO, south to *Cairo*, etc., by main line of the Illinois Central road.] Vandalia, by *Greenville, Highland*, etc., *to East St. Louis*, and

ST. LOUIS. [See page 221.]

Division G.

PITTSBURG BY FORT WAYNE TO CHICAGO.

[See Route 13—pages 209 to 211; also same route, pages 212 to 216, for

CHICAGO.]

ROUTE NO. 13.—WESTERN.

NEW YORK TO EASTON (PA.), HARRISBURG, PITTSBURG, FORT WAYNE AND CHICAGO; BY THE ALLENTOWN ROUTE.

Division A.

NEW YORK TO EASTON, HARRISBURG AND PITTSBURG.

Leave New York, by boats of New Jersey Central Railroad, from foot of Liberty Street to *Communipaw* (lower Jersey City); thence by the cars of that road, by *Bergen Point*, and over *Long Bridge* across Newark Bay; to *Elizabethport* (station—at the left the town and great coal depot of that name); and to ELIZABETH [intersection with New Jersey road, eastward to NEW YORK, and westward to PHILADELPHIA: See Route No. 8, New York to Philadelphia]. Elizabeth, by other stations, to

PLAINFIELD, pleasant village and favorite summer-residence, lying at near the foot of the Orange Mountains, a minor spur of the Blue Ridge, and with a remarkable eminence at a short distance to the north, called "Washington's Rock," from which that general is said sometimes to have watched the movements of the British forces. By *Bound-Brook*, on the Raritan River, and at the opening of the Valley of the same name, to

SOMERVILLE, county seat of Somerset County, very handsomely situated, with fine quiet scenery in the neighborhood, some copper and iron mines, and much general prosperity. [Connection by South Branch Road to *Flemington* and *Lambertville.*] By other stations to the

High Bridge, (or rather very long and high *embankment*) over the South Branch of the Raritan River, with fine view in crossing, and large Iron-Works in the neighborhood, for railroad-founding. Very soon is reached

Hampton Junction [connection with the Delaware, Lackawanna and Western Railway, for the *Delaware Water Gap, Scranton,* the Coal Regions of Pennsylvania, and the Erie road at Binghampton.] By *Bloomsbury* and other stations, to

PHILIPSBURG, on the New Jersey side of the Delaware, with heavy iron-manufactures, and three bridges connecting it with *Easton,* on the opposite side of the river. Also with important railway connections, for Central New Jersey, *Philadelphia,* and northward to the *Delaware Water Gap* and the Coal Regions. Crossing the river by bridge, the train reaches

EASTON, Pennsylvania, on the western bank of the Delaware, at the double junction of the Lehigh and the Bushkill, and one of the most important of the coal and railway centres of the two adjoining States, with extensive mills, distilleries and general manufactures. It is also the seat (on an eminence known as Mount Lafayette, at the east of the town) of *Lafayette College*, a flourishing and well-endowed institution, rapidly growing in influence. [Extensive railroad connection, apart from the line of route being traversed; as in addition to that mentioned by both the New Jersey Central and the Delaware and Lackawanna to NEW YORK, it has also connection northward to the *Water Gap* and the Coal Regions; southward to PHILADELPHIA; the Lehigh Valley road northward to *Pittston*; the Lehigh Canal in the same direction; and the Morris Canal through the State of New Jersey to Raritan Bay.]

Leave Easton by Lehigh Valley road; by BETHLEHEM, pleasant town on the Lehigh river; seat of *Lehigh University*; and long celebrated as the principal abode of the Moravians, or United Brethren, in the United States. [Connection southward with North Pennsylvania road for PHILADELPHIA, and northward for *Scranton* and the Coal Regions.]

From Bethlehem, by *E. Penn. Junction* [connection with East Pennsylvania road]; to

ALLENTOWN, handsome town on high ground near the Lehigh river, with large iron and other manufactures, and much charm as a residence. Has *Big Rock* and several popular mineral springs in the neighborhood. Hotel: the *American*. [Connections, northward by the Lehigh Valley road to the Coal Regions and the Erie road; westward by present route to *Reading*, etc.]

Allentown, by East Pennsylvania road, to

ROUTE NO. 13.—WESTERN.   209

READING, large and important manufacturing town on the Schuylkill river, especially notable for mills, iron-furnaces and railroad work. It has a high and handsome sloping location, with a considerable eminence, *Penn's Mount*, near, commanding fine view. It has a noble *Court House;* two or three *Churches* of especial beauty; and *Mineral Springs* in the neighborhood, with hotels of popular resort. Leading Hotel (in the town), the *Mansion House*. [Connection, northward, to *Catawissa* and *Hazleton* (Coal Regions), and southeast to PHILADELPHIA by the Philadelphia and Reading road.] Reading to

LEBANON, on the Swatara Creek, county seat of Lebanon County, and a prosperous town, with the most immense (Cornwall) Iron Ore Beds in the neighborhood, known to exist in the world; also Copper Ore in large quantities, and Marble. From Lebanon to

HARRISBURG. (For notes on Harrisburg, see previous Route, No. 12.)

[Harrisburg to *Pittsburg*, as by Route No. 12, preceding; whether for *Chicago*, *Cincinnati*, or *St. Louis*.]

Division B.

PITTSBURG TO FORT WAYNE AND CHICAGO.

[At Pittsburg, previous route, No. 12, may be pursued, from that point to *Columbus* and *Cincinnati*, with extension to *St. Louis;* or other lines pursued (see that route) northward to the Lakes, southward to the Baltimore and Ohio road, etc.]

Leaving Pittsburg, for ·CHICAGO or places on that line, by Pittsburg, Fort Wayne and Chicago road ; by *Rochester* (small town on the Beaver Creek—with connection southwestward, by Cleveland and Pittsburg road, to *Wheeling* and West) ; by Homewood [connection northward for *Newcastle*, etc.] ; by *Leetonia* [connection southward to New Lisbon, etc.] ; by *Salem*, very handsome small town, with fine suburbs, and manufactures ; to

Alliance, important station [connection northward, by Cleveland and Pittsburg road, to *Cleveland;* southward to *Steubenville*, etc.] From Alliance, by *Canton* and *Massillon*, handsome manufacturing towns ; by *Orrville* [connection northward to AKRON and *Cleveland*] ; by *Mansfield*, another handsome manufacturing town [connections northward to *Sandusky*, southward to *Zanesville*, southwestward to *Dayton, Hamilton* and CINCINNATI] ; to

Crestline, another important railway town. [Connections southward by the Cleveland, Columbus, Cincinnati and Indianapolis road, to *Columbus;* northward by the Sandusky road to *Sandusky;* northeastward to *Cleveland* by the Cleveland, Columbus, Cincinnati and Indianapolis road ; northwestward to *Toledo* and *Detroit* by same road and connections]. From Crestline, by *Bucyrus*, thriving village on the Sandusky River ; by *Forest* [connections north to *Cleveland* south to *Cincinnati*] ; by

Lima, manufacturing village on the Ottawa river [connections southward by Cincinnati, Hamilton and Dayton road, to *Dayton* and *Cincinnati*; northward by the same road to *Toledo* and *Detroit*]; by minor stations, to

FORT WAYNE, Indiana, on the Maumee river—called the "Summit City;" because it lies at the highest point of the water-shed. It is passed through by the Wabash and Erie Canal, and is an important railway centre as well as a manufacturing town of promise. [Connections: northeastward to *Toledo*, Lake Erie and *Detroit*, by Toledo, Wabash and Western road; westward by the same road and connections, to *Logansport*, and thence to *Peoria* and towns of Central Illinois; northward to the Michigan Southern road, at *Waterloo*, etc.] From Fort Wayne, by *Columbia:* by *Warsaw;* by *Plymouth* [connection southward to INDIANAPOLIS, capital of the State, by Indianapolis, Peru and Chicago road]; by *Wanatah* [connection southward by the Louisville and New Albany road, to *Lafayette* and to LOUISVILLE, Ky.]; by Valparaiso, to that city which has furnished, both in fortune and misfortune, the best possible type of American capacities in either direction, and which has been, and will continue to be, quite as often in men's mouths as any other on the Western Continent—

Chicago, Illinois.

Division C.

CHICAGO AS IT WAS, HAS BEEN, AND IS.

The history of the world furnishes no parallel to the change between the three conditions above named, in connection with the "Giant of the West" city of Chicago, an exaggerated type of the whole continent, in the "was," the "has been" and the "is."

Up to the fall of the eventful year, 1871, Chicago stood, as it had been for thirty or forty years growing up to be, the actual Queen City of the West, one of the most important of the Union, and the greatest grain mart and depot of the world, as well as one of the most important railroad centres of the entire continent. It lay on the western shore of Lake Michigan, at near the southern boundary of that Lake, at the entrance of the Chicago river into it. It had its first white settlement in 1804, by Col. John Kinzie; and so late as 1830 contained only 15 houses. It was incorporated as a city, seven years later, in 1837—the population at that time being 4,170. In 1843 this had increased to 7,580; in 1847 to 16,859; in 1850 to 23,269; in 1855 to 80,023; in 1860 to 109,263; in 1865 to 178,539; and in 1870 to the round figures of 300,000, while the suburban population was supposed to raise it to 350,000.

The site of the city was admirably chosen, on ground sloping up from the Lake, and with the

ROUTE NO. 13.—WESTERN. 213

Chicago River, dividing into two branches, running through the entire city, at once adding to commercial convenience and healthfulness. Numerous costly bridges and many tunnels made the connection across the rivers. The city was divided into 20 wards, with nearly 800 streets. The river and the ship canals afforded many miles of excellent harbor, to which came vessels from all parts of the great lakes, with and for produce of every description. The grain warehouses were of such extent as to accommodate 8,000,000 to 10,000,000 bushels; while the yearly exportation had reached to about 60,000,000 to 65,000,000 bushels. It had also a most extensive trade in cattle and stock, the whole yearly number handled, reaching 2,500,000; besides provisions, lumber, and transportation trade to immense amounts. Within the last year or two, on the completion of the Pacific Railway, Chicago had commenced to import her teas and silks direct from India, and was arranging a heavy trade in that direction. There were several of the largest and finest railway-depots on the continent, to accommodate its immense connection as the very largest of the railway-centres. It had streets among the most elegant in the West, in Michigan, Wabash and other avenues: and many of the houses of residents were princely in their luxury. There were more than 200 Churches; 12 or 15 of the largest and finest of Hotels, some of them marvels of size and cost; an Opera-House and 5 Theatres of good class; an University; Medical Colleges, splendid public Parks and Cemeteries; and a wilderness of scientific, social and benevolent institutions, second to none in the Western World. In addition to this, and a feature unequalled elsewhere—a Tunnel had been constructed to a Tower two miles distant in the Lake, whence the water-supply of the city was derived.

Such, hastily sketched, was the position of Chicago on the 8th of October, 1871. On the night of that day, a fire broke out at near the centre of the city, though in an older and wooden portion. A fierce wind made vain all efforts for staying the flames, which extended on every side, and eventually acquired such force that buildings considered fire-proof could not resist the heat five minutes when attacked. By the morning of the 10th the city was literally destroyed—the whole central and business part of it entirely so. Some 10,000 buildings were burned; 500 to 1,000 persons are supposed to have lost their lives; 50,000 to 75,000 persons were rendered houseless; and the pecuniary loss was estimated to have reached $200,000,000. Chicago, the Queen of the West, was no more—*for the time.*

A most gratifying spectacle of general benevolence, however, was exhibited, in connection with this great calamity, not only in all the cities of America, but in those of England and of all Europe; and the extremity of suffering at once materially

ROUTE NO. 13.—WESTERN. 215

relieved by contributions from all quarters, which not only smoothed the then painful present, but gave opportunity and hope for the future. Rebuilding was at once commenced with marvellous energy; and so rapidly was it continued, that within a year from the great catastrophe, more than two-thirds of the marks of the visitation were obliterated, public and private erections of more than the original splendor taking the places of those destroyed, and the fact being made certain that within two years from the fatal 8th of October not a mark of the calamity would be visible, except in the absence of the trees and shrubbery impossible to be replaced within a limited period.

It may even now be said, indeed, that Chicago, as a city, has entirely recovered from the shock temporarily prostrating it, spite of a second destructive fire in 1874,—supplying quite its previous charm to the visitor, while an exceptional interest is found in the virtual death and marvellous resurrection of the place of such varied fortunes.

Among the objects of greatest interest in what the proud citizens call the "New Chicago," may be named the large and beautiful

Lincoln Park, lying on the Lake Shore, north of the city, with charming drives along the Lake, a Zoological Garden, a Lake,. Fountains, fine shade, and all the attractions for the corso and the promenade ;

Union Park, in the West Division, older than Lincoln and more completely finished, with Lakes,

Fountains, Zoological collection, pagodas, a music-pavilion, and great popularity as a place of promenade and for the open-air concerts given every evening during the summer. There are also, of public grounds, *Lake Park*, only partially improved, but with wonderful location, running down the Lake Shore, south of the city, to *Hyde Park* and *Hyde Park House*, favorite driving and bathing resort, at the southern extremity ; the *South* and *West Side Parks*, one day to be very extensive and beautiful ; *Dearborn*, *Jefferson*, and other minor parks ; and *Dexter Trotting Park*, in connection with the great Stock Yards, at the west of the city. Principal Cemeteries, *Graceland, Rose Hill, Calvary* and *Oakwoods*, and the old *Catholic*, on the Lake Shore, near Lincoln Park, with interesting marks of the Great Fire. Among other leading objects of interest are the

Great Stock Yards, lying at some distance west of the city, and among the most extensive and commodious in the world, with Hotel, Bank, Telegraph-offices, and all other facilities (Dexter Park in connection) ; the

Water Works, with their extensive and ingenious Lake connection, unparalleled on the continent ; the many *Bridges*, and the costly Tunnels for their avoidance ; the *Chicago River*, its port, and Lake shipping ; the great

Grain Warehouses and *Elevators*, capable of containing and handling more grain than those of any other city on the globe ; the very large and fine

ROUTE NO. 13.—WESTERN. 216a

Railway Depots, of the many and extensive roads finding their centres or termini here ; the McCormick Reaper Factory, largest in the world (Blue Island and Western avenues) ; Bridge Building Works of the American Company (Egan avenue); Union and other Foundries, Wagon Factories, &c. ; and many magnificent

Mercantile Buildings, Banking Houses, &c., in which detail the rebuilt city far excels even its ambitious predecessor, and rivals all others. The most notable among the new structures is the

Chamber of Commerce, corner of Washington and La Salle Streets, considered one of the noblest and most complete buildings of its class in the world. Also may be mentioned the

Exhibition Building, an erection of size and taste, standing on Michigan avenue and the Lake Shore, used for frequent exhibitions and as a Rink in winter. The *Churches* were many of them destroyed, and are not as yet generally rebuilt.

Of Streets, the most typical and best worthy of observation, will be found Michigan and Wabash avenues, State, Dearborn, Clark, La Salle, and Wells streets, running parallel with the Lake Shore ; and Jackson, Adams, Monroe, Madison, Washington, Randolph and Lake streets, crossing them at right angles, and extending across the city from the Lake.

Prominent Hotels (most of them built since the fire and finished with lavish cost and great completeness) : the *Grand Pacific, Gardner, Potter Palmer,*

Brevoort, Tremont, &c. Theatres: *McVicker's, Aiken's, Hooley's,* with a *Grand Opera House,* soon to be erected.

[Among the widely-extended railway connections of Chicago, are the following of most importance: Northward to *Milwaukie,* thence to *Green Bay,* and beyond, to the Lake Superior sections, by the Chicago and Northwestern road and its connections; north-westward to MADISON (capital of Wisconsin), Baraboo, Devil's Lake, Eau Claire, and Hudson; and to ST. PAUL and the *Falls of St. Anthony,* by the same road and its connections: westward to Clinton and *Cedar Rapids* (Iowa), by the Iowa division of the same road; south-westward to *Burlington* (Iowa), and the Mississippi River, by the Chicago, Burlington and Quincy road: southward to ST. LOUIS, by the Chicago and Alton road; southward to *Cairo* (junction of the Ohio and Mississippi rivers), and to ST. LOUIS, by the Illinois Central road; westward to *Omaha,* and thence to SALT LAKE CITY and SAN FRANCISCO, by the Chicago and Northwestern, Chicago and Rock Island, and Chicago, Burlington and Quincy routes; south-eastward to CINCINNATI, by the Columbus, Chicago and Indiana Central road; eastward to PHILADELPHIA and NEW YORK by the Pittsburg, Fort Wayne and Chicago road,— as also by *Toledo, Cleveland* and the Lake Shore road—as also (with all Canadian cities and connections) by *Detroit* and the Grand Trunk Railway of Canada. Also, steamers on the Lakes, to all important points, in the season.]

ROUTE NO. 14.—WESTERN.

CINCINNATI TO LOUISVILLE (MAMMOTH CAVE), NASHVILLE, CAIRO, ST. LOUIS AND CHICAGO.

Division A.

CINCINNATI TO LOUISVILLE, NASHVILLE AND ST. LOUIS.

Leave Cincinnati by the Louisville, Cincinnati and Lexington road (from *Covington*—opposite side of the river); by *Walton, Sparta, Lexington Junction* [connection southward for LEXINGTON and *Ashland*, old home of Henry Clay, near it; and, by stage from *Eminence*, for Shelbyville]; by *Lagrange*, and *Anchorage* [connection with Shelby road], to Louisville. (Or, steamer down the Ohio from Cincinnati, in the pleasant season).

LOUISVILLE, located on the Ohio river, at the Falls and near the entrance of Bear-Grass Creek, is the largest and most important city of Kentucky. It is well located and shaded; and the views of the Falls, from various points of the city, are much admired. The most important trade of the city is in *tobacco*, of which it is one of the central marts: also extensively in flour, provisions, hemp, etc. The most interesting public buildings are the *City Hall*,

Court House, Custom House (with Post-office), *University Medical College, Masonic Temple, Blind Asylum, the Cathedral, St. Paul's Church,* etc. Principal Theatre : the *Louisville.* Leading Hotels : the *Louisville,* and *National.* Principal Cemetery : *Cave Hill,* with many monuments of merit. At the opposite side of the river is JEFFERSONVILLE, Indiana [railway connection to Indianapolis].

[It is from Louisville that detour may be most conveniently made to visit the

Mammoth Cave of Kentucky, one of the most extensive subterranean passages in the world, and considered among the most interesting. Or, it may be taken on the way from Louisville to *Nashville,* as at present to be considered].

Leave Louisville by the Louisville and Nashville road, to *Cave City,* whence stage or carriage, 9 miles to the Cave (or, steamer from Louisville, on the Green River, to within 1 mile of the Cave—thence on foot). A Hotel, the *Cave House,* affords facilities for stoppage, during the exploration, which may be brief, but must, for any approach to thoroughness, require days of interest and toil, always accompanied by a guide, and with lights and means of relighting, without either of which it is not safe to enter. For particulars of the chambers, passages, and various points of interest in this wonderful cave, which is believed to extend eight or nine miles back from the entrance, dependance may be made entirely upon the capable and instructed guides, procurable at the

ROUTE NO. 14.—WESTERN. 219

hotel or the entrance. Three other Caves—the *Indian*, *White's*, and *Diamond*, may be found in the vicinity: the two former with peculiarly handsome stalactite and stalagmite formations, miniatures of those in the great cave.

From Cave City (after return from the Cave) continue route by Louisville and Nashville road; by *Bowling Green* ; *Memphis Junction* [connection southwest for *Memphis* and the Mississippi river] ; by *Junction* [connection northwest by Henderson road to *Henderson*, and *Evansville* (Ind.); to

NASHVILLE, Capital of the State of Tennessee, and one of the most important cities of the middle southwest. It lies on the Cumberland river, on elevated ground, much of the city lying nearly or quite 100 feet above the water level, and being considered very healthy. The most prominent building, the *State Capitol*, is considered one of the finest in the Union, having admirable legislative halls, splendid material of native marbles, a tower, State Library, etc. Other buildings of prominence are the *University*, the *City Hall*, *Lunatic Asylum*, *Penitentiary*, etc. Theatres : the *Nashville* and *Duffield's*. Prominent Hotels : the *St. Cloud* and *Stacey*. Nashville has many handsome residences ; and the tone of its society is considered equal if not superior to that of any other city of the South. Very near it may be visited the *Hermitage*, old seat of Andrew Jackson. [Extensive railway connections ; east to *Knoxville;* southeast to *Stevenson;* southward, by

Nashville and Decatur and connecting roads, to *Montgomery* (Ala.), and thence to the Gulf Cities; northward, by Evansville road to *Vincennes* and *Terre Haute*; south-westward to *Memphis* by Nashville and North Western road, and connections; north-westward to *St. Louis*, etc.]

From Nashville, by North Western road, by *Waverley*; *Johnsonville*; *McKenzie* [connection south-westward, by Memphis and Louisville road, for *Memphis*, and for *Little Rock* (Arkansas); by *Paducah Junction* [connection north to *Paducah*]; to

Union City, where connection is made with the Mobile and Ohio road. By that road to

Columbus, on the Mississippi river; with *Belmont*, Missouri, opposite, connecting the route just traversed with the St. Louis and Iron Mountain road to *St. Louis*.

From Columbus the Mississippi may be ascended, by boat, to

CAIRO, modern town, very low-lying, on the point formed by the confluence of the Ohio and the Mississippi, with costly levee against inundations by the river, and much prominence as a steamboat port of the Mississippi, vessels from and to all ports stopping here to land and receive passengers and freight. Has some noble buildings; among the best, the *Custom House*. [Railway connection, from Cairo, or from *Mound City*, immediately above, with the Illinois Central Road, direct for CHICAGO. Or, steamboat may be taken for ST. LOUIS or any other point on the Mississippi. Or, steamboat may be taken for *Louisville* or CINCINNATI.]

For St. Louis, from *Bird's Point* (opposite Cairo) to *Charleston;* where the St. Louis and Iron Mountain road is taken. By *Glen Allen, Marquand,* and other stations, to *Bismarck* (where pause should be made, if time allows, to visit, by a spur of the same road, *Iron Mountain, Pilot Knob* and *Ironton,* with some of the most extraordinary developments of richness in iron mines, on the continent.) Bismarck, by *Mineral Point* [spur to *Potosi*] and other stations, to ST. LOUIS.

Division B.

AT ST. LOUIS; AND BY TWO ROUTES TO CHICAGO.

ST. LOUIS, Missouri, is one of the largest and most important cities of the West, focus of mercantile supply for a wide extent of country, virtual Queen of the Mississippi, and often spoken of as the point for removal of the National Capital. It lies on the west bank of the Mississippi river, at what is supposed to be about half-way between St. Paul, at the head of navigation on the Mississippi, and New Orleans, at the mouth of that noble river. It occupies elevated ground, though uneven; has a very long extent on the river, and an imposing appearance from it. It has wide streets, with good shade; handsome parks; substantial residences; and one feature commanding unmixed admiration, in the *Levee* at which the most immense number of steamboats can at any time be seen lying, loading, discharging, arriving and departing, observable at any one spot on the globe. *Front Street*, along the Levee, is one of the finest of mercantile and warehouse streets in the Union; while *Washington* and *Grand Avenues*, and *Fourth Street*, are among the most fashionable thoroughfares.

St. Louis is singularly rich in Parks; the most notable being *Lafayette*, *Hyde*, *Laclede* and *Gravois Parks*, in the outskirts; *Washington* and *Missouri*, and smaller squares; with *Tower Grove* only partially completed, to contain more than 3,000 acres and rival the *Fairmount* at Philadelphia. The *Fair Grounds* are also very beautiful and perfect, as well as popular, with an *Amphitheatre* for spectators, estimated to accommodate 80,000 to 90,000 persons; and *Shaw's Gardens* (botanical) are the very finest on the continent. The Principal Cemeteries are the *Bellefontaine* and the *Calvary*.

Among the Buildings best deserving attention, are the *Custom House*, Third Street; the *Court House*, Fourth Street; *Temple of Justice*, Clark avenue; *Arsenal*; *Merchants' Exchange*, Main street; *Masonic Hall*, Market street; and some of the innumerable Hospitals, Asylums, Educational Institutions, and Roman Catholic Convents. Among Churches, the *Catholic Cathedral*, Walnut street, takes the lead; followed by *St. George's*, (Epis.) Locust street; *First Presbyterian*, Fourteenth street; *Church of the Messiah*, (Unitarian) Oliver street, etc. Theatres: *De Bar's Opera House, Olympic* and *Varieties*. Prominent hotels: the *Lindell, Planters, Laclede*, &c.

Other objects of interest at St. Louis: the *Steel Bridge*, not long since completed across the Mississippi, from the Illinois shore to Washington Avenue, for railroad and general use, and having the reputation of being one of the world's master-works in bridge-erection; the magnificent *Union Depot*, accommodating all railroads centering in the city, and being among the largest and most commodious, as well as most important, on the continent,—with Tunnel leading to it from the western end of the Steel Bridge; and the *City Water Works*.

[Connections from St. Louis: by rail, east to *Indianapolis* by the St. Louis and Terre Haute road, and to *Cincinnati* and eastward by the Ohio and Mississippi road; southeastward to *Tennessee Cities* by the route just traversed; south to *New Orleans* and the Gulf by the Mobile and Ohio road; west to *Jefferson City*, to *Topeka*, and other towns of Kansas, by the Pacific and Missouri road; northwestward to *St. Joseph, Omaha*, and the Pacific Railroad for *Salt Lake City* and San Francisco, by the same and St. Joseph roads; north to *Chicago* and the Lakes and Canada, and south to Cairo and New Orleans, by the Illinois Central and Alton roads. In addition, steamboat communication to all navigable points on the Mississippi, the Missouri and Ohio rivers.]

Leave St. Louis by Chicago, Alton and St. Louis road ; by ALTON, loftily located at just above the junction of the Missouri and Mississippi Rivers, with grand and notable scenery at that point, and much general charm in situation [connection eastward to *Indianapolis* by the Indianapolis and St. Louis road] ; to

SPRINGFIELD, capital of the State of Illinois, a thriving and handsome town standing on the margin of a wide and fine *prairie*. It has a very handsome *Capitol, State Arsenal, Court House, Custom House*, etc. ; extensive *Water Works*, on the Sangamon River ; and will always enjoy an additional celebrity as the residence and burial place of *Abraham Lincoln*, a noble monument to whom marks his tomb in *Ridge Cemetery* Hotel : the *Leland House*. [Connection westward to *Quincy*, and eastward to *Logansport* and *Fort Wayne*, by the Toledo, Wabash and Western road.]

Springfield to BLOOMINGTON, capital of McLean county, and a large town of much commerce and many manufactures, besides having the great engine-shops of the Chicago and Alton Company. [Connection southwestward to *Jacksonville;* west to *Pekin;* southeast to *Champaign* and the Illinois Central road.] To *Chenoa* [connection west to *Peoria;* east to *Warsaw* and *Logansport*]. By other stations to JOLIET, large and thriving town on the Des Moines river, with State Penitentiary of noble construction, immense fine building-stone quarries

ROUTE No. 14.—WESTERN.

near, valuable water-power, and extensive trade and manufactures. [Connection west to *Rock Island*, by the Chicago, Rock Island and Pacific road.] Joliet to CHICAGO.

Or, leave St. Louis by the Illinois Central road (St. Louis and Chicago Through Line), to East St. Louis ; thence to *Greenville*, VANDALIA (see Division F., Route 12, pp. 205 A and B), EFFINGHAM, *Mattoon, Tolono, Champaign, Gilman, Calumet*, etc., across one of the richest ranges of the great prairie lands of Illinois, to

CHICAGO.

(For notes on Chicago, see Route No. 13, Division C.)

ROUTE No. 15.—NORTHERN AND WESTERN, (SEMI-SKELETON.)

BUFFALO TO CLEVELAND AND CHICAGO, BY LAKE SHORE ROAD.

Leave Buffalo by Lake Shore road; to *Dunkirk*, on Lake Erie, terminus of lower branch of the Erie road [connection eastward to *Salamanca*, for the Oil Regions.] Dunkirk to

ERIE, (Pa.), on the shore of Lake Erie, with fine harbor (a U. S. Naval Station); *Court House* and other good buildings; extensive iron rolling-mills, and the connection of the Erie Extension Canal with the Ohio River and Beaver Canal. Hotel: the *Reid House*. [Connection southeast to *Corry* and the Oil Regions]. By *Girard* [connection southward to Pittsburg]; and Painesville to

CLEVELAND (Ohio) on Lake Erie, with harbor at mouth of Cuyahoga River, heavy lake shipping trade, much prosperity in business aspects; and so pronounced a shaded beauty, especially in the fine elms lining its wide streets, that it bears the name of the "Forest City." It has a *Medical College:* a *Marine Hospital;* several handsome Churches; a splendid *Union Railway Depot*, of great size; *Monumental Park* (with monument to Commodore Perry); *Woodlawn Cemetery;* noble *Water Works;* and many other attractions. [Connections southeast to

ROUTE NO. 15.—NORTHERN AND WESTERN. 227

Pittsburg and *Wheeling;* south to *Coshocton* and *Zanesville*; southwest to *Columbus, Cincinnati,* etc.]

From Cleveland, by *Oberlin* (seat of the celebrated "Oberlin College," which admits blacks as well as whites); by *Monroeville* [connection northward to Sandusky] ; by *Clyde* [connection south to CINCINNATI]; *Fremont,* etc., to

TOLEDO, on the Maumee River, near Lake Erie, with considerable lake trade (principally in grain), much domestic commerce, many handsome buildings, rapid progress, great educational facilities, and an almost matchless location as a railway centre. Hotels: *Oliver House, Island House, American,* and *St. Charles.* [Conections: southeast to *Clyde* and (opening) to Wheeling; South to *Lima, Dayton* and CINCINNATI; southwest to *Logansport, Springfield* (Ill), the Mississippi river, and *St. Louis;* northward to *Detroit* and the Canadian lines; etc.]

From Toledo, by the Michigan Southern and Northern Indiana road; by ADRIEN (Michigan), with water-power; some manufactures; repair-shops of the railroad-division; a handsome Soldiers' Monument, and many attractions as a residence. Hotel: the *Lawrence House.* By *Hillsdale; Jonesville* [connection south to *Fort Wayne*]; *Sturgis* [connection north to *Grand Haven* and south to *Fort Wayne*]; *White Pigeon* [connection north to *Kalamazoo*]; *Elkhart* [junction with Air-Line of same road, to TOLEDO] ; *South Bend* and *Laporte;* to

CHICAGO. (For notes on Chicago, and connections, see previous route, No. 13.)

ROUTE NO. 16.—NORTHERN (SEMI-SKELETON).

NEW YORK OR PHILADELPHIA TO THE LACKA-
WANNA COAL REGIONS, AND THE OIL CREEK
OIL REGIONS.

New York, by the New Jersey Central road to *Hampton Junction* (see Route No. 13); to *Manunkachunk* (New Jersey).

Or by the Delaware, Lackawanna and Western road—Morris and Essex Division from New York: from foot Barclay Street to Hoboken; thence by rail, by *Orange* [connection to NEWARK]; by *Madison*, location of Drew Theological Seminary; by MORRISTOWN, thriving town of New Jersey, and capital of Morris County, on the Whippany Creek, with handsome residences, a "Washington's Head Quarters" and other Revolutionary remains; by *Boonton, Rockaway* and *Dover*, all towns in the iron-region, with extensive iron mills and foundries; by *Chester*, Drakesville, *Stanhope* [connection by stage or boat to *Lake Hopatcong* and to *Budd's Lake*]; by *Waterloo* [connection north to *Newton*, by Sussex road]; by *Hackettstown*, handsome town of Warren County, with flouring mills and a Methodist Episcopal Seminary of eminence [connection by stage to *Schooley's Mountain* (see Excursions from New York)]; to *Washington*. At Washington connect with the Delaware, Lackawanna and Western road, and by that road to *Manunkachunk*.

Or, from Philadelphia, by the Northern Pennsylvania road, or the Belvidere Delaware road, to *Easton;* thence to *Manunkachunk*.

Manunkachunk to the *Delaware Water-Gap* (see Excursions from New York). Water-Gap to *Stroudsburg*, (Pa.), and by several minor stations to

SCRANTON (Pa.), important heavy-manufacturing town, and great centre of the coal operations of the Lackawanna district. In brief excursions from Scranton, locally directed, may be observed all the details of mining and transportation, of the immense coal trade and the iron trade accompanying. [Connections southwest to *Pittston* and *Wilkesbarre;* north to *Great Bend* and the Erie road; east to *Carbondale, Honesdale,* etc]. Scranton to

Pittston, another important coal centre. Pittston, by *Rupert* [connection southward with the wildly-grand Catawissa road, for *Reading*, etc.]; by *Milton* and other stations, to

WILLIAMSPORT, capital of Lycoming County, on the Susquehanna river, with much industry and miscellaneous business, and the most extensive lumber trade of any town in America. Among the curiosities of the place, is the *Great Timber Boom* in the Susquehanna, capable of holding millions of logs at a time; the many saw-mills and other lumber works. There are also extensive Black Marble

Quarries in the neighborhood. Hotels: the *Herdic, Crawford, City,* and *American.*

From Williamsport by the Philadelphia and Erie road; by

LOCK HAVEN, another great lumber centre, also with immense Timber-Boom, saw-mills, etc., and fine scenery in the neighborhood. Hotels: the *Fulton, Irving,* and *Montour.* Lock Haven, by *Renovo, Emporium,* Wilcox and other stations; to

Irvineton, whence should be taken the Oil Creek and Alleghany road, to *Tidioute, Oleopolis, Pithole, Oil City, Titusville,* or any of those great oil centres, from which short excursions, locally directed, can be made with most profit and satisfaction. Thence to CORRY, for *Salamanca* and the Erie road, going east; or for *Erie* and the Lake Shore road, for the north or West.

ROUTE NO. 17.—CANADIAN AND WESTERN.

NIAGARA FALLS, BY HAMILTON AND LONDON TO
DETROIT AND CHICAGO, BY GREAT WESTERN
AND MICHIGAN RAILWAYS.

Leave Niagara Falls (Suspension Bridge), by rail on the Great Western road of Canada; by *Thorold* (crossing of the Welland Canal around the Falls of Niagara), to

St. Catharine's, pleasant small town, favorite as a residence, and with Mineral Springs of much celebrity. Thence by *Grimsby*, lying near the shore of Lake Ontario, to

HAMILTON, on Burlington Bay, at the extreme western end of the Lake, with very handsome coast-scenery in the neighborhood; a magnificent harbor, with heavy lake trade and fine fishing; and the town itself very prettily laid out, with elegant residences and other buildings, well shaded and attractive. Very fine views are to be obtained from the *Mountain*, where also stands *Dundrum Castle*, erected by Sir Allan McNab, when Governor-General; and there are many favorite resorts in the neighborhood, among others the *Beach*, *Oaklands*, *Flamborough Heights*, etc. Prominent Hotels: the *Anglo-American* and *City*. [Connection eastward (*Hamilton Junction*) with the Grand Trunk Railway for *Toronto* and all the Eastern Canadian cities; also, by boat on the Lake, for *Toronto* and the same]. Hamilton to DUNDAS, with many manufactures and much fine scenery at and near the Desjardines Canal, here commencing; to *Harrisburg* [connection northward to *Berlin, Guelph*, and the Grand Trunk road] ; to

PARIS, a thriving town, with important water-power and manufactures, at the junction of the Grand and Nith rivers, with mineral springs and a petrifying spring in the neighborhood [connection northwestward to *Goderich* and Lake Huron, and southeastward to *Dunville* and BUFFALO, by Goderich and Grand Trunk road]. Paris to

LONDON, considered the metropolis of South Western Canada—with handsome location, streets well laid out and shaded, costly buildings, and all the attractions for residence. [Connection northward to *St. Mary's* and the Grand Trunk road; southward to *Port Stanley*, on Lake Erie, with boat connection to BUFFALO]. London, by *Komoka* [connection westward to *Petrolia* (oil-centre), and *Port Sarnia*, at the entrance of the St. Clair river into Lake Huron] ; and by Glencoe; to

Bothwell, principal town of the Canadian oil-regions, in the neighborhood of which those who have not visited the Pennsylvania oil-sections, may derive a very good idea of the petroleum wells and processes.

Bothwell to *Chatham*, with the distinction of very

large percentage of negro population. [Connection with *Detroit*, by steamers down the Thames river and across Lake St. Clair to Detroit river]. Chatham by unimportant stations to

WINDSOR, very old town on the eastern side of the Detroit river, with many French peculiarities and but moderate prosperity. From Windsor, ferry, carrying over cars on boats, to

DETROIT, Michigan, lying on the west bank of the Detroit river, strait connecting Lake St. Clair with Lake Erie. This is the largest city of the State; one of the oldest in any of the Western States, and one of the most wealthy and influential of all. The city front extends along the river at great length, with most of the location elevated, and the streets well shaded and broken up into many small parks and public grounds. The most important of the latter is the *Grand Circus*, park and promenade, from which radiate many of the finest avenues; among others, *Woodward, Jefferson*, etc. There is also a large Plaza, called the *Campus Martius*, around which are grouped many of the finest buildings in the city. Without the town, the favorite public resorts are *Fort Wayne*, on the river, three miles from the city; *Belle Ile, Grosse Pointe* and *Grosse Ile*, more distant. The principal Cemeteries are *Elmwood* and *Woodlawn*.

Among the prominent buildings in the city, are the *Michigan Central Freight Depot*, of immense size and costly construction, with the great *Loco-*

motive Round House and *Grain Elevator*, near it; the *Custom House* (with Post Office); the *Opera House;* the *Board of Trade Building*, etc. The most notable churches are *St. Paul's* (Epis.), with the peculiarity of a roof without columns; *Christ, St. John's* and *Grace* (all Epis.); *Fort Street Presbyterian; Central* (Meth.-Epis.); *St. Peter* and *St. Paul* (Cath.); *St. Anne's* (Cath.), with very fine choir; etc. Detroit has also elaborate Water-works; large manufacturing and lake-shipping interests, in grain and provisions, etc. Theatre: the *Opera House*. Prominent Hotels: The *Russell, Biddle,* and *Michigan Exchange*.

From Detroit may be visited, north, *Lake St. Clair*, with many attractive features in scenery; and southward, the *Put-in-Bay Islands*, below the mouth of the Detroit river, in Lake Erie, near which occurred Commodore Perry's victory in 1813; now famous as bathing and fishing resort, etc. [Boat from Detroit to Kelly's Island, largest of the group, every day during warm season.]

[Railway connection from Detroit: north to *Port Huron*, foot of Lake Huron: northwest to *Saginaw, Wenona*, etc.; west to *Kalamazoo*, etc.; east by route just traversed, and by Toledo and Lake Shore road; west to CHICAGO, etc., as see route to be pursued. In addition, it has steamboat communication on Lake Erie to BUFFALO and other ports; and to all ports on Lake Huron and Michigan.]

Leave Detroit by Michigan Central road, by *Yp-*

silanti, pleasant small town of Michigan, seat of the State Normal School; thence (along the Huron River), to

ANN ARBOR, handsome large town, on elevated plateau, with fine shade and many handsome buildings; and seat of the *University of Michigan*, an institution of wide influence, with varied courses, a fine Observatory, etc. Hotel: the *Gregory House*. By *Dexter* and *Chelsea* to

JACKSON, large and thriving town, with many manufactures, an important coal-trade from mines in the immediate neighborhood, and seat of the *Michigan State Prison*. [Connections, northward to LANSING (capital of the State); southward to *Adrian* and *Toledo*, etc.] From Lansing, by *Parma*, on the Kalamazoo river; by *Albion* (seat of Albion College, of the Meth. Epis. Church); by *Marshall* (large paper manufactories, and railway repair-shops); to BATTLE CREEK, manufacturing town, especially with extensive flour-mills [connections north to LANSING, and south to *South Bend*, etc.]; to

KALAMAZOO, largest town in the State, after Detroit. It is a thriving manufacturing and commercial town, with much shaded beauty and many handsome residences; and the seat of a *Baptist College* and the *State Insane Asylum*. Hotels: the *Kalamazoo* and *Burdick*. [Connections: northwest to *Grand Haven* and Lake Michigan; also to *Grand Rapids*; southeastward to *Fort Wayne*, etc.] From

Kalamazoo, by *Lawton* (with extensive iron works); *Niles*, small town of commercial and industrial importance on the St. Joseph River; *New Buffalo* and *Michigan City* (both modern towns, on the immediate shore of Lake Michigan); to

CHICAGO.

ROUTE NO. 18.—NORTH-WESTERN (SEMI-SKELETON.)

CHICAGO TO ST. PAUL (MINN.) AND FALLS OF ST. ANTHONY; WITH OPTIONAL RETURN DOWN THE MISSISSIPPI OR BY LAKE SUPERIOR.

Leave Chicago by the Chicago, Milwaukie and St. Paul Railroad ; by *Waukegan;* KENOSHA [connection west to *Genoa, Rockford,* etc.]; RACINE [connection west to *Elkhorn* and *Freeport*]; to MILWAUKIE. (Or by Chicago and N. W. Railroad, or daily steamer on the Lake.)

MILWAUKIE, commercial capital of the State of Wisconsin, one of the largest cities of the northwest, considered very handsome and attractive as a residence, and so healthful in reputation, as to have originated the jest that "people are obliged to go away from Milwaukie, when they wish to die!" Hotels: the *Plankinton, Walker,* and *Newhall.* [Connections, northwest to *Horicon, Portage City,* etc.; southwest to *Milton, Janesville,* etc.]

Leave Milwaukie by the Milwaukie and St. Paul road ; *Waukesha* and *Palmyra,* famed for their mineral springs and attractive resorts ; by *Watertown* [connection north to *Horicon;* northwest to Portage City, etc.]; to

MADISON, capital of the State, and a very thriving and handsome town, with the *Capitol, University of Wisconsin,* many other local attractions, and the notably-beautiful *Four Lakes* in the immediate neighborhood. [Connections southeast to CHICAGO, by the Chicago and North-western road; and to *Plymouth, Beloit*, etc., by the Madison division of the same road]. Madison, by many minor stations, to

PRAIRIE DU CHIEN, important town on the Mississippi river, with a considerable river-trade, many steamboats making stoppage, and *prairies* in the neighborhood, as the name indicates. By ferry to

McGregor, small town on the opposite side of the river; where the route by rail is continued. By *Colmar* [connection westward to *Charles City* and the Missouri river]; to AUSTIN [connection southward by the Burlington and Cedar Rapids road, to *Cedar Rapids, Burlington*, and the Mississippi]; to *Ramsey* [connection west with Southern Minnesota road]; to *Owatona* [connection west for *Mankato, St. Peter*, etc.]; by *St. Paul* and *Mendota Junctions* [connection southwest to *Mankato*,] etc.; to

ST. PAUL, capital of Minnesota, and the largest town in the State; on the Mississippi river, at the virtual head of navigation; with *State Capitol; State Reform School; St. Joseph's Academy* (Catholic); a *Bridge* of great length, over the Mississippi; *Carver's Cave* and *Fountain Cave* in the immediate vicinity, etc. Theatre: the *Opera House.* Leading Hotel: the *Merchants'*. [Connections: north to *Duluth*, on Lake Superior; northwest to *St. Cloud;* west to *Breckenridge;* southwest to *St. Peter* and *Mankato;* southeast to *Milwaukie* and CHICAGO, by route just traversed; also southeast to *Red Wing,* and Lake Pepin. Also by steamer to all Mississippi ports, ST. LOUIS and NEW ORLEANS.] It is from St. Paul that visit will be paid (short ride by carriage, by *Fort Snelling*) to the

Falls of Minnehaha, very beautiful small fall of the Minnesota river, made famous by Longfellow in the poem of the same name, with the Indian derivation, "Laughing Water." Also will be visited, by rail from St. Paul, the

Falls of St. Anthony, and *Minneapolis,* formerly ST. ANTHONY, a few miles above. The town is a thriving one, at the actual head of navigation of the Mississippi, with *State University,* and connection by bridge with *Minneapolis.* The Falls, though with very mean surroundings, are grand, especially in the feature of Rapids, and show to best advantage by *moonlight.*

From St. Paul descent of the Mississippi may be made, by steamboat, by *Red Wing* (Minn.); *La Crosse* (Wis.); *Prairie du Chien* (Wis.); *Dubuque* (Iowa); *Galena* (Ill.), centre of the lead-trade; *Davenport* (Iowa); *Rock Island* (Ill.); *Burlington* (Iowa); *Nauvoo* (Ill.), original seat of the Mormons; *Keokuk* (Iowa); *Hannibal* (Mo.); *Alton* (Ill.), and many other interesting river ports, with stoppages, to ST. LOUIS for the South or return eastward.

Or, northern route may be taken, leaving St. Paul by the Lake Superior and Mississippi road, to

DULUTH, new but important town at the extreme southwest point of Lake Superior, with good harbor, heavy lake trade and rapidly increasing prosperity, Hotel: the *Clark House.* At Duluth, steamer to be taken (depending on local direction for the most reliable particulars) on Lake Superior, to the *Ontonagon Copper Region,* on the south shore of that Lake; thence to the *Marquette Iron Region,* on the same shore; thence to the *Pictured Rocks,* also on the same shore. Thence route may be continued. through the *Sault St. Marie* (Strait) into *Lake Huron,* and to *Bay City* for rail to DETROIT; or to DETROIT by boat direct; or to *Goderich,* for return by rail through Canada; or through the St. Clair River and Lake, and the Detroit river, to *Lake Erie,* for *Toledo, Cleveland, Erie,* or BUFFALO, on that Lake.

[Another popular route from Milwaukie to the North-West is as follows: From Milwaukie, by the Chicago, Milwaukie and St. Paul Road, by *Watertown, Portage,* Tomah (connection to Grand Rapids and lumber region), *Sparta* (noted mineral springs), *Winona Junction,* over the Mississippi River at *Lacrosse,* by fine scenery of Upper Mississippi, by *Winona,* passing *Red Wing,* to *Minneapolis* and ST. PAUL.]

ROUTE NO. 19.—CANADIAN.

NIAGARA FALLS TO TORONTO, OTTAWA, MONTREAL, QUEBEC, AND THE SAGUENAY RIVER; BY GRAND TRUNK RAILWAY, AND BOAT-CONNECTIONS.

Division A

NIAGARA FALLS TO TORONTO AND OTTAWA.

Leave Niagara Falls (Suspension Bridge) by Great Western Railway, by *Thorold*, to *St. Catharine's* (see Route No. 17); and to

HAMILTON (also see Route No 17.)

From Hamilton, continuing by Toronto branch of Great Western Railway, at near the upper coast of Lake Ontario, by *Oakville* and other stations, to

TORONTO, most populous city of the Western province (Ontario), and one of the handsomest in America, though excelled in size by many. It lies on the Northern shore of Lake Ontario; is well laid out and finely shaded; and has one thoroughfare, *Yonge Street*, actually extending northward as an unbroken drive, the whole distance to the foot of *Lake Simcoe*, some 35 miles. Among the prominent buildings is the *University of Toronto*, a noble structure with lofty tower, and fine park surrounding. Scarcely second is *Osgoode Hall*, the law-court building, with the distinction of not only being one of the most tasteful in the world for legal purposes, outside, but one of the most completely and tastefully arranged, within. There are also the *Exchange, Provincial Lunatic Asylum, Trinity College, Normal School,* etc., all worthy of visit. Of the many Churches, three have especial prominence: the *Cathedral of St. James* (Epis.); that of *St. Michael* (Catholic); and the (new) *Wesleyan Church.* Prominent Hotels: the *Rossin House,* and the *Queen's.* Those who have abundant leisure, should make the drive before spoken of, to *Lake Simcoe,* with wild beauty; those with less time will find drives through some of the main avenues, and along the shore of the Lake, amply repaying them.

[Connections by rail, north to Lake Simcoe; west to *Guelph, Berlin,* and other towns on the Grand Trunk road. Also, by boat with *Niagara Falls,* by *Lewiston* and rail along the Niagara River. Also, by daily boat along Lake Ontario and down the St. Lawrence River to MONTREAL. Also, to ports on the New York side of the Lake.]

From Toronto by the Grand Trunk Railway; by *Frenchman's Bay, Bowmanville* and other stations, to

Port Hope, pleasant little town, on the Lake, with hill suburbs and some lake-trade. [Connection northwestward to *Beaverton,* on Lake Simcoe; and with Lake ports, by boat.] Port Hope to

Cobourg, important station as well as handsome

town, with fair trade, a pleasant residence, and the seat of *Victoria College* (Wesleyan). [Connection northward to *Peterboro* and Rice and Salmon Trout Lakes.] Cobourg, by *Colborne* (not to be confounded with " Port Colbourn," on the Great Western road); by *Trenton* (on the little river Trent); by *Belleville*, pleasant small town on Moira river (actual inlet from the Lake); by *Napanee, Collins' Bay* and other stations; to

KINGSTON, very old town at the entrance of the St. Lawrence river, and once capital of Canada; with very heavy fortifications, in *Fort Henry* and several other works; seat of *Queen's College University*, the *Regiopolis Catholic College, Provincial Penitentiary*. Hotel: the *British American. Cape Vincent*, on the New York shore, lies opposite. [Steamer connection from Kingston up the Lake to Toronto, down the Lake to MONTREAL and other ports. Also, by Rideau Canal, with *Ottawa*. From Cape Vincent, by rail to *Watertown*, and thence to *Rome* and other points on the New York Central road.]

From Kingston, by *Gananoque* and *Mallory Town*, to BROCKVILLE, a town of pleasant location and some commercial importance, on the St. Lawrence river [connection northward to *Carleton Place, Arnprior*, etc.; and from Carleton Place, by Canada Central road, to OTTAWA]. Brockville to

PRESCOTT (Junction), small town, principally of transit importance, also on the St. Lawrence. [Connections, north to Ottawa, as see route to be pursued; east direct to Montreal, continuing by Grand Trunk road; across the river to *Ogdensburg,* on the New York side, whence connection south to the New York Central road and towns on that line, by the Rome, Watertown and Ogdensburg road, for southward; or eastward by Ogdensburg and Champlain road to *Rouse's Point,* Lake Champlain and *St. Albans* for all Eastern States].

From Prescott, by St. Lawrence and Ottawa road, through a region comparatively unbroken, but with many features of beauty in natural scenery, to

OTTAWA, Capital of the Dominion of Canada. It lies on the Ottawa river, and on the Rideau Canal, running to Lake Ontario at Kingston. The scenery in the district is somewhat wild and untamed, but very picturesque; and in the immediate neighborhood may be witnessed some of the most extensive operations in the rafting and sawing of lumber and timber, on the whole range of the continent. The *Chaudiere Great Falls* (of the Ottawa) lie within the city proper, at the west, are some 200 feet in width by 40 in depth, and have many features of grandeur; while the *Little Falls,* handsomer though smaller, lie at the east. The *Rideau Falls,* at the northeast, and the *Remoux* and *De Cheyne Rapids,* some miles above, are all worthy of visit and notice.

The feature of Ottawa is of course to be found in the *Parliament Houses* and government buildings connected. They are of native stone, lately erected, at great cost, and truly magnificent in size, design and arrangement—promising, when fully completed, with their grounds, to be worthy of the Dominion and command great admiration. The respective *Chambers* of the Senate and House of Commons are of the same size as those at Westminster Palace, and quite as handsomely finished; and there is an immense *Library*, not yet finished, to be capable of accommodating half a million volumes. They stand at the height of an elevation known as "Barrack Hill," forming the apex of the higher ground on which the Upper Town is built, being divided from the Lower Town by the Rideau Canal and its handsome stone bridge. The *Queen's Printing House*, near the Parliament Houses, the *Catholic Cathedral*, and other prominent buildings, demand attention. Leading Hotel: the *Russell House*. [Connection west to *Carleton Place* and the Brockville road; and to *Prescott, Ogdensburg*, etc., by the route just traversed. Direct railway along the Ottawa river, to MONTREAL, in course of construction].

Division B.

OTTAWA TO AND AT MONTREAL.

Leave Ottawa by morning boat on the Ottawa river; with fine view, soon after leaving, of the *Rideau Falls*, on the right; and not long afterwards, the entrance of the *Gatineau River*, tributary of the Ottawa, into that river, the largest on the Continent, after the Mississippi and the St. Lawrence, and very picturesque throughout, though with a beauty untamed. Various minor landings are made, before reaching

L'ORIGINAL; at which point, if time allows, the tourist should lie over for one day, to visit the

Caledonia Springs, nine miles distant, the healing qualities of which have made them very celebrated, with capacious hotel, and the presence, in summer, of a very large number of the best known people of fashion and condition, in the Dominion. Return to *L'Original.*

From L'Original, whether with or without having visited the Springs, the course is pursued by boat, down the Ottawa, to

GRENVILLE (with *Hawkesbury* opposite, with large saw mills) where the boat is left and a land ride of twelve miles taken (the *Long Sault Rapids* making navigation impossible); to

CARILLON, at the lower end of the rapids, where another boat of the line is taken. It is worthy of remark that from Ottawa to this point, the middle of the river has been the dividing line between the two provinces of Ontario (west) and Quebec (east); but that here the line leaves the river, striking southward to the St. Lawrence, and the course is taken entirely in that of Quebec.

Among the next prominent objects of interest following, is the *Mountain of Rigaud*, looming high on the southern bank, above the rough and wooded shores. Several minor landings are made on this portion of the river, after leaving which it expands into the

Lake of the Two Mountains, with the two mountains giving its name, rising on either side, one of them, *Calvary*, being held sacred by the Indians. Not long after, is reached

ST. ANNE'S, rendered so celebrated by Moore, in the "Canadian Boat Song." At this point *Mont Royale*, the height above Montreal, comes into view. The boat is taken through locks, at St. Anne's, to avoid the rapids, coming out into the

Lake St. Louis, in which the Ottawa for the first time joins the St. Lawrence. Landing from the boat is made at

LACHINE, where cars of the Grand Trunk Railway are taken to

MONTREAL, the largest and most prosperous city of the British Possessions in North America; Metropolitan See of the English Church in Canada, and seat of a Catholic Bishopric. It lies on rapidly rising ground, on the island of the same name, with the St. Lawrence immediately in front, Back River forming the sound behind it; and the mountain which gives it name, *Mount Royal*, also rising grandly at the back. There are few and unimportant fortifications, (*St. Helen's Island* being the principal); but the town has usually been garrisoned, being considered the military key of the

Dominion. The population of Montreal is wondrously mixed, there being many streets, in the higher and newer parts of the town, in which the English and Scotch elements entirely predominate, with many of the features of an English city; while in the older and lower parts of the town, many of the streets are still called "Rues," and the prevailing architecture, language and manner are all French, of not too refined an order. There are now fine quays along the river; costly and elegant residences have rapidly increased in number, stretching back towards Mount Royal; and the commercial importance and prosperity of the Northern Metropolis have quite kept pace with its growing luxury. Among other evidences of its prosperity has been the establishment of the fine *Allan line of Steamers* to Liverpool and Glasgow, coming to Quebec and Montreal during the open season, and to Portland in the winter.

First among the edifices of Montreal, comes the *Catholic Cathedral of Notre Dame*, standing on the *Place d'Armes*, in the centre of the old city, and so large that it is accredited with containing 10,000 people without difficulty. It is Gothic in architecture, with two tall towers, commanding a magnificent view from the top; and within, it has many of the features of European churches of the same faith. *Christ Church Cathedral* (Epis.) and *St. Andrew's Church* (Episcopal) rank next; and the *Church of the Jesuits*, with some fine pictures, is much visited and admired. Of public, commercial and other buildings may be especially noted the *Court House,* one of the best on the continent; the *Bank of Montreal,* near the Cathedral; *McGill College,* at the foot of Mount Royal; *Bonsecours Market,* on the quay, with large dome and excellent internal arrangements; *St. Patrick's Hall,* Victoria square; the *Albert Buildings,* same place; *Dominion Block,* McGill street, etc. There are three *Nunneries,* always exciting more or less attention among visitors, and to which admission is often granted; the *Gray,* (lately removed); the *Black,* Notre Dame street; and the *Hotel Dieu. Notre Dame* and *Great St. James Streets* may be named as the most fashionable promenades; and *St. Paul Street* as the leading commercial. The principal Cemetery is *Mount Royal,* on the mountain of that name, around which, also, is the most fashionable drive of the city. There is a handsome *Nelson Monument* at the Place Jacques Cartier. Theatre: the *Montreal.* Leading Hotels· *St. Lawrence Hall,* the *Ottawa,* the *Montreal,* etc.

Many excursions of interest can be made from Montreal, but the most indispensable one is that to

The Victoria Bridge over the St. Lawrence, at Point St. Charles, order to inspect which can be obtained from the officers of the Grand Trunk Railway, near the entrance. It is one of the immense enterprises of later times, with no less than 23 spans of 242 feet each, a centre one of 330 feet, and a total length of two miles. It is tubular, on the plan of the great bridge over the Menai Strait, in Wales; was built by Robert Stephenson and A. M. Ross; and opened by the Prince of Wales during his American visit, in August, 1860.

Another very pleasant excursion, for those reaching Montreal by rail, is to take rail to *Lachine,* and thence return to the city by boat *Down the Lachine Rapids,* with excellent idea thus obtained of that feature of the St. Lawrence.

[Connections from Montreal: westward to OTTAWA, by the route just traversed; eastward to QUEBEC, by the Grand Trunk road (from St. Lambert); southward to *Rouse's Point,* and thence to all points in the Eastern and Middle United States, (from La Prairie). Westward by steamer on the St. Lawrence and Lake Ontario, to *Toronto* and leading Lake ports; eastward by steamer on the St. Lawrence, to QUEBEC and the farther East. By Allan line of sea-steamers to HALIFAX, LIVERPOOL and GLASGOW.]

Division C.

MONTREAL TO AND AT QUEBEC, WITH EXCURSIONS

Leave Montreal (from Bonaventure Station), by train on the Grand Trunk Railway; across the *Victoria Bridge* at *Point St. Charles;* by *St. Lambert, St. Hyacinthe,* and other stations, to

RICHMOND, important railway station and point of intersection. [Connection, south-eastward, by Portland Division of the Grand Trunk road, to *Island Pond*; and thence to *Gorham* for the White Mountains and southward, or to PORTLAND and connections for BOSTON and the east.]

From Richmond, by the Quebec branch of the Grand Trunk road; by ARTHABASCA [connection northward, by *Bulstrode*, to *St. Gregoire*, on the St. Lawrence river, and *Three Rivers* (Canada)]; by *Black River* and other stations, to

Point Levi [continuation of line eastward, to *Riviere du Loup*]. From Point Levi, ferry across the St. Lawrence, to

QUEBEC, metropolis of the Province of the same name; important military station, with very strong fortifications; and with as important historical interest as any city on the American continent. It lies on the north shore of the St. Lawrence, with exceedingly picturesque location, being divided into the Upper and Lower Towns, with the very strong fortifications of the Upper Town crowning the whole; and the *Citadel of Cape Diamond*, being considered next in strength in the world to Gibraltar and Ehrenbreitstein. From the city proper, the suburbs of St. Roch and St. John extend along the river St. Charles to the *Plains of Abraham*, on the *Heights* of the same name, rendered ever-memorable by the battle fought there between the English Gen. Wolfe and the French General Montcalm, in 1759, with the death of both the commanders, but the total defeat of the French, and the final capture of Quebec and destruction of the French power in the province. The spot where Wolfe fell, near an old redoubt at the highest point, is pointed out to tourists, who have even a more singular interest in seeing the skull of Montcalm, exhumed not many years ago, now preserved in the Ursuline Convent. The joint *Monument to Wolfe and Montcalm* is to be found in the *Public Garden*, on Des Carrieres street. At the foot of the Citadel is a tower, where the American General Montgómery fell in the assault on Quebec, in 1775. Ascent from the Lower to the Upper Town is made by a very steep and winding street, through the *Prescott Gate*, by which also the fortifications may be reached on the St. Lawrence side. The Plains may be entered by the *St. Louis Gate*, nearly opposite. The *View from the Citadel*, over the city, the St. Lawrence and the opposite shore, is a truly magnificent one and not to be omitted by any one with an eye to the picturesque.

Among the most notable Buildings of Quebec, may be named the *Parliament House* (rebuilt when the city was still expected to remain the Capital); the very large *Artillery Barracks;* the immense and fine *Roman Catholic Cathedral;* the *Ursuline Convent* and *Church*, with attractive gardens; the *English Cathedral* (modern and noble); *St. Andrew's Church ;* the very old church of *Notre Dame des Victoires*, in the Lower Town; as also, in the Lower

Town, the *Exchange, Custom House, Marine Hospital, Post Office,* and many of the most extensive commercial establishments. It is worthy of remark that Quebec, even more than Montreal, has a large French admixture, and that in some of the quarters many of the lower Parisian dwellings and habits may be seen duplicated. Among the principal streets are *St. Louis; D'Auteuil* (near the Esplanade, with many fine residences); *St. Louis Road* (from the Gate of the same name); *St. Peter* (Lower Town)—commercial. Principal Cemetery: *Mt. Hermon,* elevated and handsome. Leading Hotels: the *St. Louis* and *Russell House.*

[Connections: southwestward to *Richmond* and Montreal, by route just traversed; southward by the same route, by Richmond, to *Island Pond,* Portland, the White Mountains, etc.; eastward to the *Riviere du Loup.* Also, by boat on the St. Lawrence, to Montreal, etc.]

Of short Excursions from Quebec, the most important are those to the Falls of Montmorenci, noble broken cascade, with fine surrounding scenery, reached in drive from the city, through *Beauport* (seat of the *Provincial Lunatic Asylum*); to *Lorette,* a famous Indian Village, very popular for tourists, and with a world of Indian goods for sale; to *Cape Rouge* ("Carouge"), with fine river scenery; to the *River* and *Falls of the Chaudiere,* below the city (by Point Levi); to *Lake St. Charles,* with fine scenery and good angling. Something longer is that to the

Falls of St. Anne, which may, however, be taken in connection with those of Montmorenci.

Division D.

QUEBEC TO RIVIERE DU LOUP AND THE SAGUENAY RIVER.

Leave Quebec by rail, by Point Levi, along the south shore of the St. Lawrence, by *Chaudiere Junction, St. Thomas, L'Islet* and other stations, to *Riviere du Loup.*

Or, better, if time will allow the additional day:

Leave Quebec by one of the steamers of the Canadian Navigation Company (usual trips twice a week: timely reference on this point to be made at the hotel of stoppage, at Quebec.) First object of interest, the large *Island of Orleans,* in the St. Lawrence immediately below the city, with considerable prosperity. The *Falls of St. Anne* (before referred to), and *Lake St. Charles,* celebrated for fine troutfishing, are both passed, at some miles below, though of course not visible from the boat. The first landing is made at

MURRAY BAY, on the north shore, pleasant village and attractive watering-place, much resorted to by Canadian families, and with good accomodation. Going on by steamer, an hour and a half later is reached

RIVIERE DU LOUP, on the southern side of the now rapidly-widening St. Lawrence—terminus of the easternmost branch of the Grand Trunk road. [Connection by rail, southwest to *Chaudiere Junction*, for QUEBEC; or thence to *Richmond*, for MONTREAL, or south to *Island Pond* for PORTLAND or the White Mountains]. [From Riviere du Loup, visit is paid, by stage, to the favorite watering-place of

Cacouna, with fine bathing, fishing, and much fashionable resort.]

Leaving Riviere du Loup, again by steamer, the St. Lawrence is recrossed, to the entrance of the

SAGUENAY RIVER, with scenery of such grand and stupendous wildness as is seldom encountered on either continent; the almost perpendicular cliffs at many points, and the great height of the bordering hills, combining with the darkness of the water, the frequent waterfalls, and the general aspect of wild desolation, to awe as well as enrapture. At very near the entrance of the river is passed the very old village of *Tadoussac;* and not long after, the little cove containing a fishing station, called *L'Ance a l'Eau*. The next points of interest reached, are the two frightful over-hanging cliff-mountains, *Cape Eternity* and *Cape Trinity*, beneath which, from the apprehension that they may fall at any moment, the tourist has no wish to remain for any long period, while the water seems black as ink, from the shadows. *Statue Point* and the *Tableau* are other points of special interest, approaching *Ha Ha Bay*, a beautiful village, amid softened scenery, where the route terminates.

Return by steamer to *Riviere du Loup*, whence rail to QUEBEC, or to *Chaudiere Junction* for proceeding southward.

ROUTE NO. 20.—CANADIAN.

NIAGARA FALLS TO TORONTO, MONTREAL AND QUEBEC, BY STEAMERS; WITH DIRECTION TO OTHER CITIES OF BRITISH POSSESSIONS.

Leave Niagara Falls (Suspension Bridge), by train to *Lewiston*, small town on the American shore of the Niagara River (QUEENSTON, larger town, on the Canadian side, opposite, with monument to the British General Brock, killed there in battle in 1812).

At Lewiston take Toronto boat (twice daily), on the Niagara river, with stop at

NIAGARA (Village), place of embarkation for other passengers from Falls by rail on the American side. Immediately below Niagara are passed *Fort Niagara*, on American side, and *Fort Massasauga*, on Canadian. Soon after, passing from the River into Lake Ontario, with short sail to

TORONTO (See Route No 19).

At Toronto take Royal Mail steamer for Montreal (every day, in connection with boat and train). Several hours' sail along the Lake, with shore-views, principally north—to

KINGSTON. (See Route No. 19).

(Or, leave Niagara by rail, as in Route No. 19, to

Hamilton, TORONTO and *Kingston,* first taking boat here, at very early morning or afternoon).

At Kingston the Lake narrows to become virtually the St. Lawrence River, though, still very wide, and called the "Lake of the Thousand Islands," as containing the celebrated

Thousand Islands, said to number nearly twice as many, and certainly studding the stream very thickly, in rough-tree-crowned, wild and picturesque beauty—there really seeming, at times, to be difficulty in finding passage between them.

Leaving the Lake of the Thousand Islands, entering the St. Lawrence proper, passing *Ogdensburg* on the American side, and *Prescott,* on the Canadian (connection to OTTAWA—see Route No. 19),—are soon entered the

Rapids of the St. Lawrence, among the most extended and notable to be found in any river on the globe, and some of them startling to the inexperienced who mark the rapid rush of the water and the sharp inclination of the boat, at the worst moments; though the amount of danger involved, with good boats and the inevitable skilful pilotage, must be almost nothing, as accidents are literally unheard of. The different Rapids follow each other in the succession named : the *Gallopes* (4); the *Plate*; the *Depleau*; the *Long Sault*; the *Coteau*; the *Cedars* (considered by many the finest); the *Cascades;* and the *Lachine* (shortest of all, but more sensational than any of the others). Im-

ROUTE NO. 20.—CANADIAN. 259

mediately after passing the Lachine, is in sight, and soon after reached,

MONTREAL. (See Route No. 19).

From Montreal (every evening) by boats of the Richelieu Company, making the whole passage during the night (little interesting scenery offering), and landing in the morning at

QUEBEC. (See Route No. 19; as also for excursion to Riviere du Loup and the Saguenay River).

SKELETON ROUTES TO OTHER TOWNS OF BRITISH POSSESSIONS.

HALIFAX, Capital of Nova Scotia. Reached by steamers of the Allan line, from Montreal or Portland; or by packet-steamer or rail from Portland; or from St. John, N. B., by steamer to Windsor, N. S., and rail thence to Halifax. Hotels: the *Waverley*, *Stewart's*, *Halifax*, and *International*.

ST. JOHN, New Brunswick. From Boston, by steamer, or from Portland by rail. From Halifax by rail and steamer, by Windsor, N. S. Hotels: *Waverley* and *Stubbs'*.

FREDERICTON, Capital of New Brunswick. From Boston, by steamer to St. John's, and rail, or rail from Portland.

WINDSOR, Nova Scotia. By rail from Halifax.

SIDNEY, Cape Breton. By boat from Halifax.

SHEDIAC, New Brunswick. By rail from St. John, N. B.; also by steamer from Quebec.

CHARLOTTE TOWN, Prince Edward's Island. By

rail from St. John, N. B., to Shediac, N. B.; thence boat.

PICTOU, Nova Scotia. By rail from St. John, N. B., to Shediac, N. B.; thence boat.

BATHURST, New Brunswick. By boat from Shediac; also from Quebec.

ROUTE NO. 21. FAR-WESTERN (SEMI-SKELETON.)

CHICAGO TO OMAHA, SALT LAKE CITY, SAN FRANCISCO, BIG TREES AND YO-SEMITE VALLEY.

Division A.

CHICAGO TO OMAHA, BY OPTIONAL ROUTES.

By Chicago and North-Western road.

Leave Chicago by Chicago and North-Western road, to

Junction [connection north-westward to MADISON; westward to *Dunleith* and *Dubuque*]. Junction, by *Geneva* and other stations, to

Dixon [connection northward to *Freeport*; southward to *Bloomington*, SPRINGFIELD, *Alton* and ST. LOUIS]. By other stations to

Sterling [connection south-westward to Rock Island]; to

CLINTON, on the Mississippi River, entering the State of Iowa [river connections north and south. Connections to Dubuque, McGregor, Prairie du Chien and Lacrosse]. Clinton, by various stations, to

CEDAR RAPIDS, railway centre on the Cedar River. [Connections, northeast to *Dubuque*; north to *Waterloo*, *Austin* and ST. PAUL; south to *Burlington* and *Keokuk*]. Cedar Rapids, by various other stations, to

Marshall, [connections northward to *Mason City, Austin* and ST. PAUL; southward to *Ottumwa, Keokuk*, &c.]; to *Boone*, thriving town and coal centre, to

GRAND JUNCTION [connection north to *Fort Dodge*]. Grand Junction, by many other stations, through the Valley of the Des Moines, to

MISSOURI VALLEY JUNCTION. [Minor connections north to *Sioux City;* westward by California Junction, across the Missouri River to *Fremont* and the Union Pacific road, for California and the Pacific coast]. By other stations to

COUNCIL BLUFFS, on the eastern side of the Missouri River. [Connections north to *Sioux City*, &c.; south to *Nebraska City* (by branch), LINCOLN, Capital of Nebraska, ST. JOSEPH, on the Missouri River, &c]. From Council Bluffs, bridge-transfer (railroad), to OMAHA.

By Chicago and Rock Island road.

Leave Chicago by the Chicago and Rock Island road; by *Englewood* [connections eastward to all cities on the Michigan Southern and Lake Shore roads; southeastward to *Fort Wayne, Pittsburg,* &c.]. By other stations to

JOLIET, large town on the Des Moines River, with State Penitentiary, extensive stone-quarries, &c. [Connections, eastward to Michigan Southern and Lake Shore roads; southwestward to *Blooming-*

ROUTE NO. 21.—FAR-WESTERN. 263

ton and *Springfield;* also by Canal with CHICAGO]. By other stations to

LA SALLE, flourishing town and coal centre on the Illinois river. [Connections, north to *Mendota* and *Freeport*, south to *Bloomington* and SPRINGFIELD, by Illinois Central road; also by steamer to ST. LOUIS]. La Salle, by *Bureau* [connection southward to *Peoria*] ; by *Pond Creek*, and other minor stations to

ROCK ISLAND, important town on the Mississippi, with extensive manufactures and river trade. [Connections northeast to *Freeport*, etc.; southeast to *Peoria;* south to *Alton* and ST. LOUIS; also by steamboat to ST. LOUIS]. From Rock Island, by bridge over the Mississippi, to

DAVENPORT (Iowa), large town on the western bank of that river, with water-power, manufactures, *Griswold* and other *Colleges*, an *Opera House*, etc. [Connections, substantially same as Rock Island]. Davenport to *Wilton* [connection southwestward to *Muscatine, Washington*, and the Kansas Pacific road] ; to *Moscow* [connection, by Ashland, with Des Moines Valley road] ; to

West Liberty [connection south to BURLINGTON; north to *Cedar Rapids*, etc.] ; to

Iowa City, on the Iowa river, formerly capital of the State, and now with State University, manufactures, etc. By other stations to *Grinnell*, seat of Iowa College [connections north to *Mason City*, etc.; south to *Ottumwa*, etc.] By other stations to

DES MOINES, capital of the State of Iowa, thriving manufacturing town and coal centre, at the confluence of Des Moines and Raccoon rivers, with magnificent State House in course of erection. [Connections, northwest to *Fort Dodge* and *Sioux City;* southeast to *Ottumwa, Keokuk,* etc.] Des Moines, by *Dexter, Casey, Atlantic,* and other stations, to

COUNCIL BLUFFS and OMAHA. (See Chicago and Northwestern route over the same distance, immediately preceding.)

By Chicago, Burlington and Quincy road.

Leave Chicago by the Chicago, Burlington and Quincy road, by *Aurora*, on Fox river; by *Mendota*, agricultural and manufacturing town, seat of Mendota College, and of a Wesleyan Seminary [connection south to *Bloomington,* etc., north to *Freeport,* etc., by the Illinois Central road]; by *Princeton, Galva;* by *Galesburg*, seat of Knox and Lombard Colleges [connection south-eastward to *Peoria,* etc.]; by *Monmouth,* to

BURLINGTON, on the Mississippi river, one of the largest and most important towns of Iowa, with fine river scenery, extensive commerce, by river and otherwise, seat of *Burlington University* (Baptist), and a great railway centre. [Connections very general; principally by the Chicago, Burlington and Quincy road and its branches; and Mississippi river may be

ROUTE No. 21.—FAR WESTERN.

ascended to *Rock Island, Dubuque,* etc., or descended to St. Louis, etc.]

From Burlington by the Iowa Division C. B. & Q. road, by the important stations of *Ottumwa* [connections north to *Cedar Rapids,* southward and eastward to St. Louis, etc.]; Chariton, Osceola, Creston, *Red Oak, Pacific Junction,* etc., to

COUNCIL BLUFFS and OMAHA. (See Chicago and North Western route.)

Division B.

OMAHA TO OGDEN, SALT LAKE CITY, AND SAN FRANCISCO.

OMAHA, Nebraska, on the western side of the Missouri river, opposite Council Bluffs, well located, and unprecedentedly rapid in growth, though deriving its principal importance from the great Pacific transit through it, and the commercial supply of a wide section, making it the central point between Chicago and San Francisco. Communication with Council Bluffs by ferry boat, and by the magnificent iron bridge now crossing the Missouri. [Connections: (besides the routes just traversed) south-east to *Ottumwa, Keokuk,* BURLINGTON & St. LOUIS by the Chic., B. & Q. road; north to *California Junction* and *Sioux City;* south to St. JOSEPH, *Kansas City,* and TOPEKA, capital of the State of Kansas ; &c.]

[Before proceeding westward from Omaha, on the great Pacific Route, a few observations are worthy of notice. *First,* no apprehensions of the length of the road need be entertained, as to anything more than easily-endurable fatigue—the road, throughout, from Omaha to the Pacific, being thoroughly well laid, a large proportion of it straight and level, and the moderate rate of speed making the motion smooth and easy, so that reading, writing, card-playing, conversation or eating (if lunch is carried), are all practicable and easy throughout. *Second,* to secure the full charm of the route, berths in the Pullman Sleeping Carriages, advisable elsewhere, are almost indispensable for the night-and-day travel on the Union Pacific road, as are the Silver Palace Cars of the same character correspondingly necessary beyond Ogden, on the Central Pacific road. The cost of using these coaches, with freer room and greater privileges by day and comfortable sleeping-accommodations by night, will be found but a trifle added to the price of tickets (only $8.00, Omaha to Ogden; $6.00, Ogden to the Pacific); and no wiser additional outlay can be made, as no more complete luxury can be found in any line of travel. *Third,* the trains stop at convenient stations for meals, which will be found good enough for all practical purposes, and many excellent; though parties of several persons will probably add to their comfort by taking lunch-baskets, prepared food, and what drinks they may prefer, and having tables set for them in the cars, at leisure, by the stewards or porters. *Fourth,* at some portions of the long ride there is always dust, and linen or other dusters (wraps) are indispensable; while the same stout clothing needed nearly all the year at San Francisco and other places on the immediate Pacific coast, is often found pleasant at that point of the route which crosses the Rocky Mountains. *Fifth*, to the intelligent and observing, the ride is by no means monotonous, at least on the first crossing—the infinite variety of scenery making such monotony impossible. The first few hours from Omaha show the Prairies, in perfection, with an absolute level, fertility, though without wood, the Platte river on the left, and a sea of living green; the second day changes the prairies to the Plains, with less fertility, some bluffs, and low river scenery; while, also on the second day, the snow-crested Rocky Mountains are seen, the route of travel roughens, and the mountains themselves are crossed; to these succeed the High Plains of Laramie; then the Desert, with rocky bluffs; then the Wahsatch Mountains, generally snow-crowned, and the grand scenery of Echo and Weber Cañons, penetrating through them, to Ogden (with its detour of Salt Lake City). Beyond Ogden occurs, first, grand scenery on the left, of the Wahsatch, the Great Salt Lake, etc.; then succeed the Great American Desert, with its characteristics of desolation indicated by the name—the Valley of the Humboldt, with some approach to fertility— followed by the Great Nevada Sandy Desert, more desolate than any preceding, but curious in its bluffs and rock-formations. Then follow the noble and wild scenery of the Sierra Nevada Mountains, nearly always snow-crowned, the tremendous passes over and around the summits of those mountains, with nearly forty miles of snow-sheds, views of the great gold-mining sections and operations, the thrilling descent of the Sierras, to the English-looking and fertile plains of California.]

The following table shows all the stations between Omaha and San Francisco, on both the Union and Central Pacific roads, with the distances from Omaha, and the altitudes of all points above sea-level. Those in capitals are the more important stations; and in notes following, and marked by reference letters (*a, b, c*, etc.) will be found some of the notable features of the route, the connections, etc. General eating-stations are designated, in the notes, by the initials " G. E. S."

Distances from OMAHA.	STATIONS.	Elevations.
	..............OMAHA DEPOT..............	966
4	...., ...Summit Siding..............	1142
10	...................Gilmore *a*.................	976
15	......................Papillon..................	972
29	...................Elkhorn *b*..................	1150
35	........·...........Valley..................	1120
47	..........·......Fremont *c*.................	1176
54	..................Ketchum..................	1270
62	..............North Bend *d*......	1259
69	....................Rogers..................	1359

ROUTE NO. 21.—FAR WESTERN.

Distances from OMAHA.	STATIONS.	Elevations.
76	Schuyler	1335
84	Richland	1440
92	Columbus *e*	1432
99	Jackson	1470
109	Silver Creek	1534
121	Clark's	1610
132	Lone Tree	1686
142	Chapman's	1760
148	Lockwood	1800
154	GRAND ISLAND *e†*	1850
162	Alda	1907
172	Wood River	1974
183	Gibbon	2046
191	Kearney *f*	2106
201	Stevenson	2170
212	Elm Creek	2241
221	Overton	2305
230	Plum Creek *g*	2370
240	Cayote	2440
250	Willow Island	2511
260	Warren	2570
268	Brady Island	2637
278	McPherson *h*	2695
285	Gannett	2752
291	NORTH PLATTE *i*	2789
299	Nichols	2882
308	O'Fallon's	2976
315	Dexter	3000
322	Alkali	3038
332	Roscoe	3105
342	Ogalalla	3190
351	Brule	3266
361	Big Spring	3325
369	Barton	3421
377	Julesburg *j*	3500
387	Chappel	3702
397	Lodge Pole	3800
408	Colton	4022

Distances from OMAHA.	STATIONS.	Elevations.
414	SIDNEY *k*	4073
423	Brownson	4200
433	Potter	4370
442	Bennett	4580
451	Antelope	4712
463	Bushnell	4860
473	Pine Bluffs, W. T. *l*	5026
484	Egbert	5272
496	Hillsdale *m*	5591
508	Archer	6000
516	CHEYENNE *n*	6041
523	Hazard	6325
531	Otto	6724
536	Granite Canon	7298
542	Buford	7780
549	Sherman *o*	8242
558	Harney	7857
564	Red Buttes	7336
570	Fort Saunders	7163
573	LARAMIE *p*	7123
581	Howell	7090
587	Wyoming	7068
602	Cooper's Lake	7044
606	Lookout	7169
638	Como	6680
645	Medicine Bow	6550
656	Carbon *q*	6750
662	Simpson	6898
669	Percy *r*	6950
675	Dana	6875
680	St. Mary's *s*	6751
688	Walcott	6800
690	Fort Steele	6840
704	Grennville	6560
709	RAWLINS	6732
716	Summit	6821
723	Separation	6900
730	Fillmore	6885

ROUTE NO. 21.—FAR WESTERN.

Distances from OMAHA.	STATIONS.	Elevations.
737	Creston t	7030
744	Latham	6900
752	Wash-a-kie	6697
761	Red Desert	6710
775	Table Rock	6890
785	Bitter Creek	6685
794	Black Buttes	6600
798	Hallville	6590
805	Point of Rocks	6490
817	Salt Wells	6360
825	Baxter	6300
831	Rock Springs	6280
839	Lawrence	6200
845	GREEN RIVER u	6140
858	Bryan v	6340
867	Marston	6245
876	Granger	6270
887	Church Buttes w	6317
896	Hampton	6500
904	Carter x	6550
913	Bridger	6780
928	Leroy	7123
937	Piedmont	6540
944	Aspen	7835
950	Millis	6790
614	Miser	6810
623	Rock Creek	6690
630	Wilcox	7033
957	EVANSTON, Utah y	6870
966	Wahsatch	6879
975	Castle Rock z	6290
982	Hanging Rock	5974
991	Echo	5315
999	Weber Quarry	5250
1007	Weber	5130
1015	Peterson	4963
1019	Devil's Gate	4870
1024	Uintah	4560

Distances from OMAHA	STATIONS.	Elevations
1032	OGDEN *aa*	4340
1040	Bonneville	4310
1055	Corinne *bb*	4294
1073	Blue Creek	4360
1084	Promontory *cc*	4943
1092	Rozel	4600
1105	Monument *dd*	4290
1123	Kelton *ee*	4500
1139	Matlin	4821
1153	Terrace	4450
1178	Lucin	4400
1187	Tecoma, Nevada	4600
1197	Montello	4800
1206	Loray	5409
1215	TOANO *ff*	5964
1227	Pequop	6180
1236	Independence	6115
1251	Wells *gg*	5650
1259	Tulasco	5418
1283	Halleck	5220
1297	Osino *hh*	5100
1307	Elko *ii*	5030
1319	Moleen	5000
1330	CARLIN *jj*	4930
1339	Palisade *jj**	4870
1358	Be-o-wa-we	4717
1368	Shoshone	4665
1379	Argenta *kk*	4575
1391	Battle Mountain *kk* †	4534
1410	Stone House	4449
1434	Golconda	4419
1451	WINNEMUCCA *ll*	4355
1472	Raspberry	4354
1492	Humboldt *mm*	4262
1514	Oreana	4206
1525	Lovelock's	4100
1541	Brown's	3955
1553	White Plains	3921

ROUTE NO. 21.—FAR WESTERN.

Distances from OMAHA.	STATIONS.	Elevations.
1568	Hot Springs	4098
1587	WADSWORTH nn	4104
1602	Clark's	4290
1614	Vista	4400
1622	Reno oo	4525
1633	Verdi, California pp	4915
1648	Boca	5560
1657	TRUCKEE qq	5866
1671	Summit rr	7042
1684	Cisco	5911
1692	Emigrant Gap ss	5309
1697	Blue Canon	4700
1706	Alta	3625
1709	Dutch Flat	3425
1711	Gold Run tt	3245
1722	Colfax uu	3448
1740	Auburn	1385
1745	Newcastle	920
1754	Rocklin	269
1758	Junction uu*	189
1768	Arcade	76
1776	SACRAMENTO vv	56
1803	Galt	73
1824	Stockton ww	46
1834	Lathrop xx	48
1867	Livermore	520
1893	Niles	148
1914	San Jose yy	114
1909	Oakland zz	0
1914	SAN FRANCISCO	0

NOTES.

a. *Gilmore*, entrance of the Papillon Valley.

b. *Elkhorn*, entrance of the Platte Valley, and crossing of the Elkhorn river.

c. *Fremont*, connection with the Chicago and North-Western road, by California Junction. G. E. S.

d. *North Bend*, with first views of the Platte river on the left.

e. *Columbus*, with bridge across the Platte, and railroad crossing the Loup Fork near.

e†. *Grand Island*, important station. G. E. S.

f. *Kearney*, supply station for Fort Kearney, in the immediate neighborhood.

g. *Plum Creek*, scene of the Plum Creek Massacre of railroad employees, 1868.

h. *McPherson*, supply station for Fort McPherson on the opposite side of the river.

i. *North Platte*, with extensive machine-shop of the railway company.

j. *Julesburg*, with Fort Sedgwick near—the place having some activity and the reputation of being the wickedest in the world, during the railway building, but now stripped and in decay.

k. *Sidney*, important station, with railway repair-shops, and Sidney Barracks, military station, adjoining. G. E. S.

l. *Pine Bluffs*, with singular rock scenery in the neighborhood.

m. *Hillsdale*, with first views, near, of the Black Hills, the snow-crowned peaks of the Rocky Mountains; and Pike's Peak, Long's and Spanish Peaks, of the Colorado Mountains, often visible at the south-west, at the incredible distance of 170 miles.

n. CHEYENNE, principal station between Omaha and Ogden, with railway shops. Point of connection, by the Denver Pacific road, with *Denver;* and thence, by the Kansas Pacific road, with *Topeka, Lawrence* and other Kansas towns, and ST. LOUIS. Also, by the road to Denver, and stages thence, with *Central City, Golden City, Pike's Peak,* and other mountain and mining centres of Colorado. Also, central military station of the Plains. G. E. S.

o. *Sherman*, highest point of the railway over the Rocky Mountains, and also highest railway-station in the world, with altitude of 8,242 feet.

p. *Laramie*, important station, with railway machine-shops, near the North Park on the south and the Black Hills on the north, and very favorable for residence and mountain rambles. G. E. S.

q. *Carbon*, with coal-mines in the neighborhood.

r. *Percy*, with fine views of Elk Mountain.

s. *St. Mary's*, with wild and rugged scenery in the vicinity, and a crossing of the Laramie river.

t. *Creston*, at the summit of the dividing-ridge of the continent, though really lower than Sherman.

u. *Green River*, thriving village, fording-place of the old Overland Stage line, and with fine views of the Uintah Mountains at the south, and the Wind River Mountains at the north. G. E. S.

v. *Bryan*, important station, and point of connection, by stage, with the Sweet Water mining region and the once popular South Pass of the Overland emigration.

w. *Church Buttes*, with singular rock formations in the neighborhood, giving it the name; and the chief place of supply of the celebrated moss-agates of the section.

x. *Carter*, supply station for Fort Bridger, near.

y. *Evanston*, new but thriving town of Utah, with reputation for supplying the alkali bread, of peculiar excellence; and the point at which, when available, the open "observation car" is attached to the westward-bound train, for favorable views of the snow-crowned Wahsatch mountains, and through Echo and Weber Cañons. G. E. S.

z. *Castle Rock*, entrance to the grand rock scenery of Echo Cañon, and of Weber Cañon, following, with Pulpit Rock, the Thousand Mile Tree, the Devil's Gate, Devil's Slide, and other notable features of one of the most remarkable passes on the continent.

aa. OGDEN, termination of the Union Pacific road, and commencement of the Central Pacific; Mormon town of some prosperity, and with grand scenery at the north, in in Ogden and other Cañons. Also, point of departure, by the Utah Central railroad, for Salt Lake City (see that detour, Division D, following), and for northern points by the Utah Northern road. G. E. S.

bb. *Corinne*, important station near the Great Salt Lake, with stage connection to the Lake, and by boat to Salt Lake City; also stage connection to Virginia, Helena, and other mountain and mining towns of Nevada and Montana.

cc. *Promontory*—Promontory Point, so called from strange rock protuberances near it; the spot where the "last spike" of the connecting roads was driven on the 10th May, 1869, and where the connection of the two roads was expected to be made, until transferred to Ogden by Act of Congress.

dd. *Monument*, commencement of the Great American Desert.

ee. *Kelton*, with connection by stage to Boise City, Rocky Bar, and other mining sections in Idaho, and thence to cities of Oregon.

ff. *Toano*, important station, at near the entrance to the Humboldt Valley. G. E. S.

gg. *Wells*, with the Humboldt Wells and their fertile oases in the neighborhood, and point of stage departure for Pioche, Nevada, and northern mines.

hh. *Osino*, western termination of the Humboldt Valley.

ii. *Elko*, important station and thriving town of Nevada, with stage and wagon connections to White Pine, Wyoming, Cape District, and other mining districts.

jj. *Carlin*, another important station, and rival of Elko. G. E. S.

jj*. *Palisade*, connection with Eureka and Palisade R. R., and with stage for White Pine district.

kk. *Argenta*, with stage connections to Austin and Belmont, and distributing trade to Reese river and White Pine mining districts.

kk. *Battle Mountain*. G. E. S. Stage for Austin City, Nevada.

ll. *Winnemucca*, with railway shops and mining trade and stage connection to Boise City, Paradise, Silver City, etc. Also, virtual commencement of the Great Nevada Sandy Desert.

mm. *Humboldt*, with bridge crossing of the Humboldt river, and Sink of the Humboldt visible at the left. G. E. S.

nn. *Wadsworth*, western termination of the Great Nevada Desert, and commencement of ascent of the Sierra Nevada Mountains. Also, with extensive workshops, and with Pyramid Lake at some twenty miles due northward.

oo. RENO, important station, on the Truckee river, and great mining center of supplies and transportation, with Virginia & Truckee R. R., to Carson City, Virginia City, Gold Hill, Washoe, etc.

pp. *Verdi*, point of entering California.

qq. *Truckee*, thriving town, with numerous saw mills and many characteristics of the early California towns. Point of detour from the railway, by stage to *Lake Tahoe*, 15 miles southward (see Division E), and to *Lake Donner*, at a short distance northward. Has fine mountain scenery in the neighborhood, and thence westward up the Sierra, though with many interruptions from the snow-sheds. Not far westward from Truckee are caught noble views of Lake Donner, lying far below, to the right.

rr. *Summit*, highest point of the railway over the Sierra Nevada, almost always with much snow in the neighborhood, and surrounded by snow-sheds. G. E. S.

ss. *Emigrant Gap*, at and beyond which may be said to commence the grand scenery of the descent of the Sierras,

ROUTE NO. 21.—FAR WESTERN. 276a

of which the two most striking points are the great American Canon, and Cape Horn.

tt. *Gold Run*, in the neighborhood of which, from the road, may be surveyed many of the effects and some of the processes of hydraulic gold-mining in California.

uu. *Colfax*, important station, and point at which ceases the very steep descent of the Sierras. G. E. S.

uu*. *Junction*, connection with Oregon Division for Marysville, Chico, Red Bluff, and Redding.

vv. SACRAMENTO, capital of California, lying on the Sacramento river, with a very handsome *Capitol* not yet finished, a large amount of trade by river and otherwise, the *Yolo Bridge* over the river, *Central Pacific Railway Works*, and many attractions as a residence. [Steamboat communication down the Sacramento river, by *Amador*, *Benicia*, *Vallejo*, etc., supplying very pleasant transit to SAN FRANCISCO.] Connection with California Pacific R. R. G. E. S.

ww. *Stockton*, large town of the San Joaquin Valley, at the head of navigation on the San Joaquin river, mining emporium, wheat-center, and one of the points of departure for the Big Trees of Calaveras, the Yo Semite Valley, etc., Stockton & Copperopolis, and Stockton & Visalia R. R's., for Milton and Oak Dale.

xx. *Lathrop*, thriving town of San Joaquin Valley, point of junction of the Visalia Division of the C. P. R. R., and another of the favorite points of departure for the Yo Semite. G. E. S.

yy. *Niles*, connection by branch rail to *San Jose*, pleasant town south-east of San Francisco, thence to the latter city by all-rail.

zz. *Oakland*, thriving town and favorite residence, celebrated for its growth of live oaks, and as being the site of the University of California. Terminus of the Central Pacific road, whence ferry to San Francisco.

Division C.

SAN FRANCISCO, WITH SHORT EXCURSIONS.

SAN FRANCISCO, called the "Metropolis of the Pacific," as well as the "Golden City," lies on the western side of the Bay of the same name, with entrance to the Pacific Ocean through the "Golden Gate." It is immense in trade and wealth, with singularly varied and sometimes-trying climate, and a dashing enterprise unparalleled elsewhere. *California, Montgomery, Clay, Bush, Washington, Kearney, Stockton* and *Dupont*, are among the principal streets; and *Market street* divides them between north and south, as in Philadelphia. *Montgomery Avenue*, recently opened, supplies one of the finest thoroughfares through the city. *Telegraph Hill*, at the northern side, gives a splendid view of the city and harbor, and many of the distant mountains.

Among the leading Public Buildings are the *U. S. Mint*, new and magnificent, at Mission and Fifth streets; the *Custom House* (with Post Office), *Merchants' Exchange*, California street; *Nevada Bank; Safe Deposite Company's Building*, &c.; *New City Hall* (building, Yerba Buena Park); *U. S. Marine Hospital*, Mission street; *Roman Catholic Orphan Asylum*, Market street; *St. Ignatius College*, Market street, etc. Prominent Churches: *Grace Church* (Epis.); *Rev. Dr. Stone's; St. Mary's* and *St. Patrick's Cathedrals* (Cath.); *Calvary Presbyterian; First Methodist; First Baptist; Jewish Synagogue Emanuel; Mariners' Church*, etc. Leading Theatres: the *California*, and two additional, of elegance and completeness, recently erected. Chinese Theatres: Dupont street, and Jackson street. Leading Hotels: the *Occidental, Palace, Cosmopolitan, Grand, Lick House*, &c.

Other Features of Interest will be found, *The Chinese*, whose head-quarters in the Western World are at San Francisco, and in whose "quarter," "Joss House" or Temple, and Theatre, much experience may be gained; *Woodward's Gardens*, with very fine

ROUTE No. 21.—FAR WESTERN. 276c

collections in Natural History and a Hall for public amusements; the *City Water Works*, etc.

Near Excursions will include those to *Lone Mountain Cemetery*, with fine outlook, tombs of Broderick, Col. Baker, and others; to *Golden Gate Park*, recently opened, and one of the just prides of the city; to the *Cliff House* and *Seal Rock*, with the seals always crowning the latter (favorite drive or horse-cars, with stages connecting); to the *Ocean House* and *Race Course*, near the latter; to the *Hunter's Point Dry Docks;* to the *Mission Dolores* (street car); to the *Presidio, Fort Point*, etc., (drive or street car); and many others, locally directed, for longer sojourners. There are also ferries to *Oakland, San Antonio, Alameda, Contra Costa, San Quentin* and *Saucelito.*

[Connections from San Francisco. By rail to SACRAMENTO, *Marysville, Oroville, Shasta*, (Shasta Butte-Mountain) *Vreka* and other towns north; to *Stockton, San Jose, Visalia*, and other towns, and *New Almaden Mines*, south; eastward to SALT LAKE CITY, *Omaha*, and the East, by route just traversed. (Railway being laid, further north, to *Oregon City*, PORTLAND, *Vancouver*, etc.) By river-steamer to SACRAMENTO. By sea-steamer on the Pacific, to *Monterey, St. Luis, Santa Barbara, Acapulco*, and other towns on the Pacific, southward; with connection at PANAMA with the Panama Railway and steamers on the Atlantic from ASPINWALL to NEW YORK. Also by sea-steamer north to PORTLAND and other towns of Oregon. Also by sea-steamer to the *Sandwich Islands*, with connection thence to AUSTRALIA. Also by Pacific Mail steamers to JAPAN and CHINA, with connections to BRITISH INDIA, the Peninsular and Oriental steamers and overland route to EGYPT, *Mediterranean* and EUROPE.]

Division D.

DETOUR FROM OGDEN TO SALT LAKE CITY.

Leave Ogden by cars of the Utah Central Railway, down the Great Salt Lake Valley, with the Wahsatch Mountains (a part of them always snow-crowned) rising boldly on the left and forming the eastern rim of the valley; and the Great Salt Lake, with encircling mountains and bold islands, forming the western boundary. The valley is very fertile, though needing and receiving constant irrigation on account of deficient rain; and the Mormon farms and homesteads line the eastern side of the valley, and nestle under the mountains the whole distance. Passing through the settlements of *Kaysville, Farmington, Centreville,* and *Bountiful,* at 36 miles from Ogden is reached

SALT LAKE CITY, lying at the southern extremity of the fertile portion of the Valley, with marshy ground extending for some miles southward from it and westward to the lake. It is well laid out, with broad and well-shaded streets, streams of water running through many of them, though little that is complimentary can be said of the houses, a large proportion of them ill-built of adobe or wood. A full view of the noble Wahsatch Range is commanded from every portion of the town. Two wagon roads, leading southward and eastward to the mines and mountain settlements, enter the city at the eastward, through Emigrant and Parley Cañons. There is also stage connection from the City, for *Provo, Fillmore, San Bernardino,* and other towns in Lower California, and for *Stockton* and *Rush Valley* in the West. Salt Lake City, from its commencement, the home of the Mormon religion and ascendancy, is now growing to be a great mining exchange, its character becoming Gentilized and revolutionized.

Among the most notable buildings in the city are the *Tabernacle*, an immense, oval, round-roofed structure, with very large organ and wonderfully good acoustic properties, in which the denominational services of the Mormons are held; the *Old Tabernacle* near the other, and much smaller, for use in winter; the *Bee Hive* and *Lion Houses* of Brigham Young, standing near together, with the *Eagle Gate* between them; the *City Hall*, a very creditable structure; the *Theatre*, one of the most commodious in the West, and noted for the boxes devoted to President Brigham Young's extensive family; the foundations of the *Temple*, near the Tabernacle; some of the shops, with the "Z. C. M. I." (Zion's Co-operative Mercantile Institution) on their signs, showing the Mormon proclivities of the dealers. The principal business street is *Main* or *East Temple street.* Visits may profitably be paid to *Camp*

Douglas, the U. S. Military Station, three miles from the city, eastward, on a fine elevated plateau under the mountains; to the *Cemetery*, north-east of the city, and remarkable for being without shade; to the *Tithing Store*, where the denominational dues are paid; to *Ensign Peak*, for fine views: to the *Warm Springs*, the *Hot Springs*, the *Canyons*, etc., near the City. Hotels: the *Walker* (new), *Salt Lake* and *Townsend*.

Return to Ogden for pursuance of route westward.

Division E.

DETOUR TO LAKE TAHOE.

For this halt is made at Truckee (see that point in Division B); and the lying over of one train, or one day, will allow of a hurried visit to it, though much more time should be consumed.

From Truckee by stage fifteen miles, along the banks of the bright little Truckee river the whole distance, and over a very fair mountain road. An object of great interest is passed on the way, and should receive attention—the *Tahoe Fisheries*, at which, in pools, fine trout of all sizes and ages may be seen, while in a building adjoining, the whole process of incubation is shown.

LAKE TAHOE (often called by Californians "Lake Bigler," and so officially named), is undoubtedly one of the most beautiful bodies of water in any land, as it is the highest-lying large lake in the world. It is thirty-two miles in length, by ten in breadth, and lies bosomed in the snow-clad Sierras, which inclose it on the east, south and west, noble pine forests forming the border. The water of the lake is wondrously clear and blue, so that, when in repose, fish and other objects can be readily discerned at a depth of thirty or forty feet. It is also very cold, but has the peculiarity of never freezing in winter—possibly on account of the depth, which has been found to be 1,700 feet in the middle.

There are two small but commodious steamboats on the lake, besides sail and row-boats; and a variety of excursions, in these, to Cornelian and Emerald Bays, and other points of interest, may be made; or the whole lake may be ridden around by carriage, passing the same Bays, Lake Valley, Tahoe City, etc. Hotel: the *Tahoe House*.

Return to Truckee, for pursuing route by rail.

Lake Donner (much smaller than Tahoe, and seen from the rail) may also be reached from Truckee in a comparatively brief ride by carriage.

Division F.

TO THE BIG TREES AND YO-SEMITE VALLEY.

For this double visit (the two great natural curiosities lying in such directions that they should be taken in connection), several different routes offer themselves to the tourist. To the Yo-Semite, without the Calaveras Big Trees being always considered, three principal routes are in popular use, known as the "Big Oak Flat," the "Coulterville" and the "Mariposa" routes.

Big Oak Flat Route.

The easiest route is considered to be the "Big Oak Flat," the upper or north route. For this, the point of departure is STOCKTON, and the Big Trees of Calaveras lie very nearly on the way to the Valley.

Leave Stockton by cars of the Copperopolis road, to *Peters'*, and (with change) to *Milton*. At Milton take stages for *Murphy's* (Hotel, at Murphy's Camp), reached the same night. Proceed next day, by stage, fifteen miles, to the

BIG TREE GROVE OF CALAVERAS, where the *Sequoia gigantea* may be seen in their matchless glory, largest of all the arboreal products of earth. In the Mammoth Grove proper, there are nearly 100 trees, amid other trees that would be gigantic elsewhere; the heights of those standing ranging from 180 to 350 feet, circumference from 30 to 93 feet; estimated ages, from 1,400 to 2,500 years. Most of the largest are named after distinguished statesmen and generals. On the smoothed stump of one of the largest, now covered with a building, in front of the hotel, sixty persons have danced in a set; and through the hollow remains of the fallen "Father of the Forest," believed to have measured 420 feet in height, tall men walk erect and short ones ride on horseback. The largest still standing erect, the "Mother of the Forest," is dead and naked of its salable bark, some portions of which measured 30 inches in thickness. (Hotel, at the Calaveras Grove, the *Mammoth Grove House.*)

Six miles distant from the Mammoth Grove (reached on horseback), is the *South Grove*, of which some of the trees are alleged to be larger than any of the others, while the number reaches over 1,300.

Return to *Murphy's* from the Big Trees, and proceed thence, next morning, by stage, to *Sonora, Chinese Camp, Garote, Big Oak Flat, Hardin's* and *Hodgdon's,* to *Hutchings'* (Hotel), in the Valley, two days being consumed in the transit from Murphy's, with only eighteen miles of saddle. This brings the now celebrated

Yo-Semite Valley, on the Merced river, with scenery alleged to be more grand than any other on the globe, in many particulars. Special points of interest: *El Capitan,* gigantic separated rock; the *Three Brothers,* also rocks; the *Bridal-Veil Fall,* 940 feet; the *Royal Arches,* rocks; the *Great-Yosemite Fall,* in three leaps of 1,600, 434, and 600 feet; the *North* and *South Domes,* rocks; *Mirror Lake;* and the stupendous but frightful view of the whole Valley, from *Inspiration Point.* (Depend upon guide, necessary and always in readiness, for route and particulars.) Hotels at the Valley: *Hutchings', Lydig's,* and *Black's.* Proceed to *Clark's,* and thence make detour, a few miles, to the

Big Trees of Mariposa, with no less than 427 of the monsters, varying from twenty to thirty-four feet in diameter, and from 275 to 325 feet in height —many of them estimated to be 1,500 to 2,500 years old.

Return may be made from the Valley, by the same route by which it was entered, with the exception of not returning to Murphy's, on the way back to Stockton, and thus shortening the ride. But, unless special reasons offer for such a course, a greater variety of scenery will be secured, by adopting the reverse of one of the other following routes; or, if the visitor has entered the Valley by either of the following, the same advantages, with the glance at the Big Trees, will be secured by coming out by the reverse of the preceding.

Coulterville Route.

For this route, whether proceeding eastward or westward, the Central Pacific road is left at LA-THROP, cars being changed for *Merced*. Stage from Merced to *Coulterville*, and to *Gobin's Ranch*, at Crane's Flat. From Gobin's, saddle-train to *Black's*, in the Valley, with same features to be observed as those noted in the previous route, though some changes in the order of visiting them, from different points of arrival. This route is considered to have especial beauty in scenery along the route, as much of it lies along the dividing ridge between the Tuolumne and Merced rivers, giving fine views of the Sierra Nevada, the Coast Range, San Joaquin Valley, etc.

ROUTE NO. 21—FAR WESTERN.   276½

Mariposa Route.

This route, the southernmost, is identical with the Coulterville, in departure and detail, so far as *Merced*, by rail. Thence stage to *Snelling's*, *Hornitos*, *Bear Valley*, *White and Hatch's*, and *Clark and Moore's*. Thence into the Valley, by saddle, some thirty miles—the distance on horseback being greater than by any of the other routes, but with the advantages claimed of bringing both the Mariposa Big Trees and the stupendous view from Inspiration Point, into more convenient access.

Two additional routes have lately been opened, known as the *Mokelumne Hill* and *Hamilton's New*. For the former, stage from *Mokelumne Hill* Station of the Central Pacific road, to the Calaveras Big Trees, and thence to the Yo-Semite Valley as by the Big Oak Flat route; for the second, stage from the railroad station at *Galt*, by Ione City and Valley, Jackson, Mokelumne Hill and Railroad Flat, to the Big Trees; and thence to the Yo-Semite as by the Big Oak Flat route.

Division G.

EXCURSION TO THE GEYSERS

Visit may be paid to the wonderful steam-springs, known as The Geysers, and considered as among the greatest of California curiosities—most conveniently by the following route:

Steamer from San Francisco (twice a day), or from Sacramento, to

VALLEJO, (pronounced "Val-lay-o"), [see "vv.," p. 276a], important town on the Straits of Carquinez, with Mare Island Navy Yard in the immediate neighborhood, and terminus of the California Pacific Railway. Thence rail on the Napa Valley Railway, by *Napa City* (stage to Sonoma), St. Helena (stage to White Sulphur Springs), and minor towns, to

Calistoga (whence conveyance to *Calistoga Springs*, Mount St. Helena, the Petrified Forest, etc.) From Calistoga, Foss' stages, daily, by Ray's Ranch, Godwin's Peak (with fine and very extensive view over Russian River Valley, the Coast Range and distant Pacific), and the picturesque ridge of Hog's Back, to the

Great Geyser Canon and Springs, exhibiting some of the most startling phenomena in nature, in the wildness of the scenery, and the heat, varied mineral impregnation, and terrific force of outburst, of the various springs included. Among the most notable exhibitions are those of the "Witches' Cauldron," throwing up mingled pitch and ink, with clouds of steam; the "Steamboat Geyser," throwing out steam of the most intense heat, with such force as to imitate the blowing off of the most powerful boiler; the "Scalding Steam Iron Bath;" the "Mountain of Fire," with hundreds of vomiting fissures; the "Alkali Lake," the "Boiling Black Sulphur Springs," and many others that can only be intelligently or even safely visited under capable guidance—the whole maintaining, and well deserving, the reputation of being one of the most interesting and altogether the most diabolical, of the natural wonders of the continent.

Division H.

RETURNING EASTWARD FROM CALIFORNIA.

Overland return from California must necessarily be made, until the completion of the Northern Pacific road, and that of the California and Oregon road, running northward to meet it at Portland—by the same route pursued in going westward to the Pacific, over the Central and Union Pacific roads, at least so far as Cheyenne, Wyoming Territory; and the return ride will be by no means monotonous or without use, so many of the points passed over needing at least a second observation to measure them properly.

At Cheyenne, however (see "n," p. 274), much additional variety may be secured by taking the Denver Pacific road to

DENVER, capital of Colorado, as well as its commercial centre, with much beauty in location, a U. S. Branch Mint, magnificent views of the great snow-capped Colorado mountains from the rail, the city and neighborhood, and numerous rail and stage connections with all the great mining-centres of the territory, Golden City, Central City, Boulder City, etc., and with New Mexico, Arizona, and the South-West. It is also from Denver that excursions may best be arranged, to the famous Parks of Colorado, to the best points of view of Pike's, Long's, the Spanish Peaks, etc., among the grandest mountains of the central continent.

From Denver the route eastward may be pursued, by the Kansas Pacific road, by Kit Carson, (Col.) Sheridan, Fort Hays, Brookville, Salina (on the Smoky Hill Fork of the Kansas), *Junction City* (connection with the Missouri, Kansas and Texas railway, southward), Manhattan, and other more-or-less important towns of Kansas—to TOPEKA, capital of that State, and *Lawrence*, seat of the State University, directly eastward, or by *St. Joseph* ("St Joe") important town of Missouri, and old starting-point of the overland emigration—to ST. LOUIS, for pursuance of any route eastward, northward or southward (see Route No. 14, p. 223.)

[Of course, for the California-bound traveller finding himself previously at St. Louis, and desiring to traverse both routes, the course of this Division will be reversed so far as Cheyenne, and the route thence eastward to **Omaha and Chicago,** be taken on the return.]

OFF-ROUTE AND MINOR PLACES.

[TOWNS AND OTHER PLACES NOT INDEXED OR MENTIONED IN ANY OF THE ROUTES, OR WITH OPTIONAL ROUTE HERE INDICATED.]

Adrian (Mich.) by rail from Detroit.
Afton (N. Y.) on Albany and Susquehanna road, from Albany or Binghamton.
Allentown (N. J.) from Trenton or Bordentown.
Amenia (N. Y.) Harlem railroad from New York.
Amherst (Mass.) from New London by New London Northern road.
Ansonia (Ct.) from Bridgeport by Naugatuck road.
Antietam [Battle Field] (Md.) from Harrisburg to Hagerstown ; or from Harper's Ferry.
Appleton (Wis.) by rail from Milwaukie.
Ashley Falls (Mass.) from Bridgeport by Housatonic road.
Aspinwall (Isthmus, for *California*) from New York by Pacific Mail Steamers, 1st and 15th of every month.
Ashburnham (Mass.) from Fitchburg.
Atchison (Kansas,) by rail from Kansas city, (see this list.)
Aurora (N. Y.) on Cayuga Lake, (see this list.)
Avon (N. Y.) by rail from Rochester or Batavia.
Bainbridge (N. Y.) on Albany and Susquehanna road, from Albany or Binghamton.
Bath (Me.) by rail from Portland.
Bath (N. H.) from Wells River.
Bath (N. Y.) on Buffalo Division of Erie road, from Batavia or Corning.
Baton Rouge (La.) by steamer from New Orleans.
Beaufort (S. C.) from Charleston.
Belfast (Me.) by rail from Waterville, (see this list.)

Bennington (Vt.) by rail from Bellows Falls; or from Chatham Four Corners, (see this list.)
Benicia (Cal.) by boat from San Francisco.
Bethel (Me.) by rail from Portland or Gorham.
Bethel (Vt.) from White River Junction or Burlington.
Bethlehem (N. H.) from Littleton.
Beverly (Mass.) by rail from Salem.
Bolton [and *Falls*] (Vt.) from Ridley's Station, (see this list.)
Booneville (Mo.) by rail from Jefferson City, (see this list); or from St. Louis, by boat.
Booneville (N. Y.) from Utica.
Bowdoin College (Me.) at Brunswick, (see this list.)
Bradford (Vt.) by rail from Wells River or White River Junction.
Brandon (Vt.) by rail from Rutland or Burlington.
Braintree (Mass.) from Boston by South Shore road.
Bridgewater (Mass.) from Boston by Old Colony road.
Bristol (Ct.) by rail from Waterbury, (see this list), or Providence.
Bristol (N. H.) from Concord by N. New Hampshire road.
Bristol (R. I.) by rail from Providence.
Brookfield, (Ct.) from Bridgeport by Housatonic road.
Brunswick (Me.) by rail from Portland.
Canaan (Ct.) from Bridgeport by Housatonic road.
Cairo (N. Y.) by stage from Catskill.
Camel's Hump [Mountain] (Vt.) by carriage from Ridley's Station, (see this list.)
Canton (Mass.) by rail from Providence or Boston.
Carlisle (Pa.) by rail from Harrisburg.
Caseyville (Ill.) by rail from St. Louis.
Castine (Me.) by boat from Belfast, (see this list.)
Carbondale (Ill.) by rail from Cairo.
Centralia (Ill.) by rail from Cairo or Chicago.
Chateaugay Woods (N. Y.) from Rouse's Point, or from Plattsburg.

Chatham (N. J.) by Morris and Essex road from New York.
Chatham (N. Y.) Harlem railroad from New York, or Boston and Albany road from Boston.
Charlemont (Mass.) from North Adams.
Charleston (S. C.) from New York by steamers twice a week or oftener.
Cheat River (W. Va.) by rail from Wheeling; or from Harper's Ferry.
Cheshire (Ct.) from New Haven by Northampton road.
Chester (Vt.) by rail from Bellows Falls.
Chicopee (Mass.) by rail from Springfield.
Chilicothe (O.) by rail from Cincinnati.
Circleville (O.) by rail from Cincinnati or Zanesville.
Clarendon [*Springs*] (Vt.) by stage from Rutland.
Clarksburg (W. Va.) by rail from Harper's Ferry; or from Wheeling by Grafton.
Clifton Springs (N. Y.) on Auburn Branch of New York Central road, from Syracuse or Rochester.
Coatesville (Pa.) from Philadelphia by Pennsylvania Central road.
Collinsville (Ct.) from New Haven by Northampton road.
Cooperstown (N. Y.) by Susquehanna road from Albany.
Crawfordsville (Ind.) by rail from Indianapolis.
Crooked Lake (N. Y.) from Penn Yan, (see this list.)
Croton Falls (N. Y.) Harlem railroad from New York.
Dalles of St. Louis River (Minn.) by rail from St. Paul or Duluth.
Danbury (Ct.) from Norwalk.
Danielsonville (Ct.) by rail from New London or Worcester.
Deal (N. J.) from Long Branch.
Deerfield [and *South*] (Mass) by rail from Northampton, (see this list.)
Delaware (O.) by rail from Columbus.
Derby (Ct.) from Bridgeport by Naugatuck road.
Dexter (Me.) by rail from Bangor.

Dover Plains (N. Y.) Harlem railroad from New York.

Downington (Pa.) from Philadelphia by Pennsylvania Central road.

Easthampton (Mass.) from New Haven by Williamsburg road.

Eastport (Me.) by steamer from Boston and from St. John's, N. B.

Eatontown (N. J.) by New Jersey Southern road from New York; or New Jersey Central for Long Branch.

Effingham (Ind.) by rail from Terre Haute or St. Louis.

Englewood (N. J.) from New York by Northern New Jersey road.

Essex Junction (Vt.) from Burlington.

Falls Village (Ct.) from Bridgeport by Housatonic road.

Farmingdale (N. J.) by New Jersey Southern road (boat and rail) from New York.

Fitchburg (Mass.) by rail from Boston.

Fitzwilliam (N. H.) by rail from Fitchburg, Mass.

Flint (Mich.) by rail from Detroit.

Florence (Mass.) from New Haven by Williamsburg road.

Flushing (L. I.) from New York by 34th street ferry and Flushing railroad.

Fond du Lac (Wis.) by rail from Milwaukie or Duluth.

Fort William (Canada), by boat from Duluth.

Foxborough (Mass.) by rail from Providence or Boston.

Franklin (Ind.) by rail from Indianapolis.

Franklin (N. H.) from Concord by Northern New Hampshire road.

Freehold (N. J.) from New York by Pennsylvania, N. J. Central or N. J. Southern roads; or from Long Branch.

Galveston (Texas), by steamer from New Orleans.

Gardiner (Me.) by rail from Portland.

Gettysburg (Pa.) by rail from Harrisburg, by York.

Glassboro (N. J.) by rail from Camden.

Gloucester (Mass.) by rail from Salem.

Grafton (N. H.) from Concord by N. New Hampshire road.
Great Barrington (Mass.) from Bridgeport by Housatonic road.
Greensburg (Pa.) from the Pennsylvania Central road at Blairsville.
Greenfield (Mass.) from New Haven, by Northampton.
Greenport (Long Island), from New York by Long Island road.
Greenwich (Ct.) from New York by New Haven road.
Hackensack (N. J.) by Erie road from New York.
Hadley (Mass.) from Northampton, (see this list.)
Hagerstown (Md.) by rail from Baltimore, or Harrisburg by Chambersburg.
Hamilton (O.) by rail from Cincinnati.
Hammondsport (N. Y.) on Crooked Lake, (see this list.)
Hannibal (Mo.) by rail from Springfield, Ill.; or by river from St. Louis.
Hanover (N. H.) from White River Junction.
Havana (Cuba) from New York by Atlantic Mail Steamers, every Thursday; and by Vera Cruz Steamers, every 10 days.
Haydenville, (Mass.) from New Haven by Williamsburg road
Highgate Springs (Vt.) from Rouse's Point.
Hingham (Mass.) from Boston by South Shore road.
Hinsdale (Vt.) opposite Brattleboro.
Holmdel (N. J,) by steamboat from New York to Keyport (see this list,) thence by stage; or N. J. Central R.R.
Holyoke (Mass.) by rail from Springfield.
Honesdale (Pa.) by rail from Lackawaxen, on Erie Road.
Hoosac Tunnel (Mass.) from North Adams.
Housatonic (Mass.) from Bridgeport by Housatonic road.
Houston (Texas) by rail from Galveston (see this list.)
Howe's and *Ball's Caves* (N. Y.) from Schoharie (see this list.)
Ipswich (Mass.) by rail from Salem.
Isle Royal (Mich.) by boat from Duluth.

Ithaca (N. Y.) on Cayuga Lake (see this list.)
Jacksonville (Florida) from Savannah.
Jacksonville (Ill.) by rail from Springfield.
Jamaica (Long Island) from New York by Long Island road.
Jefferson City (Mo.) by rail from St. Louis.
Jonesboro (Ill.) by rail from Cairo.
Kane (Pa.) from Ridgeway or Irvineton, on Philadelphia and Erie road.
Kansas City, (Mo.) by rail from St. Louis, or from Omaha.
Kearsarge Mountain (N. H.) from Concord by Northern New Hampshire road.
Keene (N. H.) by rail from Fitchburg or Bellows Falls.
Kenoska (Wis.) by rail from Chicago.
Kent (Ct.) from Bridgeport by Housatonic road.
Keyport (N. J.) by steamboat from New York, or N. J. Central rail from Matawan.
Killington Peak (Vt.) from Rutland.
Knightstown (Ind.) by rail from Dayton (O.) or Indianapolis.
Lafayette (Ind.) by rail from Logansport.
Lake Dunmore (Vt.) by stage from Brandon (see this list.)
Lake Luzerne (N. Y.) from Saratoga.
Lake Pleasant (N. Y.) from Amsterdam, New York Central road.
Lake Temisconata (Canada) from Riviere du Loup by Grand Portage road.
Lake Umbagog (Me.) from Gorham, N. H.
Lambertville (N. J.) from Trenton by Belvidere Delaware road.
Lancaster (O.) by rail from Columbus or Zanesville.
Lawrence, (Kansas) from Kansas City (see this list).
Lawrenceburg (Ind.) by rail from Cincinnati.
Leavenworth (Kansas), by rail from Kansas City (see this list.)
Lebanon (N. H.) from White River Junction.
Lee (Mass.) from Bridgeport by Housatonic road.
Lehigh Water-Gap and *Lehighton* (Pa.) from Easton by Lehigh Valley road.

OFF-ROUTE AND MINOR PLACES. 283

Lenox (Mass.) from Bridgeport by Housatonic road; or from Albany by Boston and Albany road to Pittsfield.
Lexington (Mo.) by rail from Sedalia and Jefferson City (see this list).
Litchfield, (Ct.) from Bridgeport by Naugatuck road.
Little Rock (Ark.) by rail from Memphis, Tenn.
Logan (O.) by rail from Columbus.
London (O.) by rail from Springfield.
Long Branch (N. J.) from New York by N. J. Central R.R., or N. J. Southern, boat and rail.
Ludlow (Vt.) by rail from Bellows Falls.
Mackinaw (Mich.) from Detroit, by boat.
Manchester (Ct.) by rail from Hartford.
Manchester (N. J.) by New Jersey Southern road from New York.
Manchester (Vt.) by rail from Rutland.
Mansfield (Ct.) by rail from Hartford or Providence.
Marblehead (Mass.) by rail from Salem.
Marietta (O.) by rail from Wheeling.
Martha's Vineyard (Mass.) by steamer from New Bedford.
Martinsburg (W. Va.) by rail from Harper's Ferry.
Martinsville (Ind.) by rail from Indianapolis.
Massena Springs (Canada), from Louisville, on the St. Lawrence, near Prescott.
Matawan (N. J.) by rail from New York, on New Jersey Central road for Long Branch (also Keyport).
Mauch Chunk (Pa.) from Easton by Lehigh Valley road.
Maysville (Ky.) by rail, or the Ohio river from Cincinnati.
Meadville (Pa.) from Corry, Oil-Regions.
Medford (Mass.) from Boston by Lowell road.
Middleboro (Mass.) from Boston by Old Colony road.
Middleburg (Vt.) by rail from Burlington.
Middletown (N. J.) by New Jersey Central rail for Long Branch, from New York.

Middletown (Pa.) from Harrisburg.
Milford (Ct.) from New York by New Haven road.
Milford (O.) by rail from Columbus.
Minnesota Lakes (Minn.) from St. Paul.
Missisquoi Springs (Vt.) from St. Albans, by stage.
Mitchell (Ind.) by rail from Louisville.
Mound City [and *Mounds*] (Ill.) by rail from Cairo.
Monroe (Mich.) by rail from Detroit.
Montpelier (Vt.] from Burlington.
Mount Desert [and *Rock* and *Island*] (Me.) by steamer from Boston, Portland or Bangor.
Mount Diablo (Cal.) from San Francisco, by San Francisco and Oregon Railway, and connections.
Mount Holly (N. J.) by rail from Camden or Burlington.
Mount Holyoke (Mass.) from Northampton, (see this list.)
Mount Katahdin (Me.) by stage from Bangor; or partially by rail from same place.
Mount Mansfield (Vt.) by carriage from Waterbury, (see this list.)
Mount Tom (Mass.) from Northampton, (see this list.)
Mount Vernon (N. Y.) from New York by New Haven road.
Mount Vernon (O.) by rail from Newark.
Nantucket (Mass.) by steamer from New Bedford.
Narragansett Pier (R. I.) from Kingston, on Stonington and Providence road.
Nassau (New Providence) from New York, by Atlantic Mail steamers, irregularly.
New Britain (Ct.) by rail from Waterbury (see this list) or Providence.
Newburg (O.) by rail from Cleveland.
Newburg (Vt.) by rail from Wells River.
New Egypt (N. J.) by rail from Hightstown, Mt. Holly or Burlington.
New Milford (Ct.) from Bridgeport by Housatonic road.

New Monmouth (N. J.) from New York by New Jersey Central road for Long Branch—stage from Middletown.
New Orleans (La.) from New York by steamers, every Saturday or oftener.
New Philadelphia (O.) by rail from Pittsburg.
New Rochelle (N. Y.) from New York by New Haven road.
Newtown, (L. I.) from New York by 34th street ferry and Flushing railroad.
Norfolk (Va.) from New York by steamer, every Saturday or oftener.
Normal (Ill.) by rail from Chicago.
North Adams (Mass.) from Bridgeport by Housatonic road, or from Boston, Albany or Troy by Troy and Boston road.
North Derby (Vt.) from Lenoxville, Canada, by Massiwippi road.
Northampton, (Mass.) by rail from New Haven.
Northfield (Mass.) from New London by New London Northern road.
Northfield (Vt.) from Burlington.
Northumberland (Pa.) from Harrisburg by Northern Central road.
Norwich (Vt.) by rail from White River Junction.
Oceanport (N. J.) by New Jersey Southern road from New York; or from Long Branch.
Oshkosh (Wis.) by rail from Milwaukie.
Otsego Lake (N. Y.) by Susquehanna road from Albany.
Otter Creek Falls (Vt.) from Vergennes (see this list.)
Oxford (Me.) by rail from Portland.
Oxford (O.) by rail from Cincinnati.
Owasco Lake (N. Y.) from Auburn (see this list.)
Parkesburg (Pa.) from Philadelphia by Penn. Central road.
Parkersburg, (W. Va.) by rail from Wheeling, or from Columbus, O.
Passumpsic (Vt.) by rail from Wells River.
Phœnixville (Pa.) from Philadelphia by Reading road.

Patchogue (Long Island) from New York by South Side road.
Pemberton (N. J.) by rail from Hightstown, or from Camden Burlington, or Long Branch.
Penn Yan (N. Y.) by Northern Central road, from Elmira.
Perth Amboy (N. J.), from New York by N. J. Central, Long Branch line.
Peru (Ind.) by rail from Logansport.
Pittsfield (Mass.) from Bridgeport by Housatonic road, or from Albany or Boston by Boston and Albany road.
Piedmont (W. Va.) by Balt. and Ohio road from Harper's Ferry.
Pittsford (Vt.) by rail from Rutland.
Piqua (O.) by rail from Columbus.
Plainville (Ct.) from New Haven by Northampton road.
Pontiac (Ill.) by rail from Chicago.
Pontiac (Mich.) by rail from Detroit.
Port Huron (Mich.) by rail from Detroit.
Port Kent (N. Y.) by boat on Lake Champlain, going to or from Burlington, Vt.
Pottsville (Pa.) from Reading.
Poultney (Vt.) by rail from Rutland.
Putney (Vt.) by rail from Bellows Falls.
Quincy (Mass.) from Boston by Old Colony road.
Racquette Regions (N. Y.) in connection with Adirondacks from Crown Point.
Ravenna (O.) by rail from Cleveland.
Readville (Mass.) by rail from Providence or Boston.
Red Bank (N. J.) by New Jersey Central rail for Long Branch, from New York; or boat direct.
Riceville (N. J.) by New Jersey Southern road from New York.
Richfield Springs (N. Y.) from Sharon Springs; or from Utica or Binghamton by the Utica, Chenango and Susquehanna road.
Richmond (Ind.) by rail from Xenia or Indianapolis.
Ridley's Station (Vt.) from Essex Junction, (see this list.)

OFF-ROUTE AND MINOR PLACES. 287

Richmond (Va.) from New York by steamer every Saturday or oftener.

Rio Janiero (Brazil) from New York by United States and Brazil steamers, 23rd of every month.

Rockville (Ct.) by rail from Hartford.

Rockville (Ind.) by rail from Terre Haute.

Royalton [and *South*] (Vt.) from White River Junction.

Sackett's Harbor (N. Y.) by rail from Rome, on New York Central road.

Saginaw (Mich.) [and *East*] by rail from Detroit.

Salem (Ind) by rail from Louisville.

Salem (N. J.) by rail from Camden.

Salem (N. Y.) by Troy and Boston road, from Troy.

Salisbury (Ct.) from Bridgeport by Housatonic road.

Salisbury [*East* and *Beach*] (Mass.) by rail from Salem.

San Francisco (Cal.) from New York by Pacific Mail steamers, 1st and 15th of every month.

San Rafael and *San Quentin* (Cal.) by boat from San Francisco, and horse.

Sault Ste. Marie (Mich.) [Rapids and Canal], by boat from Detroit.

Savannah (Ga.) from New York by steamer several times a week. [Connection for *Florida cities*.]

Schoharie (N. Y.) on Albany and Susquehanna road, from Albany or Binghamton.

Schuylkill Haven (Pa.) from Reading.

Scotch Plains (N. J.) by New Jersey Central road from New York.

Seabrook (N. H.) from Boston or Portsmouth.

Sedalia (Mo.) by rail from St. Louis.

Seneca Lake (N. Y.) on Auburn Branch of New York Central road, from Syracuse or Rochester.

Seymour (Ct.) from Bridgeport by Nangatuck road.

Shark River (N. J.) by New Jersey Southern road from New York.

Sharon (Vt.) from White River Junction.
Sheboygan (Wis.) by rail from Milwaukie.
Shelburne N. H. from Gorham.
Shelburne Falls (Mass.) from North Adams.
Shelbyville (Ind.) by rail from Indianapolis.
Sheffield (Mass.) from Bridgeport by Housatonic road.
Sheffield (Pa.) from Ridgeway or Irvineton, on Philadelphia and Erie road.
Shrewsbury (N. J.) by New Jersey Southern road from New York ; or N. J. Central, Long Branch line.
Skeneateles (N. Y.) on Auburn Branch of New York Central road, from Syracuse or Rochester.
Sorel (Canada), by steamer from Quebec.
South Hadley (Mass.) by rail from Springfield.
South Paris (Me.) by rail from Portland.
Squan [*Beach*] (N. J.) by New Jersey Southern road from New York to *Shark River*, thence stage.
Squankum (N. J.) by New Jersey Southern road from New York.
Stafford (Ct.) by rail from Hartford or Providence.
Stanstead (Canada), from Newport, Lake Memphremagog, or from Lennoxville.
St. Augustine (Florida), from Savannah, Ga.
St. Charles (Mo.) by rail from St. Louis.
Sterling (Ct.) by rail from Hartford.
Stillwater (Minn.) from St. Paul.
St. John Falls (Canada), from Riviere du Loup or from Cacouna.
St. Johnsburg (Vt.) by rail from Wells River.
Stockbridge [and *West*] (Mass.) from Bridgeport by Housatonic road.
Stratford (Ct.) from New York by New Haven road.
St. Thomas (W. I.) from New York by Brazil steamers, 23d of every month.
Sunbury (Pa.) from Harrisburg by Northern Central road.

Superior City (Wis.) by boat from Detroit or Chicago.
Sutherland Falls (Vt.) by rail from Rutland
Terryville (Ct.) by rail from Waterbury (see this list) or Providence.
Thetford (Vt.) by rail from White River Junction.
Thompson (Ct.) by rail from New London or Worcester.
Thunder Bay (Lake Superior) by boat from Duluth.
Tiffin (O.) by rail from Sandusky.
Tolland (Ct.) by rail from Hartford or Providence.
Tom's River (N. J.) by New Jersey Southern road from New York.
Topeka (Kansas) from Kansas city (see this list.).
Troy (O.) by rail from Dayton.
Urbana (O.) by rail from Columbus.
Valley Forge (Pa.) from Philadelphia, or from Reading.
Vandalia (Ind.) by rail from St. Louis.
Van Deusenville (Mass.) from Bridgeport by Housatonic road.
Vera Cruz (Mexico), from New York by Mexican mail steamers, every 10 days.
Vergennes (Vt.) by rail from Burlington.
Vicksburg (Miss.) by river from New Orleans; or rail from Jackson.
Waltham (Mass.) from Boston by Fitchburg road.
Warren (O.) by rail from Cleveland.
Warren (R. I.) by rail from Providence.
Warren (Pa.) from Ridgeway or Irvineton, on Philadelphia and Erie road.
Waterbury (Ct.) from Bridgeport by Nangatuck road.
Watertown (Mass.) from Boston by Fitchburg road.
Waterville (Ct.) by rail from Waterbury, (see this list,) or Providence.
Waterville (Me.) by rail from Portland by Augusta.
Watkins Glen (N. Y.) from Elmira, Erie road.
Waukegan (Ill.) by rail from Chicago.

Waukesha (Wis.) by rail from Milwaukee.
Wellsville (O.) by Ohio river from Pittsburg.
West Burke (Vt) by rail from Wells River.
Westfield (Mass.) from New Haven cy Williamsburg road.
Westminster (Vt.) by rail from Bellows Falls.
West Randolph (Vt.) from White River Junction or Burlington.
Weymouth (Mass.) from Boston by South Shore road.
White Plains (N. Y.) Harlem railroad from New York.
Wilkesbarre (Pa.) from Easton by Lehigh Valley.
Williamsburg (Mass.) from New Haven by W. road.
Williamstown (Mass.) from Albany, Troy or Boston, by Troy and Boston road.
Williston (Vt.) from Essex Junction.
Willoughby Lake (Vt.) from West Burke, (see this list.)
Wilmington (O.) by rail from Cincinnati.
Winstead (Ct.) from Bridgeport by Nangatuck road.
Woburn [East] (Mass.) from Boston by Lowell road.
Wolcotville (Ct.) from Bridgeport by Nangatuck road.
Woodbury (N. J.) by rail from Camden.
Woodstock (Vt.) from White River Junction.
Woodbridge (N. J.) from Rahway, by rail.
Woonsocket (R. I.) by rail from Providence or Worcester.
Wyandotte (Kansas,) opp. Kansas city (see this list).
Wyandotte (Mich.) from Detroit.
Wyoming (Minn.) by rail from St. Paul.
Wyoming Valley (Pa.) from Scranton, by the Lackawanna and Bloomsburg road.
Yankton (Dacotah), by the Missouri river from Sioux city.
Yellow Springs (O.) by rail from Xenia or Cincinnati.
York (Pa.) by rail from Harrisburg.

STEAMSHIP LINES AND BANKING-HOUSES.
STEAMSHIPS BETWEEN EUROPE AND AMERICA.
LINES BY QUEENSTOWN, LIVERPOOL AND LONDON.

Inman Line. (*Inman Steamship Company, limited.*)
The three leading vessels of this line, intended to run during the passenger-season of 1877, are the Commodore's ship, the "City of Berlin," one of the largest in the world, and one of the speediest, if not the very speediest afloat, while with comfort equalling and warranted by the size,— the "City of Richmond," and "City of Chester," only less in tonnage and without other rivals as to speed and comfort, while also exceptionally commanded. With these are still associated, of course, when additional vessels are required, the old and new favorites, the "Montreal," "Brussels," "Paris," "Brooklyn," "New York," "London," "Antwerp," &c., making up a fleet of large numbers and great capacity. The announcement of this line will show the care habitually taken to avoid northern latitudes, icebergs and collisions. Sailings from New York, on Saturdays; from Liverpool on Thursdays; and from Queenstown on Fridays. (For Special announcement see official card in its appropriate place.)

Guion Line. (*Liverpool and Great Western Steamship Co.*)
It has for some time been an admitted fact, that the Williams & Guion boats, especially of the later build, have established a high reputation for comfort, convenience, and sea-worthiness, and that they, consequently, deserve the patronage they receive. The ships of this line now number the exceptionally large and powerful "Montana," "Wyoming," "Wisconsin," "Nevada," and "Idaho," every one of which has won commendation for sea-going qualities and comfort of the first order, while some of them are among the very race-horses of the ocean for speed. The U. S. Mail Service has added materially, as deserved, to the capacity and popularity of a commendable line, continually growing better, year by year. Sailings from New York on Tuesdays, and from Liverpool on Wednesdays. (For special announcements see official card.)

National Line. (*National Steam Navigation Company.*)

With their boats always large and burthensome, self-insured, and sailed on lines especially calculated to avoid ice and collisions; now the National Line not only make the well-founded boast of employing the largest vessels in the trade, but the rate of speed has wonderfully increased, and the fleet can boast the presence of some of the speediest as well as noblest vessels afloat. This is especially the case with the "Spain" and the "Egypt," closely followed by the "Italy," the "Greece," "Canada," "England," "France," "The Queen," &c.; and higher commendation is seldom bestowed upon passages by any line, than by old voyagers, on some of the National ships during late years. Sailings from New York on Saturdays; from Liverpool on Wednesdays; and from Queenstown on Thursdays. From New York for London direct, every Saturday.

White Star Line. (*Oceanic S. S. Co.*)

Principal vessels employed, leaving New York on Saturdays and Liverpool on Thursdays, the "Britannic," "Germanic," "Celtic," "Adriatic," &c.

Cunard Line. (*British and North American Royal Mail Steam Packet Company.*)

Principal vessels employed, leaving New York on Wednesdays and Liverpool on Saturdays, the "Scythia," "Bothnia," "Russia," "Algeria," "Abyssinia," &c.

LINES BY LONDONDERRY, GLASGOW AND LONDON.

Anchor Line. (*Henderson Bros., New York: Handyside & Henderson, Glasgow.*)

Principal vessels employed, leaving New York for Glasgow every Saturday, the "Devonia," "Circassia," "Anchoria," "Ethiopia," "Bolivia," "California," "Victoria," &c.; for London, every alternate Saturday, the "Alsatia," "Anglia," "Australia," "Elysia," "Utopia," &c.

State Line to Glasgow, by Larne. (*Austin Baldwin & Co., New York.*)

Principal vessels employed, leaving New York on Thursdays, the "States" of "Indiana," "Georgia," "Pennsylvania," and "Virginia."

LINE BY HAVRE AND PLYMOUTH.

French Line. (*Compagnie Générale Transatlantique.*)

Principal vessels of this line, now leaving New York for Havre, by Plymouth, every Wednesday, with materially reduced rates, the "Pereire," "St. Laurent," "Canada," "Labrador," "Ville de Paris," "St. Germain," "Amerique," and "France."

LINE BY SOUTHAMPTON AND BREMEN.

Bremen Line. (*North German Lloyd.*)

We continue this year the list of vessels engaged in the North German Lloyd service, by which it will be seen that the fleet is one of the most extensive in the world, and the connection almost literally world-wide. The "Rhein," "Main," "Donau," "Weser," "Oder," "Neckar," "Mosel," and many other vessels of this line, have proved themselves first favorites as to speed and sea going qualities, with exceptionally good accommodations and service, while especially supplying a virtual connection direct to London (by Southampton); and all the old facilities will be retained during the current year. Sailings from New York to Bremen, *via* Southampton, on Saturdays, with others from Baltimore and New Orleans. From Bremen for New York on Saturdays, with call at Southampton on Tuesdays.

STEAMSHIPS TO CALIFORNIA, CHINA, AND INDIA.

LINES TO CALIFORNIA AND CHINA.

Pacific Mail and Panama Transit Steamship Service.

This magnificent line now employs one of the largest fleets in any service, and among the vessels many alike reflecting credit on American ship-building, and supplying the extreme of comfort in transit. Among the noblest of these are the "City of Peking," and "City of Tokio," so much talked of as illustrating the growth of American enterprise, with many others only less commanding in size and appearance. Among the connections with this California line, leaving foot of Canal Street semi-monthly (see current time-tables), are those to Japan, China, Australia, New Zealand, British Columbia, Oregon, &c; and the enterprise, now managed by Messrs. W. P. Clyde & Co., necessarily commands even more than the old confidence.

BANKING-HOUSES.

Exchange may be bought, Letters of Credit taken, and all other financial business connected with European tours and mercantile operations, safely and profitably transacted, as well as many of the details of correspondence and requirements abroad--with the following first class houses, particulars of whose special lines will be found in their announcements.

Brown Brothers & Co., 59 Wall Street, New York, whose very name suggests Liverpool, Parliament, British solidity married to American thrift, the Bank of England, and everything else connected with moneyed intercourse between the nations, and who notably share in the supplying of foreign credit as well as keeping up the true commercial status between the continents;

Morton, Bliss & Co., Broad Street, New York, in connection with Morton, Rose & Co., Bartholomew Lane, London, who largely enjoy, with other leading houses named, the confidence of the government in the arrangement of its financial concerns abroad, and who have long since attained a leading place in the corresponding confidence and patronage of the traveling community.

John Munroe & Co., 8 Wall Street, New York, and No. 4 Post Office Square, Boston, who not only effect exchange for thousands upon thousands of Europe bound travelers, but lay them under obligations by care of their letters, free use of reading-rooms, &c., at their banking-house, No. 7 Rue Scribe, Paris, which has long been and will continue to be one of the "homes" of Americans in that pleasant city, always holding its position as the great European resort of Americans.

AMERICAN HOTELS FOR TRAVELERS,
AND SUMMER RESORTS.

[In the list of American Hotels following, no attempt is made at supplying a complete chain in any direction, though such an arrangement may be gradually made in following years. Of the Hotels, however, it is necessary to say that none have place except such as have been personally tested, and found well located and capable of supplying excellent accommodation; and upon the special features ascribed to each, the utmost dependence can be placed by all interested. For locations, names of proprietors, &c., official cards must be referred to. It will be observed that the alphabetical arrangement of *places* has been adopted, as most convenient for the traveler.]

ALBANY, *N. Y.—Delavan House.—Stanwix Hall.*

BALTIMORE, *Md.—Mt. Vernon House.*

Located in the most elevated and fashionable part of the city and contiguous to the Union Depôt, the Mount Vernon Hotel is now open for the reception of guests, its appointments of the most modern and approved character, and its tables furnished with every domestic and foreign luxury.

BALT. & OHIO R. R. HOTELS.—*Deer Park, &c.*

One of the specialties of the Baltimore and Ohio Railroad, elsewhere noticed as one of the leading trunk lines of the United States, is to be found in the excellent line of Hotels at different points of its route, erected, owned and managed by the Company, and having the reputation of supplying the very best of transient or resident accommodations. Among those houses may be named the " Deer Park Hotel," on the summit plateau of Big Savage Mountain (of the Alleghenies, in Maryland), with great elevation, high reputation as a health resort, capital facilities for reaching, and all the advantages; the "Queen City Hotel," at Cumberland, Md.; and the "Viaduct Hotel," at Relay Station, near Baltimore. All are of the best, in location and management; and they add in no small degree to the travel reputation of the line.

BERKELEY SPRINGS, *Va.*—*The Pavilion.*

As elsewhere noted, in the "Special Virginian Tour," the Berkeley Springs are among the best known, as well as the oldest in Virginia, having enjoyed the patronage and residence of Washington, Jefferson, and many others of the old-time magnates. Of this very charming place the Pavilion is the centre and chief resort, offering airy rooms, the finest baths in the world, and profuse Virginia hospitality, in a mountain-valley air equal to that of Florence. It passes, this year, under new management calculated to add to its well-deserved popularity.

BIG TREES OF CALAVERAS, *Cal.*—*Mammoth Grove Hotel.*

This house forms, with *Sperry's Hotel*, Murphy's, an important link in the chain of California travel, to the Big Trees, by the Big Oak Flat route to the Yo Semite, &c.

BOSTON.—*Parker House.*—*American House.*

CHARLESTON, *S. C.*—*The Charleston Hotel.*

This hotel has the reputation of being one of the most magnificent structures of its kind, on either continent, well built, well kept, and satisfactory to travelers as well as for residence.

CHICAGO.—*Grand Pacific Hotel.*

This house, with central location, and under most efficient and capable management, is justly considered to be one of the most striking marks of the wonderful enterprise and recuperative energy which have, within a short period, built the "New Chicago" on the site of the great fire, and one of the evidences of the perfection to which hotel-keeping has reached in America.

CINCINNATI, Ohio.—*Burnet House.*

For many years past, the Burnet has been *the* house of Cincinnati, and among the first in the Middle West; and now that it has been thoroughly renovated and refurnished, and is under the control of a firm, the members of which have made themselves enviable reputation in management elsewhere, in some of the very best hotels of the Continent, the Burnet is fully maintaining its old status as the best located and most desirable house in Cincinnati, and even adding materially to reputation and popularity.

DELAWARE WATER-GAP, Pa. — *Kittatinny and Water-Gap Houses.*

This side of paradise there is not probably finer air to be found, than that of the Pennsylvania Mountains of the Upper Delaware,—as there are few reaches of finer scenery than can be found in that neighborhood. In the midst of that noble scenery are located the Kittatinny and Water-Gap Houses, admirable hostelries, and the former for many years one of the favorite resorts of those who wish to blend the Rhine and the Bavarian Highlands, without crossing the Atlantic, while the latter is rapidly growing into corresponding public favor and patronage.

DETROIT, *Mich.*—*The Russell House.*

Beyond question, one of the most admirable houses of the North-West, is the Russell, standing in one of the handsomest localities, as well as in one of the most convenient for reaching from any quarter, that could have been afforded by the pretty little "City of the Straits."

LAKE GEORGE.—*Fort William Henry Hotel.*

A very large and admirably kept summer hotel, standing on the southern shore of the lake, commanding the finest of views over it, and in the immediate vicinity of old Fort George and the other points of historical interest of that romantic section. One of the most popular of fashionable resorts, for residence, and as on the line of travel northward from Saratoga, to Champlain and Canada—the boats up Lake George, making the connection to the larger lake and the north, taking their departure almost from the very doors. The reduced tariff of charges of this year, is very attractive to the world of pleasure-seekers. [Kept in connection with the *Arlington*, Washington, D. C., recognized as the favorite house at the Capital.]

LAKE TAHOE, Cal.—*The Tahoe House.*

A very pleasant house, with a singularly lovely location, on the north shore of Lake Tahoe, the site commanding one of the most beautiful lake views in the world.

LEXINGTON, Va.—*National House.*

As the seat of the Virginia Military Academy, as well as the spot of burial of Lee and Stonewall Jackson, Lexington presents many attractions to the tourist, apart from its nearness to Goshen Pass and the Natural Bridge; and the National is *the* hotel of Lexington.

LONG BRANCH, N. J.—*West End Hotel.*

The West End, built within a few years to meet the demand for a better and more picturesque class of hotel building on the great bluff of Long Branch, has fairly asserted its pre-eminence as the most fashionable of the houses of that unrivaled summer gathering-place, and under its present and capable liberal management may take rank with the best hotels of the cities, while unexcelled in location, nearest to the more eclectic residences of the "Branch." Important alterations and additions, made every season, make the West End continually even more capable of accommodating its immense fashionable clientelle.

Long Branch, N. J.—*Howland's Hotel.*

The oldest of the original Long Branch hotels now remaining, Howland's (very near to the West End in location), while entirely remodelled, enlarged and handsomely modernized, has lost nothing of its old reputation as among the most charming of family resorts on the coast. Its management is always excellent in every detail ; and its large clientelle of resident summer guests will not find any of its old charms lacking, under the control of proprietors so thoroughly understanding the place, their visitors, and the requirements of both.

Long Branch, N. J.—*Morris' Pavilion.*

Another of the old-time and always popular resorts of the "Branch" is the Pavilion, traditional for the solid comfort and quiet enjoyment afforded to visitors, without any pretense at the fatigue of ultra fashion.

Mammoth Grove, Cal.—*(See Big Trees.)*

Montreal, *Canada.—St. Lawrence Hall.—Ottawa House.*

Natural Bridge, *Va.—Natural Bridge Hotel.*

The opinion has been elsewhere freely expressed that the Natural Bridge is one of the grandest pieces of rock-work on either Continent ; and the desire to visit this great wonder of nature is enough to make popular the Natural Bridge Hotel, which lies beside it and affords the only gate of entrance for the view.

NEW YORK CITY.—*The Windsor Hotel.*

This magnificent house, among the largest and most perfectly built in the world, and located on Fifth Avenue, filling the entire block between and opening upon both Forty-sixth and Forty-seventh Streets, is worthy the proud name which it bears, as suggestive of much that is royal and noble in English history, and may be adduced as one of the crowning proofs of the perfection to which hotel-keeping in the larger cities of America has attained. In the management are associated (as the official card bears witness), those who have been eminently successful and popular in the gentle art of ministering to the comfort of the travel-world; and years have not been needed to place it high in confidence and distinguished patronage.

NEW YORK CITY.—*The Brevoort House.*

This house, of the first fashion, and the peculiarity of the most distinguished English patronage, stands on Fifth Avenue, in the immediate neighborhood of that handsome public ground, Washington Square, and may be said to have an exceptionally fine location, combining convenience to places of evening resort with quietness and all those nameless pleasant features distinguishing the true temporary "home" of the traveled from the mere crowded caravanserai. Every year seems to add to the charm of this unexceptionable house, and the number of its visitors of distinction.

NIAGARA FALLS.—*International Hotel.*

This large and first-class hotel offers peculiar temptations to tourists, in its possession of all those modern luxurious improvements adding so materially to the pleasure of travel, as well as in its charming location, immediately over the American Fall, at Prospect Point, with the bridge to Goat Island almost at its doors, opening all the scenic wonders of both Falls from that Island and the Sister Islands. Meanwhile, especially adding to its general charm, are the "River Parlors," extending one hundred feet over the rapids, affording unequalled view, and luxurious in every detail,—while the lodging rooms connected with them hold literally a place alone in the charm of their location.

NIAGARA FALLS.—*Clifton House.*

The Clifton, an old and excellent house, familiar for many years to the people of two continents, must ever be a favorite with those who have once known its splendid location, on the Canadian side, at the verge of the river, and with the whole marvelous panorama of the American and Horseshoe Falls fully visible from its broad piazzas and many windows. Meanwhile, though on Canada soil, it habitually flies the "Stars-and-stripes"—a fact well worth noting.

OTTAWA, *Can.*—*The Russell House.*

A first-class hotel of large size and good management, located in the immediate vicinity of the Parliament Houses, Government Buildings, and Barrack Hill, with its fine views, and indispensable to visitors to the Capital of the Dominion, of whom every year necessarily sees an augmented number, as the charms of its location and coolness as a place of summer-sojourn become more fully appreciated.

PHILADELPHIA.—*Continental Hotel.*

One of the largest and most perfectly appointed houses in America, as well as one of the best-known—holding a peculiarly central position, on Chestnut Street, and combining with its large extent all those modern improvements and luxuries which have made the American hotel of the best class world-celebrated. Not to have visited the Continental is held to be equivalent to not having known the heart of Philadelphia, and consequently of having missed many of the most charming features of the second city of America. During the Centennial year it worthily added to its popularity by accommodating all comers, apparently without trouble, and without extortion, even under the temptations of that tempting season.

Portland, Me.—*The Falmouth House.*

San Francisco, Cal.—*Palace Hotel.—Occidental Hotel.*

Saratoga Springs, N. Y.—*Grand Union.— United States.—Congress Hall.—Clarendon.*

Savannah, Ga.—*The Screven House.*

St. Louis, Mo.—*The Lindell House.*

All the modern improvements have been applied in the construction of this new and elegant house, one of the largest as well as one of the leading hotels of the West. It is located on Washington Avenue, now the thoroughfare of the city, since the opening of the Great Bridge, and stands on the site of the old house of the same name, a favorite throughout the whole country, while in no respect the equal of the present magnificent building. Few houses, in any city of the world, can so fully justify the claim of the Lindell, to be at once the "business and society hotel;" and in certain features—among others its table, its thoroughly fire-proof construction, and the running of its elevators at all hours of the day and night—it presents something unique in hotel management.

Toronto, Ca.—*The Queen's Hotel.*

One of the best-known and most complete houses in the Dominion, with a flattering and well-deserved reputation as one of the best-kept and most carefully-managed, as well as admirably located for visiting the Lake shore itself, the public buildings and fine grounds making Toronto a place of pleasant sojourn for all who once visit it. From the Queen's, the University, Osgoode Hall, and indeed all the more notable structures of the town, can be reached at very limited distances in pleasant foot-excursions. It has also the specialty of being selected by Cook as the home of the tourist. A branch house, the "Queen's Royal Niagara," is charmingly located at the mouth of the Niagara River.

TRENTON FALLS, *New York.—Moore's Hotel.*

Without doubt, one of the most capitally-located hotels on the American continent, standing within a few rods of the matchlessly-beautiful Falls of Trenton, and indeed commanding access to them, as well as supplying guides and every essential for the visit. Has noble groves and fine pleasure grounds, and a Geological Museum of the first extent and value, besides being, as a place of transient visit or longer abode, thoroughly well kept, and in every regard one of the most enjoyable of the pleasure-resorts of America. Not to have seen Trenton Falls, and *Moore's*, is to have omitted a crowning experience.

WASHINGTON, *D. C.—The Arlington.*

A house of high character and first-class patronage, seldom making any announcement to the public, from the fact that that patronage is at once assured and eclectic, composed of the most distinguished society of the two continents. Probably as many of the names of people of taste and fashion in the world of travel, can be found on the books of this house, as of any other in America. The Arlington is under the same capable management as the *Fort William Henry Hotel*, Lake George, elsewhere mentioned at length.

WATKINS GLEN, *N. Y.—Glen Park Hotel.—Lake View House.—Glen Mountain House.*

West Point, N. Y.—*Cozzens' Hotel.*

One of the most magnificently located, as well as one of the most tastefully built of all American hotels, is Cozzens', at West Point, commanding the finest part of the passage through the Hudson Highlands, and often winning the name of the "Eagle's Nest" from its height above the river, while really among the easiest of summer resorts, to reach by boat or rail. Among American retreats at once fashionable and enjoyable, Cozzens' holds a "high place" in fact, as well as in altitude. It is now in the capable hands of new proprietors, who are, however, old hotel-men, and who will not allow it to descend from its position, in any sense.

Weyer's Cave, *Va.*—*Weyer's Cave Hotel.*

Tourists visiting the Cave have all comforts, and many luxuries, spread before them at the Weyer's Cave Hotel, where guides may be procured, and where sojourn long enough to thoroughly "do" this great natural marvel, will be found pleasant and profitable.

Yosemite Valley, *Cal.*—*Hutchings' Hotel.*

Mr. Hutchings, best posted of all the pioneers of the Great Valley, has the hotel furthest up the Valley itself, nearest to most points of interest, and simply indispensable to visitors, both for convenience and comfort.

REMINDERS FOR RAMBLERS.

[See announcement cards, following at close of volume, for many particulars of value and interest—the main facts (and facts *only*) being here simply and hastily alluded to for the general information of travelers.]

SPECIAL ROUTES FOR TRAVELERS.

There is no feature so notable, in American Travel, as the great Californian Trip, by rail, by which such a wonderful space, involving the most picturesque, novel and interesting scenery, can be covered in so few days, and so much added to the previous stock of intelligence and experience—as witness the official announcement of the *Union and Central Pacific Railroads*, following, and the full particulars there given of the wonderful combinations and connections of the route, not only to San Francisco and the other Californian cities and places of interest, but the Colorado Mountain regions (the Switzerland of America), the great Mining sections, Salt Lake City, &c., and, still beyond, to Japan, China and the East.

The Pennsylvania Railroad, one of the largest undertakings of its kind in the New World, challenges favorable comparison with any in the Old, for the perfection of its construction, equipment and management; for the completeness of its service, and the consideration and accommodation it affords its patrons. Centering in Philadelphia, its colossal ramifications connect New York on the one side, with the extreme South and West on the other; and this continuity of travel shows conclusively the advantage of railway transit being in the hands of large and responsible corporations.

The New York and Philadelphia "New Line" affords a delightful variation in the route between the above cities. It is made up of portions of the well-reputed old lines, the New Jersey Central and the North Pennsylvania, and a new link from Bound Brook, in the former, to the River Delaware, where it forms a junction with a new extension of the latter road. This portion will be a first class double track, stone-ballasted, built and equipped with all the latest improvements, and run with especial regard to speed and safety. Its passengers during the Exposition will land conveniently at the Penn. Depôt, main entrance of the grounds, thus securing all advantages.

The North Pennsylvania Railroad, running from Philadelphia northwards, to the crossing of the Lehigh River at Bethlehem, is one of the best equipped and arranged in the State. It affords a most picturesque route of travel, and connects, at this point, with the Lehigh Valley roads; passing through the coal districts of the State and the historic Valleys of Wyoming, Susquehanna, &c. Scenes of unequalled beauty and originality are thus afforded to the tourist; and Niagara Falls are reached without change of cars. Passengers by this line are also taken to the Main Entrance of the Exposition at Philadelphia.

The card of the *New Jersey Southern Railroad*, for the present season, shows that the Company has now two fast and splendid boats on the line, to Sandy Hook, in the *Jesse Hoyt* and *Crystal Wave*, supplying the pleasantest of transits to the Hook, Highlands of Navesink, Long Branch, &c., and thence on to Philadelphia by that and connecting roads, twice a day, and in "good form," as our English cousins say.

Of the more prominent roads of the country the *Baltimore and Ohio* ranks among the first for the excellence of its management, the extent and perfection of its equipment and accommodation, and for the magnificent scenery through which it passes. Connecting Baltimore and Washington with the far West, its wide-reaching arms extend to Cincinnati, St. Louis, Chicago, and by its connections to the whole of the West, South, and South-West. From Harper's Ferry, crossing the Allegheny Mountains to the Ohio River, the road goes through the best of American scenery, illustrating the Railroad construction of this country by some of its most stupendous works. As a pendant, the management have made arrangements for admirable hotel accommodations along the line, duly referred to in the chapter on "American Hotels."

The *Great Atlantic Coast Line Railway* is one of the representative roads of America, connecting the Great North with the whole of the Southern Seaboard States to its objective point—Florida. At Portsmouth joining the steamship lines, and at Weldon the Northern Railroads, passengers are luxuriously conveyed by the shortest direct route to Columbia, Aiken, Charleston and Savannah. With its connections, the Atlantic and Gulf R. R., &c., it forms the special route to Florida, whose just claims to be considered the Italy of the New World are now fully recognized. For tourists and others seeking this resort, especial and careful accommodations are most complete. Tickets to all points can be obtained in New York, Philadelphia, and chief cities.

The *Chicago and North-Western Railroad* is at once one of the greatest and best-managed enterprises of the North-West, a great trunk-line leading from Chicago, by Fulton, Clinton, Cedar Rapids, Boone, &c., to Council Bluffs, Omaha, and connecting there with the Pacific roads for California; also with lines leading directly from Chicago by Kenosha, Racine, &c., to Milwaukee; and to Fort Howard, Green Bay, or direct connection to St. Paul and Lake

Superior, with numberless other ramifications, of the first interest to travelers, and which only the official announcement can fully explain. It is the well-founded boast of the C. & N. W., among other things, that it supplies the most magnificent Pullman Drawing Room and Hotel Cars, to be found on any line in America, thus adding to the speed of travel a luxury otherwise unattainable.

The *Chicago, Burlington and Quincy Railroad* claims, and justly, to be among the leading lines of the Continent, affords a favorite route from Chicago to Omaha, and thence by its connections to San Francisco and the Pacific slope. Its equipment and careful consideration for its patrons are unsurpassed; and among the announcements of the Company, that "Pullman's palatial dining and breakfasting saloon on wheels," furnishing "sumptuous meals at 75 cents while traveling at the rate of thirty miles an hour," is the climax of railroad accommodation—is a fact endorsed and verified by the many who have partaken of it.

The *Chicago, Milwaukee and St. Paul Railway* is the representative line of the district through which it runs. With Chicago north and north-westward it connects Milwaukee, and in its immediate vicinity the far-famed Mineral springs of Bethesda, &c., and a neighborhood unrivalled for its beautiful scenery and as a summer resort; thence westward to Madison, the State Capital, Prairie du Chien, St. Paul, Minneapolis, the Falls of St. Anthony, &c. An alternative route through Portage City, by Lacrosse, passes up the valley of the Mississippi to St. Paul, and affords scenic views of unequalled grandeur and beauty. The equipment and accommodation of this road are unsurpassed.

The *Clyde Coastwise and Steamship Lines* now rank among the most prominent and numerous in America. Their ships distinguished alike for their size and full power no less than for their complete arrangements for perfect ventilation and the general wants of their passengers, they supply the pleasantest means of transit to the South-Eastern States, Havana and other West India ports. Tourists on those routes will do well to consider these advantages. The newly-established line to California, in connection, is elsewhere referred to.

The *Day Line of Steamers* on the Hudson River, from New York to West Point, the Catskill Mountains, &c., to Albany, supplies two of the fastest and most commodious steamers in the world, in the "Chauncey Vibbard" and 'Daniel Drew," carrying music on all trips, making the whole run, in either direction, by daylight, and affording opportunities for observation of the whole line of Hudson River scenery, unattainable by any other route or mode. [See map of the Hudson, accompanying announcement.]

The *People's Line of Steamers* between New York and Albany affords another splendid Centennial feature in travel on the Hudson River; leaving either place at evening and arriving at the other in the morning, in time for all railway connections; and supplying in the "St. John," "Drew," and "Dean Richmond," the three noblest and most luxurious specimens of inland marine architecture on the globe, with accommodations of perfect completeness and princely splendor, while still making no heavy draft on the purse in any detail of service. [See Map of the Hudson, accompanying official announcement for connections, &c.]

The *Mary Powell* (steamer), running as an afternoon boat from New York to West Point, Newburgh and other points on the Hudson, to Rondout (Kingston), shows still another of those "Prides of the Hudson" just referred to; passing through the Highlands by daylight, and affording the most charming of views of that splendid river scenery;

the boat herself, meanwhile, a beauty, a favorite and a celebrity.

LEADING INSURANCE COMPANIES.

The hints given in one of the earlier papers of this volume, as to the propriety of every traveler (and indeed every *man*), taking a reasonable Life Assurance, do not lose their force, year by year, but rather add new; meanwhile, the American system is the best in the world, as now admitted by the highest authorities of both continents ; and in some especial companies hereinafter named, will be found the very highest types of extensive business, reliability and usefulness. First among these may be named the *Equitable Life Assurance Society of the United States*, No. 120 Broadway, in whose remodelled building, now nearly completed, may be found the most perfect commercial structure in the world, and one of the most tastefully elegant, while its business is among the largest in the country ; and the *New York Life Insurance Company*, No. 346 Broadway, only less elegantly-lodged than the rival Company, and quite as commodiously, while its figures show the extent and soundness of its great beneficial business. In both these companies lies an absolute matter of national pride, as well as one of important knowledge to the intending investor in this most advisable of securities.

In intimate connection with the subject of Life Insurance, comes that of Accident Insurance, in which detail, too, America affords one of the noblest examples, in the *Travelers' Insurance Company*, of Hartford, Connecticut, with a New York centre, &c. The Travelers has been for years doing a noble work, meeting with very great and deserved success, and annually paying out immense sums to the families of those killed by accident, or to the disabled themselves in their day of diminished receipts and possible need. The figures of business of the past year show something of the keenness with which the American public are waking to the need and the benefit of such an institution, so indispensable among a nation of travelers—and of the amount which every late year demands from this Company, to pay for lost lives and injured bodies. This Company affords also the ordinary Life Assurance in connection, with the best advantages.

The *Hanover Fire Insurance Company*, office, 120 Broadway, New York, continues to offer the best and most reliable guarantees against loss or damage by the devouring element, one of the most satisfactory of remembrances to those who leave property behind them when traveling; while a visit to the office of the Company will show the best thing of its kind in the world, in appointments and management, especially since the late enlargement of space, rendered necessary by increase of business.

NEW YORK CITY SPECIALTIES.

At the American Branch of the house of Messrs. Thomas Cook & Son—*Cook, Son & Jenkins*, 261 Broadway, all the Cook's Tourist Tickets may be obtained, for both European and American Travel, and much money saved in going over many routes on both continents, &c.

Passports for Europe, as we all know, are convenient and profitable, if not always indispensable—as they supply identification, often save fees, &c. Arrangements have been made, by which they can be supplied at the very shortest notice, on application at *Morford's Travel Office*, 52 Broadway, or to *James Taylor*, Passport Agent, Notary and Commissioner for all the States, No. 345 Broadway, corner of Leonard Street, New York City.

Intending passengers for Europe or tourists to any part of America can examine maps, trace out routes, obtain any information desired, or have passages secured by any of the best lines of travel, with the advantages of the personal experience of an old traveler, at *Morford's Travel Office*, 52 Broadway, New York—now open in connection with the management and publication of the "Short-Trip Guides" to Europe and America.

Indispensable to those who wish to lay out routes in Europe and travel intelligently as well as comfortably and economically, will be found the companion volume to this—"*Morford's Short-Trip Guide to Europe*" (editorial office, 52 Broadway), of which a leading U. S. official said, lately, returning from a tour of the Old World, and speaking to a ship-board acquaintance : " My party, in our travels through the British Islands and on the Continent, had nearly all the Guide-Books and *all* the American ; and it is only justice to say, that after due examination, though using some of the larger and the local Guides, occasionally, for particu'ars not allowed by its limited space—*we found Morford's the book to arrange routes and travel by*, and made it our chief dependence throughout."

The *Home Journal*, the leading fashion and society paper in America, and indeed holding a corresponding place in that regard to the London "Court Journal," while it possesses a literary ability to which the English exponents of aristocracy and fashion cannot pretend, has actually become a necessity in the higher walks of American life, and is beginning to exercise no small influence as a fashion authority abroad.

That the *Mendelssohn Piano Company*, of which the office is at 56 Broadway, New York City, have in several regards deserved so well of all lovers of music and employers of musical instruments, as to be worthy of all the immense popularity they have attained. They have deserved well, in all their many improvements on and over the ordinary piano—culminating in what is undoubtedly *the best Upright Piano ever made*, as additional to their admirable Squares and Grands; and they have deserved even better in throwing overboard the whole costly system of agencies, putting themselves in immediate connection with buyers, and thus supplying $1,000 pianos at $450; $900 at $400; $850 at $350; $650 at $275, and $600 at $250!

That to no mechanician of the day is the art of printing so much indebted as to Andrew Campbell, head of the *Campbell Press and Manufacturing Company*, 39 Beekman street, New York, and Wythe avenue and Hewes street, Brooklyn. It may be said that Mr. Campbell, a thorough inventor as well as machinist, has literally revolutionized the construction of printing presses and their accompaniments, in doing away with the heavy, clumsy and needlessly-expensive, and bringing into play all the resources of engineering to produce perfect accuracy combined with comparative lightness and cheapness before unheard of. No higher proof of the excellence of the Campbell Presses is needed, than to say that the best of the splendid *Aldine* printing has been done on them—that their work done at the Centennial was universally admired—and that they, as well as the Rotary Perfecting Printing and Folding Machines, of this manufactory, received the very highest awards of the Centennial Commission.

PHILADELPHIA SPECIALTIES.

Perhaps the most perfect Drug-and-Fancy-Store in the world, as certainly one of the most beautiful in arrangement and most extensive in the variety of articles embraced, is that of *A. L. Helmbold*, Chestnut Street, between Eighth and Ninth, and within the Continental Hotel. The dispensing of medicines and chemical preparations is really made a branch of fine art, under such auspices as those enjoyed by Mr. Helmbold, whose literal bazar is open all night, and who adds to general business the specialty of supplying, at first hands, the well-known and popular Helmbold's Prepaations, now almost indispensable in the medical world.

The *Travelers' Official Guide*, published monthly, by the National Railway Publication Company, Philadelphia, is very correct, careful, and wonderfully comprehensive, and affords incomparably the best authority on the Western Continent, as to time of trains, connections, and every information necessary for the traveler.

Messrs. Claxton, Remsen & Haffelfinger, the well-known booksellers of Market Street, announce the third edition of the audacious and successful Centennial Novel, "*The Spur of Monmouth*," thus evidencing that there is a taste for historical romance in America, however that fact has been denied, at home and abroad. The book is certainly a remarkable one, like the occasion in which it originated

AMSHIP LINES.

SHORT-TRIP GUIDE.—ANNOUNCEMENTS

INMAN LINE.

NEW YORK TO LIVERPOOL

On Saturdays.

FROM PIER 45, North River, New York.

The Large, Full-Powered, Clyde-Built Steamships,

City of Chester, Sat., May 5.	City of Chester, Sat., July 14.
City of Richmond, Sat., May 19.	City of Richmond, Sat., July 28.
City of Berlin, Sat., June 2.	City of Berlin, Sat., Aug. 11.
City of Chester, Sat., June 9.	City of Chester, Sat., Aug. 18.
City of Richmond, Sat., June 23.	City of Richmond, Sat., Sept. 1.
City of Berlin, Sat., July 7.	&c., &c., &c.

With intermediate and succeeding steamers, as warranted.

The course laid down for these steamers, and followed by them for several years, is fixed to pass 250 miles south of Cape Race. Although the voyage is thus lengthened about 100 miles, better weather is met with and there is much greater freedom from fogs and floating ice and the danger of navigation consequent thereon.

RATES OF PASSAGE.

To Liverpool, $80 and $100, gold. | From Liverpool, $75 and $90, gold. (15 to 18 Guineas.)

Round Trip Tickets, $145 and $175, gold.

Steamers leave Liverpool on Thursdays.
" " Queenstown on Fridays.
" " New York on Saturdays.

For further information, apply at the Company's Offices:

Liverpool, Wm. Inman, 22 Water Street.
Queenstown, C. & W. D. Seymour & Co.
London, Eives & Allen, 61 King William Street.
Paris, A. H. Johnson, 9 Rue Scribe.
Boston, L. H. Palmer, 5 Old State House.
Philadelphia, Geo. A. Faulk, 105 South Fourth Street.
Chicago, Francis C. Brown, 32 S. Clark Street; and in
New York to

JOHN G. DALE, *Agent,*
15 Broadway.

SHORT-TRIP GUIDE.—ANNOUNCEMENTS.

This Company takes the risk of insurance (up to $500,000 in gold) on each of its steamers, thus giving passengers the best possible guarantee for safety and the avoidance of danger at sea. The most southerly route has always been adopted by this Company to avoid ice and headlands.

NATIONAL LINE.

STEAMERS WEEKLY BETWEEN

NEW YORK, LIVERPOOL AND QUEENSTOWN;
AND FORTNIGHTLY BETWEEN

NEW YORK AND LONDON DIRECT.

SPAIN, . . . 4,871 tons.	ENGLAND, . . . 4,896 tons.
EGYPT, . . . 5,089 "	THE QUEEN, . . 4,470 "
ITALY, . . . 4,341 "	HELVETIA, . . . 3,976 "
HOLLAND, . . . 3,847 "	ERIN, ... 4,040 "
FRANCE, . . . 3,676 "	CANADA, . . . 4,276 "
DENMARK, . . . 3,724 "	GREECE, . . . 4,310 "

The above powerful British-built Iron Steamships, with spar decks, and water-compartments, THE LARGEST IN THE TRADE, during the season of 1877, will form this favorite line, leaving

LIVERPOOL, ... *EVERY WEDNESDAY.*
QUEENSTOWN, ... *EVERY THURSDAY.*
NEW YORK, ... *EVERY SATURDAY.*

Weekly to and from LONDON

From the Company's Piers,

NOS. 44 AND 47, NORTH RIVER.

CABIN PASSAGE

To Liverpool, Queenstown, or London, $60 and $70, according to location of sleeping rooms. All passengers have equal privileges in the Saloon. Return Tickets by London Steamer, $100; by Liverpool Steamer, $110 and $120. For passage apply at the Company's Offices,

No. 21 Water Street, Liverpool, and at

No. 69 Broadway, New York,

F. W. J. HURST, *Manager.*

ANNOUNCEMENTS.

"GUION LINE,"
U. S. and Royal Mail Steamers.

SAILING FROM NEW YORK FOR QUEENSTOWN AND LIVERPOOL, EVERY TUESDAY.

First-Class Mail Steamships

MONTANA, - - NEVADA,
WISCONSIN, - - - IDAHO,
WYOMING,

From Liverpool every Wednesday, and Queenstown every Thursday.

DRFATS payable in all parts of England, Ireland and Scotland.

FOR PASSAGE APPLY TO

WILLIAMS & GUION,
29 Broadway.

SHORT-TRIP GUIDE.—ANNOUNCEMENTS.

STEAMERS TO FRANCE DIRECT.
General Transatlantic
COMPANY'S
FIRST-CLASS STEAMSHIPS,
Under Government Contract to carry the Mails between
NEW YORK AND HAVRE.

Leaving NEW YORK and HAVRE every WEDNESDAY, calling at
Plymouth.

PEREIRE,	SAINT LAURENT,	SAINT GERMAIN,
LABRADOR,	VILLE DE PARIS,	CANADA,
AMERIQUE,		FRANCE.

Passage Money (*Wine included*) Payable in Gold,

FROM NEW YORK, PLYMOUTH OR HAVRE,

First Cabin, $100,   Second Cabin, $65,
Third Cabin, $35,   Fourth Class, $26.
To Plymouth, $25.

Excursion Tickets issued at a reduction of 10 *per cent.*

MEDICAL ATTENDANCE FREE OF CHARGE.

American Travelers going to or returning from the Continent of Europe, by taking this Line, avoid both transit by English railway and the discomforts of crossing the Channel, besides saving time, trouble and expense. For Freight or Passage apply at the Office of

LOUIS DE BEBIAN, Agent,
55 BROADWAY, NEW YORK.

SHORT-TRIP GUIDE.—ANNOUNCEMENTS.

NORTH GERMAN LLOYD.

STEAM BETWEEN BREMEN, (via SOUTHAMPTON & HAVRE,) AND THE PORTS OF

NEW ORLEANS, HAVANA. MORE, NEW OR- NEW YORK, BALTI-

The Screw Steamers of the North German Lloyd:

RHEIN,			HABSBURG,
MAIN,	HERMANN,	HANSA,	HOHENZOLERN,
DONAU,	HANOVER,	FRANKFURT,	HOHENSTAUFFER,
KOLN,	STRASSBURG,	MOSEL,	SALIER,
NECKAR,	BALTIMORE,	BERLIN,	BRAUNSCHWEIG,
LEIPZIC,	OHIO,	BISMARCK,	NURNBERG,
WESER,	AMERICA,	ODER,	GENERAL WERDER,
KRONPRINZ FRIEDRICH WILHELM,			

These Vessels carry the German, British and United States Mails, and leave

BREMEN, for New York, by Southampton, every Saturday.
" for Baltimore, on alternate Wednesdays.
SOUTHAMPTON, for New York, every Tuesday.
" for Baltimore, on alternate Saturdays.
NEW YORK, for Southampton and Bremen, every Saturday.
BALTIMORE, for Southampton and Bremen, every alternate Saturday.

The above vessels have been constructed in the most approved manner; they are of 3 000 tons, and 700 horse-power each, and are commanded by men of character and experience, who will make every exertion to promote the comfort and convenience of passengers. They touch at Southampton, on the outward trip, for the purpose of landing passengers for England and France.
These Vessels take Freight to Bremen, London, Hull, Rotterdam, Antwerp and Hamburg, for which through bills of lading are signed.
An experienced surgeon is attached to each vessel.
All letters must pass through the post office.
Specie taken to Havre, Southampton and Bremen at the lowest rates.

For Prices of Passage, and all further particulars, apply to NORTH GERMAN LLOYD, *Bremen;* KELLER, WALLIS & POSTLETHWAITE, *Southampton and London;* PHILLIPPS, GRAVES, PHILLIPPS & CO., *London;* L'HERBETTE, KANE & CO., *Havre and Paris;* OELRICHS & CO., *New York;* A. SCHUMACHER & CO., *Baltimore;* ED. F. STOCKMEYER & CO., *New Orleans;* H. UPMAN & CO., *Havana.*

ANNOUNCEMENTS.

PACIFIC MAIL STEAMSHIP LINE
TO
CALIFORNIA.

For time of Leaving of the Magnificent Steamships of this Line, the Oldest and Most Reliable Route to California, and all Ports of the Pacific,

From Pier Foot of Canal st., N. R.,

NEW YORK,

And also for Rates of passage, made to accord with the times,

See Current and Weekly Announcements.

Close Connections made at San Francisco with China Line for

JAPAN, CHINA AND INDIA,

As also for Ports of Oregon, British Columbia and the Northwest.

For Freight or Passage pply to

WILLIAM P. CLYDE & CO.,
No. 6 Bowling Green,

Or H. J. BULLAY, *Superintendent,*
Pier Foot Canal Street, North River.

BANKING HOUSES.

BROWN BROTHERS & CO.

59 Wall Street, New York,

Issue, against cash deposited, or satisfactory guarantee of repayment, Circular Credits for Travellers, in *dollars* for use in the United States and adjacent countries, and in *Pounds Sterling* for use in any part of the world.

These credits, bearing the signature of the holder, afford a ready means of identification, and the amounts for which they are issued can be availed of from time to time, and wherever he may be, in sums to meet the requirements of the traveller.

Applications for Credits may be made to the above house direct, or through any first-class bank or banker in this country.

They also issue Commercial Credits, make Cable Transfers of Money between this Country and England, and Draw Bills of Exchange on Great Britain and Ireland.

BROWN, SHIPLEY & CO.,
Founder's Court, Lothbury, London.

BROWN, SHIPLEY & CO.,
Chapel Street, Liverpool.

DREXEL, MORGAN & CO.,

Wall Street, Corner of Broad,

NEW YORK,

DREXEL & CO.	DREXEL, HARJES & CO.
34 South Third Street,	3, Rue Scribe,
Philadelphia.	Paris.

ISSUE

COMMERCIAL AND TRAVELLING CREDITS

Available in all parts of the World.

TELEGRAPHIC TRANSFERS

TO AND FROM EUROPE, HAVANA AND SAN FRANCISCO.

Attorneys and Agents of
Messrs. J. S. MORGAN & CO., LONDON.

MORTON, BLISS & CO.,

BANKERS,

1 *Broad Street, New York,*

ISSUE

CIRCULAR NOTES AND LETTERS OF CREDIT

For Travellers; also

COMMERCIAL CREDITS

available in all parts of the world.

Negotiate First-Class Railway, City and State Loans, make Telegraphic Transfers of Money, allow Interest on Deposits and Draw Exchange on

MORTON, ROSE & CO., London,

HOTTINGUER & CO., Paris,

HOPE & CO., Amsterdam.

John Munroe & Company,

BANKERS,

No. 8 Wall Street, New York, and
No. 4 Post Office Square, Boston,

ISSUE

CIRCULAR NOTES AND CIRCULAR LETTERS OF CREDIT FOR TRAVELERS,

ON THE

CONSOLIDATED BANK, LONDON.

AND ON

MUNROE & COMPANY,

PARIS.

EXCHANGE ON LONDON AND PARIS,
Money Transferred and Credits Opened by Cable.

INSURANCE COMPANIES.

SHORT-TRIP GUIDE.—ANNOUNCEMENTS.

HANOVER
FIRE INSURANCE COMPANY,
OF THE CITY OF NEW YORK,

Office, No. 120 Broadway, cor. Cedar St.,

(EQUITABLE LIFE ASSURANCE CO'S BUILDING.)

INCORPORATED 1852.

BENJAMIN S. WALCOTT, *President.*
I. REMSEN LANE, *Secretary.*
C. L. ROE, *Ass't Secretary.*

Cash Assets,   -   -   - $1,642,882.59.

AGENCIES IN ALL THE PRINCIPAL TOWNS IN THE UNITED STATES.
Eastern Agency Department,   -   -   THOMAS JAMES, *Actuary.*
Western and Southern Agency Department, "The Underwriters Agency."   A. STODDART, *General Agent.*

ANNOUNCEMENTS.

THE
EQUITABLE
LIFE ASSURANCE SOCIETY
OF THE UNITED STATES,
No. 120 Broadway, New York.

Assets, - - $30,416,719.90
New Business of 1876, $25,020,577.00.
Surplus, - - $5,503,793.41
Policies in 1876, 7,368.

All Cash.   Purely Mutual.   Annual Dividends.

New Business among the largest of any Company in America or Europe. Average Annual Growth greater than any other leading Company. Percentage of Losses to Policies in force, less than any other. Percentage of Expenses to Income, less than the average of other New York Companies.

OFFICERS:

HENRY B. HYDE, *President.*
JAMES W. ALEXANDER, *Vice-President.*
SAM'L BORROWE, *Secretary.*
WILLIAM ALEXANDER, *Ass't Secretary.*
GEO. W. PHILLIPS, } *Actuaries.*
J. G. VAN CISE,
EDWARD W. LAMBERT, M. D., } *Medical Examiners.*
EDWARD CURTIS, M. D.

AMERICAN TRAVEL.

SHORT-TRIP GUIDE.—ANNOUNCEMENTS.

The Great Trans-Continental All-Rail
Union & Central Pacific Route
VIA COUNCIL BLUFFS AND OMAHA,

IS

226 Miles the SHORTEST,

FROM THE ATLANTIC COAST TO

SALT LAKE CITY,

SACRAMENTO,

SAN FRANCISCO,

AND ALL POINTS IN THE

SANDWICH ISLANDS,   *JAPAN,*
NEW ZEALAND,   *CHINA,*
AUSTRALIA,   *INDIA.*

Shortest and Quickest Route
To DENVER, COL., NEW MEXICO and ARIZONA.

PULLMAN'S PALACE DAY AND SLEEPING CARS are run on all Express Trains, and passengers are *cautioned* that only those who are ticketed via Omaha are sure of securing berths to points west of Cheyenne. Double Berth—Omaha to Ogden, $3; Ogden to San Francisco, $6.

To *Tourists, Pleasure* and *Health Seekers*, this Route offers unrivaled attractions in the beautiful Platte Valley; the grand scenery of the Snowy Range; the Passage of the Rocky Mountains (8,242 feet above the sea); the Laramie Plains; the Wahsatch and Uintah Mountains; the wild and weird Echo and Weber Canons; the Great Salt Lake and its Mormon City, surrounded by lofty mountains, rivers filled with trout. hunting grounds, medicinal springs, etc.; the Humboldt Sink; the Sierra Nevadas; the Palisades; the beautiful mountain lakes of Tahoe and Donner, and the passage of Cape Horn; making a two thousand mile panorama of unequalled grandeur and beauty.

Through Tickets for sale by F. KNOWLAND, General Agent, No. 287 Broadway, New York, and at all principal ticket offices in the country Members of Colonies and Excursion Parties should address the General Ticket Agent for rates and arrangements.

THOS. L. KIMBALL,
Gen'l Ticket Agent, U. P. R. R., Omaha

T. H. GOODMAN,
G. P. A., C. P. R. R., San Francisco

[SEE NEXT PAGE.]

SHORT-TRIP GUIDE.—ANNOUNCEMENTS.

THE
Union & Central Pacific Line.
TRIP AROUND THE WORLD.

From ATLANTIC CITIES to OMAHA, (Nebraska), via the Great Trunk Lines of Railway,—about 1,400 miles, in 50 hours.
From OMAHA to SAN FRANCISCO, (California), via Union and Central Pacific Railroads,—1,914 miles, in 4 days and 6 hours.
From SAN FRANCISCO to YOKOHAMA, (Japan), by Pacific Mail Line Steamers, and by Australian and American Steamships, 4,700 miles, in 22 days.
From YOKOHAMA to HONG KONG, (China), by Pacific Mail or Peninsular and Oriental Steamers,—1,600 miles, in 6 days.
From HONG KONG to CALCUTTA, (India), by Peninsular and Oriental Steamers,—3,500 miles, in 14 days.

Or from San Francisco to Calcutta via Australia, as follows:

From SAN FRANCISCO to HONOLULU, (Sandwich Islands), by United States, New Zealand and Australia Mail Steamship Line,—2,110 miles, in 10 days.
From HONOLULU to AUCKLAND, (New Zealand), by U. S., New Zealand and Aus. S. S. Line,—3,800 miles, in 14 days.
From AUCKLAND to SYDNEY, (Australia), by U. S., New Zealand and Aus. S. S. Line,—1,277 miles, in 5 days.
From SYDNEY to MELBOURNE, (Australia), by Peninsular and Oriental Steamers,—560 miles, in 3 days.
From MELBOURNE to GALLE, (Ceylon), by Peninsular and Oriental Steamers,—4,670 miles, in 21 days.
From GALLE to CALCUTTA, (India), by Peninsular and Oriental Steamers,—1,315 miles, in 7 days.

From CALCUTTA to BOMBAY, (India), by the East Indian and Great Indian Peninsular Railways,—1,400 miles, in 2 days.
From BOMBAY to SUEZ, (Egypt), by Peninsular and Oriental Steamers,—3,600 miles, in 14 days.
From SUEZ to ALEXANDRIA, (Egypt), by Rail along the Suez Canal,—225 miles, in 12 hours.
From ALEXANDRIA to BRINDISI, (Italy), by Peninsular and Oriental Steamers,—850 miles, in 3 days.
From BRINDISI to LONDON, (England), by Rail, via Paris or the P Line,—1,200 miles, in 3 days.
From LONDON to LIVERPOOL, (England), by Railway,—200 miles, in 5 hours.
From LIVERPOOL to ATLANTIC CITIES, (America), by either of the Great Atlantic S. S. Lines,—3,000 miles, in 10 days.

Total distance, 23,589 miles. Time, 81 days.

OFFICES:
No. 287 Broadway, New York.
Cor. 4th & Townsend Sts., San Francisco; and
General Foreign Agency, W. C. THOMPSON,
22 Moorgate St., London.
[SEE PRECEDING PAGE.]

SHORT-TRIP GUIDE.—ANNOUNCEMENTS.

THE PENNSYLVANIA RAILROAD
IS THE GREAT
TRUNK LINE AND MAIL ROUTE
OF THE UNITED STATES.

IT TRAVERSES the most interesting portions of the North American Continent and unites by unbroken tracks all the principal Cities on the Atlantic Coast with the Great Lakes and in the Mississippi Valley.

THROUGH TRAINS

are run between New York, Philadelphia, Baltimore and Washington, in the East, and Buffalo, Niagara Falls, Erie, Cleveland, Toledo, Chicago, St. Louis, Cincinnati and Louisville, in the North, West and South-west.

THE PENNSYLVANIA RAILROAD
IS THE
Best Constructed Railway on the American Continent.

ITS MAIN LINES are laid with a DOUBLE TRACK OF STEEL RAILS, secured on Oak Ties imbedded in broken-stone ballast, which renders them impervious to the action of frosts or freshets, and prevents annoyance from dust. All bridges are of iron or stone.

THE PENNSYLVANIA RAILROAD
RUNS THE
Most Perfect Rolling Stock in the World.

ITS ENGINES are models of mechanical excellence, and its Passenger Cars are unequalled for comfort, elegance and strength. SUPERIOR HOTELS and EATING HOUSES are provided at all essential points.

THE PENNSYLVANIA RAILROAD
ENFORCES UPON ITS EMPLOYES
STRICT COURTESY AND POLITENESS,

IN THEIR INTERCOURSE with the public, and uses every effort to secure the comfort and contribute to the enjoyment of its patrons.

THE PENNSYLVANIA RAILROAD
RUNS TRAINS FOR GREATER DISTANCES,
without stoppage, than any other line in the world.

THE PENNSYLVANIA RAILROAD
Is acknowledged to be among the most successful and beneficial enterprises of the century.

(*See current Time Tables.*)

SHORT-TRIP GUIDE—ANNOUNCEMENTS.

Baltimore and Ohio Railroad,
THE
GREAT NATIONAL ROUTE,
THE SHORTEST ROUTE
FROM
BALTIMORE AND WASHINGTON
TO

Pittsburg, Cincinnati, Columbus, Chicago, Indianapolis, St. Louis, Kansas City, Denver, St. Joseph, Omaha, San Francisco, Louisville, Nashville, Memphis, Vicksburg, New Orleans, Mobile, Galveston, and all the leading cities of the West, South-West and the North-West.

The Route passes through splendid scenery of the Potomac River, Alleghany and Cheat Mountains, West Virginia, Ohio, &c.

DOUBLE-TRACK, STEEL-RAIL AND STONE-BALLASTED ROAD.

Magnificent Day Passenger Cars, Pullman Drawing-Room Day and Sleeping Coaches, through to Cincinnati, Chicago, St. Louis and Pittsburg, without change.

The Great Public Thoroughfare between the South, South-East, West, and North-West.

L. M. COLE, Gen'l Ticket Agt.,	THOS. P. BARRY,
E. R. DORSEY, Asst. G. T. A.,	*Western Passenger Agent,*
BALTIMORE.	Cincinnati.

F. W. RANKIN, *Eastern Passenger Agent,*
315 Broadway, New York.

ANNOUNCEMENTS.

CALIFORNIA.

THE CHICAGO & NORTH-WESTERN RAILWAY

Embraces under one management the Great Trunk Railway Lines of the **WEST AND NORTH-WEST.** Its

OMAHA AND CALIFORNIA LINE

Is the shortest and best Route for all points in NORTHERN ILLINOIS, IOWA, DAKOTA, NEBRASKA, WYOMING, COLORADO, UTAH, NEVADA, CALIFORNIA, OREGON, CHINA, JAPAN AND AUSTRALIA. Its

CHICAGO, ST. PAUL AND MINNEAPOLIS LINE

Is the short line for NORTHERN WISCONSIN and MINNESOTA, and for MADISON, ST. PAUL, MINNEAPOLIS, DULUTH and all points in the great Northwest. Its

CHICAGO AND MILWAUKEE LINE

Is the old Lake Shore Route, and is the only one passing through EVANSTON, LAKE FOREST, HIGHLAND PARK, WAUKEGAN, RACINE, KENOSHA to MILWAUKEE.

Pullman Palace Sleeping Cars

are run on all through trains on all divisions of this road.

This is the ONLY LINE running these cars between Chicago and St. Paul, Chicago and Milwaukee, or Chicago and Winona.

UNRIVALLED!
PULLMAN PALATIAL DRAWING-ROOM
HOTEL CARS.

These celebrated Cars are run over the Chicago & North-Western Railway, **ALONE,** *between Chicago and Omaha.*

No other road runs this or any other form of Hotel Car between Chicago and Omaha.

This Line of Hotel Cars was built expressly for the Chicago & North-Western Railway's **CALIFORNIA LINE,** and runs over it daily each way between **CHICAGO** and **COUNCIL BLUFFS.**

No expense has been spared in the construction of these Cars, the Company being determined to excel all former productions, and present to the Traveling Public a line of Hotels on Wheels, that will embrace all the Magnificence, Comfort and Luxury of the best Hotels in the country.

Through Tickets via this Route can be procured at all Ticket Offices in the United States and Canadas.

New York Office, No. 415 Broadway; Boston Office, No. 5 State Street; San Francisco Office, No. 4, New Montgomery Street; Chicago Ticket Offices.

For rates or information not attainable from your home ticket agents, apply to

W. H. STENNETT,   MARVIN HUGHITT,
Gen. Pass. Ag't, Chicago.   Gen. Man'g., Chicago.

SHORT-TRIP GUIDE—ANNOUNCEMENTS.

HOW TO GO WEST!
TAKE THE
CHICAGO, BURLINGTON & QUINCY R. R.

THE FAVORITE ROUTE

To ALL POINTS in the WEST and SOUTH-WEST. The ONLY LINE between

CHICAGO AND OMAHA

running PULLMAN'S DINING CARS, PALATIAL DINING AND BREAKFASTING SALOONS ON WHEELS.

Sumptuous Meals for 75 cents, at thirty miles per hour, is the traveling climax of this progressive age, introducing novelty, and adding pleasure as well as comfort to the usual tedium of a long journey.

THROUGH DAY and SLEEPING COACHES by this route, without change, BETWEEN CHICAGO and OMAHA and CHICAGO and KANSAS CITY.

TRAVELERS destined to *Burlington, Council Bluffs, Omaha, Lincoln, Denver, Salt Lake, Sacramento, San Francisco, Quincy, Hannibal, St. Joseph, Atchison, Leavenworth, Lawrence, Kansas City, Topeka, or points in the Indian Territory and Texas*, should consult their safety, comfort and pleasure, by procuring their tickets via C. B. & Q. ("THE BURLINGTON ROUTE,") for sale at all ticket offices.

For rates on Freight and further information, apply at the Company's Offices:

BOSTON—222 Washington Street.
NEW YORK—317 Broadway.
CHICAGO—59 South Clark Street, and Union Depot.
LIVERPOOL, England—16 South Castle Street.
LONDON   "   —13 Queen Victoria Street.

W. B. STRONG,
Gen'l Sup't, Chicago.

E. P. RIPLEY,
Gen'l Eastern Agent, New York and Boston.

ANNOUNCEMENTS.

BOUND BROOK ROUTE,
BETWEEN
NEW YORK and PHILADELPHIA.

Fast Time! Elegant Cars! Smooth Track! No Smoke nor Dust!

Are the specialties of this Route.

SEVEN DAILY THROUGH TRAINS (EXCEPT SUNDAY)

With Parlor and Sleeping Cars,

Between Philadelphia and New York.

TRY THE NEW LINE!

Passenger Depot in New York: Central R. R. of New Jersey, foot of Liberty Street, North River.

Passenger Depot in Philadelphia: North Penna. R. R., Third and Berks Sts.

F. H. SAYLOR, *Gen. Manager.*

NORTH PENNSYLVANIA RAILROAD.

THIS SHORT AND FAVORITE ROUTE

FROM PHILADELPHIA TO NIAGARA FALLS,

Passing through the beautiful Lehigh, Wyoming and Susquehanna Valleys, contains some of the most picturesque scenery in the country. Passengers have privilege of visiting *en route* such celebrated places of resort as Bethlehem, Mauch Chunk, Switchback, Wilkesbarre, Scranton, Ithaca, Geneva, Auburn, Seneca Lake, Rochester, Buffalo, Clifton Springs, &c.

EXCURSION TICKETS AT REDUCED RATES,

to all principal Watering Places in the

NORTHERN STATES AND CANADA.

First-class equipment, Parlor and Sleeping Cars, smooth track and entire freedom from dust and smoke, are the specialties of this route.

PASSENGER DEPOT IN PHILADELPHIA,

Corner of THIRD and BERKS STS.

Ticket Offices, S. E. cor. Fifth and Chestnut Streets, 732 Chestnut St., cor. 8th St., and *1351 Chestnut St., corner of Broad.*

ELLIS CLARK, Gen. Agent.

ANNOUNCEMENTS.

New Jersey Southern
RAILROAD LINE.

The only Line between New York and Philadelphia.

VIA LONG BRANCH AND THE SEA SHORE.

Favorite Route for

MONMOUTH PARK,		HIGHLANDS,
TOMS RIVER,	**Long Branch,**	SEABRIGHT,
WARETOWN,		MONMOUTH BEACH,
BARNEGAT.	**Ocean Grove,**	RED BANK,
FORKED RIVER,		EATONTOWN,
TUCKERTON,	**Beach Haven,**	BRICKSBURG.

The fast and favorite Steamer
"JESSE HOYT."
The magnificent floating palace
"EMPIRE STATE."
Five trips per day, during the pleasure-season.
(See daily papers and bills, for time-tables.)

——:0:——

Depot in New York, Pier 8, N. R., foot of Rector Street; in Philadelphia, foot Market Street, and 700 & 732 Chestnut Street.

W. S. SNEDEN, General Manager.
CHAS. P. McFADDIN, Gen. Ticket Agent.

SHORT-TRIP GUIDE.—ANNOUNCEMENTS.

THE
ATLANTIC COAST LINE RAILWAY.

DIRECT ROUTE

TO

FLORIDA, NEW ORLEANS AND THE SOUTH.

THE QUICKEST ROUTE TO

Columbia, Aiken, Augusta, Charleston, Savannah, Jacksonville, Macon, Columbus, Montgomery, Mobile, New Orleans, South-West Georgia,

AND ALL ATLANTIC COAST LINE CITIES.

64 hours to New Orleans and 14½ hours quicker to JACKSONVILLE, Florida, than any other railway line between the *NORTH AND SOUTH.*

Pullman Sleeping Cars on all night trains, and Parlor Cars by day. Baggage checked through to destination.

TICKETS GOOD UNTIL USED.

Through Tickets *via* this Line, chairs, berths and sections in parlor and sleeping cars secured, and all information, given in

NEW YORK,

At Atlantic Coast Line Office, 229 Broadway, Opposite New Post Office,

261, 315, 526 Broadway; No, 1 Astor House; at the offices of the New York Transfer Co., 944 Broadway, and at offices of Pennsylvania R. R. Co., foot of Cortlandt and Desbrosses Sts. ; Dodd's Express, No. 4 Court St., Brooklyn.

IN JERSEY CITY, *Pennsylvania Railroad Depot.*

IN PHILADELPHIA,

700 Chestnut St.; 833 Chesnut St.; S. E. cor. B oad and Chestnut Sts., and at Philadelphia, Wilmington & Baltimore R. R. Depot, cor. Broad and Prime Sts.

IN BALTIMORE,

At Atlantic Coast Line Office, No. 9 German Street,

W. H. FITZGERALD, AGENT.

S E. cor. West Baltimore and Calvert Sts ; N. E. cor. West Baltimore and Calvert Sts.; 157 Baltimore St.; at Camden Station, Baltimore & Ohio R. R.; Baltimore & Potomac R. R.; also, at Niagara Falls, Canandaigua, Elmira, Syracuse, Buffalo, and all intermediate points on Northern Central R. R.

IN WASHINGTON,

602 Pennsylvania Ave. ; cor. Sixth St. and Pennsylvania Ave. ; cor. Thirteenth St. and Pennsylvania Ave.; Depot Alexandria & Fredericksburg Railway; on board Potomac Steamers, foot of Seventh St.

IN RICHMOND,

Apply at office of Richmond & Petersburg R. R.. or at Garber & Co.'s, No. 826 Main St., and Exchange Hotel.

A. POPE, Gen'l Pass. and Ticket Agent.

ANNOUNCEMENTS.

THE CHICAGO, MILWAUKEE & ST. PAUL RAILWAY
Is the Great Through Line!
CHICAGO--NORTHWEST,
Wisconsin, Northern Iowa, Minnesota, Dakota, Manitoba and the Black Hills,
And is the only Company owning a line of Railway
—FROM—

Chicago or Milwaukee to St. Paul or Minneapolis.

It is also the ONLY RAILWAY COMPANY by whose Line

THROUGH TICKETS
ARE OR CAN BE ISSUED

Via CHICAGO and MILWAUKEE,
—TO—

Watertown, Sparta, La Crosse, Winona, St. Paul and Minneapolis; or Madison, Prairie du Chien, McGregor, Charles City, Mason City, Austin, Owatonna, St. Paul and Minneapolis.

Tickets to St. Paul and Minneapolis by this road are good either via Madison, McGregor, Owatonna and Faribault, or via Watertown, Sparta, La Crosse and Winona.

It is the ONLY RAIL ROUTE to these celebrated SUMMER RESORTS and Business Centres, viz:

PEWAUKEE, HARTLAND, NASHOTAH, OCONOMOWOC, Portage, KILBOURN CITY, Tomah, WAUKESHA, PALMYRA, Whitewater, Brodhead, Monroe, Edgerton, Lone Rock, Boscobel, Horicon, Beaver Dam, Fox Lake, Waupun, Berlin and Winneconne in Wisconsin; Calmar, Decorah and Algona, in Iowa; Wabasha, Read's Landing, Lake City, FRONTENAC, Red Wing, Hastings, Faribault, Farmington. PRIOR LAKE and Glencoe, in Minnesota.

Watering Places and Summer Resorts in Capitals.

CHICAGO DEPOT, corner Canal and West Madison Sts. Horse Cars and Stage Lines for all parts of the city constantly passing.

CHICAGO CITY OFFICE, 61 and 63 Clark St.

☞ Palace Sleeping Cars and Day Coaches, with Westinghouse's Improved Automatic Air-Brake on all through trains.

S. S. MERRILL,
  General Manager.
              A. V. H. CARPENTER,
              Gen. Pass. and Ticket Agent.
      JNO. C. GAULT,
        Asst. General Manager.

SHORT-TRIP GUIDE—ANNOUNCEMENTS.

1877.

HUDSON RIVER
BY
DAYLIGHT.

ALBANY AND NEW YORK

DAY LINE
OF
STEAMBOATS.

The fast, commodious and favorite steamers,

"C. VIBBARD,"
AND
"DANIEL DREW,"

LEAVING NEW YORK

FROM FOOT OF VESTRY ST.,

Pier 39 North River,

AND ALBANY

FROM FOOT OF HAMILTON ST.

DAILY, SUNDAYS EXCEPTED,

(For time, see New York daily papers.)

Landing at the Principal Points on the Hudson River.

Affords the best mode of enjoying

THE UNSURPASSED SCENERY,

And of reaching the

CATSKILL MOUNTAIN HOUSE,

And all points West by
N. Y. CENTRAL R. R.

ISAAC L. WELSH,
General Ticket Agent,
NEW YORK.

ANNOUNCEMENTS.

AFTERNOON BOAT

FROM

NEW YORK TO WEST POINT, NEWBURG, POUGHKEEPSIE, RONDOUT AND KINGSTON.

THE SPLENDID AND FAVORITE STEAMER

MARY POWELL

Leaves New York, every afternoon at 3.30, from VESTRY STREET PIER, for WEST POINT, NEWBURG, POUGHKEEPSIE, RONDOUT AND KINGSTON; landing at *CORNWALL, MILTON,* and other popular places; passing

THROUGH THE HIGHLANDS BY DAYLIGHT,

and affording unequalled facilities for reaching the places named, and enjoying the noble scenery of the Hudson.

☞ This always magnificent Steamer, just refitted at great cost, and with large additional power, is now the type

FLOATING PALACE OF AMERICAN RIVERS.

Returning, leaves Rondout every morning at 5.30 A. M., reaching New York at 10.30.

SHORT-TRIP GUIDE.—ANNOUNCEMENTS.

PEOPLE'S LINE
OF
STEAMERS
BETWEEN
New York and Albany.
Rooms heated by steam during
the cool months.

New York to Albany,
STEAMERS

DREW,   **D. RICHMOND,**

Monday,	Tuesday,
Wednesday,	Thursday,
Friday,	Saturday,

FROM PIER 41, NORTH RIVER,
(Near Jersey City Ferry, Desbrosses Street.)
AT 6:00 P. M.
Connecting with Trains of New
York Central, Albany & Susque-
hanna, Rensselaer & Saratoga, and
Boston & Albany Railways; and
Lake Champlain Steamers.
☞ TICKETS at the Office on the
Wharf; also at Dodd's Express Of-
fices, 944 Broadway, New York, and
No. 1 Court Street, Brooklyn.
☞ Passengers leaving Wash-
ington at 8.00 A. M., Baltimore at
9.25 A. M., Philadelphia at 1.30
P. M., arrive in New York at 5.15
P. M., in time to connect as above.

Albany to New York,
STEAMERS

D. RICHMOND,   **DREW,**

Monday,	Tuesday,
Wednesday.	Thursday,
Friday,	Saturday,

FROM STEAMBOAT LANDING,
AT 8:15 P. M.,
On arrival of Trains from North
and West.
Cars from Saratoga and the North
go to the boats.
☞ TICKETS to Philadelphia, Bal-
timore, and Washington City, for
sale on the Boats.
HUDSON RIVER RAILROAD TICKETS
TAKEN FOR PASSAGE, including State-
Room Berth.

S. E. MAYO,
Gen'l Pass. Agt., New York.

AMERICAN HOTELS.

ANNOUNCEMENTS.

WINDSOR HOTEL, Fifth Avenue,
FORTY-SIXTH and FORTY-SEVENTH STREETS, New York City.
One of the most elegant, costly and perfect Hotels in America.
HAWK, WAITE & WETHERBEE, Proprietors.

BREVOORT HOUSE,
FIFTH AVENUE,
Near WASHINGTON SQUARE,
NEW YORK.

A quiet Hotel, with a Restaurant of peculiar excellence.

Its patrons are of the best families of this country and Europe.

C. C. WAITE,
Resident Proprietor.

SHORT-TRIP GUIDE.—ANNOUNCEMENTS.

WEST END HOTEL,
Long Branch, N. J.

PRESBURY & HILDRETH, Proprietors.

GEO. G. PRESBURY, JR.   D. M. HILDRETH.

HOWLAND'S HOTEL,

Long Branch, N. J.

HENRY HOWLAND & SON,
Managers.

One of the oldest established houses on the Long Branch shore; recently rebuilt with all modern improvements; and for many years

A FIRST FAVORITE AS A FAMILY HOTEL.

Coaches at all Trains during the Season.

PAVILION HOTEL,

Long Branch, N. J.

SAMUEL C. MORRIS, Proprietor.

This House is situated on the margin of the Atlantic Ocean, embracing a front of over two hundred and fifty feet.

Families wishing to spend the season at a watering place can be accommodated in the most comfortable manner and on moderate terms.

Particular attention paid to the comfort of Ladies.

COACHES AT ALL TRAINS.

COZZENS' HOTEL,
West Point. N. Y.

GOODSELL BROTHERS, Proprietors.

COACHES WILL AWAIT THE ARRIVAL OF EVERY TRAIN AND STEAMBOAT AT COZZENS' DOCK TO CONVEY PASSENGERS TO THE HOTEL

Passengers via Hudson River R. R. should stop at

GARRISON'S STATION,
AND TAKE FERRY BOAT TO COZZENS' LANDING.

Hotel entirely refitted and redecorated.
PRICES REDUCED TO ACCORD WITH THE TIMES.

KITTATINNY HOUSE,
Delaware Water-Gap,
PENNSYLVANIA.

The original and favorite house at the Water-Gap, with a charming location, every comfort and convenience, and a summer list of visitors averaging three thousand.

WATER-GAP HOUSE.

More modern house, erected in 1872, on ground still higher than the Kittatinny, and commanding unequalled views of the fine natural scenery of the Gap.

L. W. BRODHEAD & BRO., Proprietors.

ANNOUNCEMENTS.

THE
CONTINENTAL HOTEL
PHILADELPHIA.

J. E. KINGSLEY & CO., Proprietors.

One of the largest and most magnificent Hotels in America, located on

CHESTNUT ST., COR. NINTH,

At the actual centre of the city and convenient to places of amusement and all points of interest. Has 500 rooms; passenger elevator; two great lines of telegraph to all points; every variety of carriage facility; is passed by street cars, and offers every attention, alike for the hurried visits of the tourist or for more leisurely residence.

SHORT-TRIP GUIDE.—ANNOUNCEMENTS.

LA PIERRE HOUSE,
BROAD ST., NEAR CHESTNUT, PHILADELPHIA.

J. B BUTTERWORTH, Proprietor.

☞ Passenger Lift, Telegraph Office, and all modern improvements and luxuries.

MOUNT VERNON HOTEL,

81 West Monument Street,

BALTIMORE.

Conducted on the European Plan.

This superb edifice, located in the most fashionable part of the city, is now open for the reception of guests. Its appointments are of the most approved character, and the tables are supplied with every luxury this and foreign markets afford. It has heretofore been patronized extensively by European travellers, as well as by men of eminence and distinction of this country.

SHORT-TRIP GUIDE—ANNOUNCEMENTS.

THE ARLINGTON,
WASHINGTON, D. C.

Admitted to be the most thoroughly enjoyable of all the hotels of the National Metropolis, in location, arrangement and management.

T. ROESSLE & SON,
Owners and Proprietors.

IN CONNECTION, THE

Fort William Henry Hotel,
LAKE GEORGE, N. Y.

This magnificent house is located at the most beautiful spot on the shore of "Horicon" (the site of old Fort William Henry); is fitted with all modern conveniences, and has accommodation for nine hundred persons.

Open June 1st, 1877, with Reduced Terms.

TO BOARDERS FOR THE SEASON, $15.00, $17.50 and $21.00 per week, according to location of rooms; TRANSIENT GUESTS, $4.00 per day.

ANNOUNCEMENTS.

MOORE'S HOTEL.
TRENTON FALLS,
New York.

This first-class hotel is located immediately in the neighborhood of these, the handsomest Falls in America, and among the finest in the World; and from it every facility is to be obtained for viewing them to advantage.

M. MOORE, Proprietor.

ANNOUNCEMENTS.

INTERNATIONAL HOTEL,
Niagara Falls.
(AMERICAN SIDE.)

WITH NEW PARLORS ON THE RAPIDS.

J. T. Fulton Jr.

Largest and most pleasantly situated of any at Niagara; nearest to the Falls, and the only one containing all modern improvements. New RIVER PARLORS extending 100 feet over the Rapids, and commanding unequalled view.

OMNIBUSES AND PORTERS AT ALL TRAINS.

Railroad, Steamboat and Telegraph Offices in the Hotel.

PRICES REDUCED TO SUIT THE TIMES.

SHORT-TRIP GUIDE—ANNOUNCEMENTS.

THE

RUSSELL HOUSE,

DETROIT,

Michigan.

WITBECK, CHITTENDEN & CO.,
Proprietors.

This House, handsomely as well as conveniently situated in the most eligible portion of the admittedly beautiful "City of the Straits," enjoys the reputation of being one of the

HOTEL ATTRACTIONS OF THE NORTH-WEST,

And the peculiarity of being visited by

People of Distinction, American and Foreign,

To a degree seldom equalled elsewhere.

All Modern Conveniences and Elegancies

SHORT-TRIP GUIDE.—ANNOUNCEMENTS.

THE
GRAND PACIFIC HOTEL,
CHICAGO, ILLINOIS,
U. S. A.

One of the largest (having over 500 rooms), best arranged, finest ventilated and most elegantly furnished Hotels in America. Has all the different safeguards against fire, which makes it
PRACTICALLY FIRE PROOF.
With a frontage east, south, west and north of over 1,000 feet.

Prices according to location of rooms, but on moderate scale to accord with the times.

JOHN B. DRAKE & CO., *Proprietors.*

ANNOUNCEMENTS.

SHORT-TRIP GUIDE—ANNOUNCEMENTS.

THE LINDELL HOTEL.
BUSINESS AND SOCIETY HOTEL OF
St. Louis, Missouri.
GRISWOLD, CLEMENT & SCUDDER, *Proprietors.*

CLIFTON HOUSE,

Niagara Falls.

(*Canada Side.*)

COLBURN & McOMBER, Proprietors.

Has advantages over all others, in the unequaled view of the Falls and Rapids, to be obtained from the windows and piazzas of the Hotel.

Rooms en suite or singly. Superior accommodations for families spending the season. Transient board at reasonable terms. Commutation Tickets for passing over the New Suspension Bridge, immediately adjoining.

Attendance excellent, and rates moderate.

THE

Russell House,

OTTAWA,

Canada.

This Hotel is the largest and only first-class house in the city. It is fitted, furnished and kept as an unexceptional first-class Hotel, combining modern elegance, comfort and economy. It has ample accommodation for five hundred guests, and is delightfully and centrally situated, being in close proximity to the Parliament Buildings, the Post Office, and all the points of interest.

ANNOUNCEMENTS.

THE QUEEN'S HOTEL,
McGAW & WINNETT, Proprietors.
TORONTO (Ontario), CANADA.

One of the Largest Hotels in the Dominion of Canada, and the most convenient to the Great Western, Union and Northern Railway Stations, Steamboat Piers, and the business portion of the city. Stands on Front Street, between Bay and York; has every modern convenience, accommodation for 500 guests; Lawn, Croquet Grounds, &c.; has received the Grand Duke Alexis, Lord Dufferin (Governor-General), and many other distinguished persons; and is selected by Cook for reception of his tourists in Canada.

SHORT-TRIP GUIDE—ANNOUNCEMENTS.

NATURAL BRIDGE HOTEL,

ROCKBRIDGE CO., VIRGINIA.

A. LEAR, Superintendent.

This commodious and well-situated Hotel is in the immediate neighborhood of that *unparalleled wonder of nature*, the NATURAL BRIDGE, admitted to be among the grandest of the rock-works of the continent and far superior to the world-famed Giant's Causeway of Ireland.

The Hotel offers comfortable accommodations for 100 guests, and offers a pleasant Summer Home for families.

Connections to the Bridge and Hotel, by stage from Goshen Depot of the Chesapeake and Ohio Railroad; by stage from Bonsack's, Ohio and Mississippi Railroad; by stage from Gilmore's Mill, Chesapeake and Ohio Canal, from Lynchburg and Richmond.

PAVILION HOTEL,
BERKELEY SPRINGS,
WEST VIRGINIA.

JOHN T. TREGO, Proprietor.

The Pavilion is the leading house of this old and justly celebrated Bathing and Watering Place; is large, commodious and well kept, and supplies the

PLEASANTEST SUMMER RESORT IN VIRGINIA.

☞ The most extensive and perfectly arranged Medicinal Baths in America, connected with the Hotel.

☞ Accessible by stage-ride of 2½ miles, from SIR JOHN'S RUN, station of the Baltimore and Ohio Railroad, from Baltimore, Washington, or the West.

AMERICAN SPECIALTIES.

ANNOUNCEMENTS.

COOK, SON & JENKINS,
TOURIST OFFICE,
No. 261 Broadway, New York City.

Excursion Tickets for *all Routes in America*, (including CALIFORNIA, with SALT LAKE CITY, YOSEMITE VALLEY, the GEYSERS, &c., and all the wonderful scenery of COLORADO); to

ALL POINTS OF INTEREST IN THE WEST AND SOUTH

THE WHITE MOUNTAINS,

AND

ALL POINTS OF INTEREST IN THE EAST AND NORTH

AT

Rates below those Otherwise Attainable,

AND WITH

Combinations and Privileges Peculiar to their Arrangements,

TICKETS TO AND THROUGH EUROPE AND THE EAST, WITH OCEAN-CROSSING BY ALL LINES OF STEAMERS, AND AT MARKED REDUCTIONS FROM ORDINARY RATES.

"COOK'S EXCURSIONIST," published monthly, price 10 cents, with nearly one thousand specimen Tours and Combinations.

Branch Offices: BOSTON, 197 Washington St.; PHILADELPHIA, 1251 Chestnut St.; WASHINGTON, 820 F St.; SAN FRANCISCO, 3 New Montgomery St.; NEW ORLEANS, 35 Carondelet St.

THOMAS COOK & SON, Ludgate Circus London.

ANNOUNCEMENTS.

A. CAMPBELL, President.

A. F. BROWN, *Treasurer.* JNO. R. CAMPBELL, *Secretary.* J. L. BROWER, *Asst. Sec'y*

CAMPBELL PRINTING PRESS

AND

MANUFACTURING COMPANY.

OFFICE,
No. 39 Beekman Street, New York.

FACTORY,
Wythe Avenue, Hewes and Penn Streets, Brooklyn, E. D., N. Y.

MANUFACTURERS OF

Rotary Perfecting Printing & Folding Machines.

ALSO

Cylinder Presses

FOR

Book, Newspaper, Job, Color & Wood-Cut Printing.

The Campbell Presses are Endorsed by the Leading Printers and Publishers in the United States.

Highest Award at the Philadelphia Centennial.

SEND FOR ILLUSTRATED CATALOGUE.

SHORT-TRIP GUIDE—ANNOUNCEMENTS.

1846.   THIRTY-SECOND YEAR.   1877.

THE
HOME JOURNAL,

ENLARGED AND IMPROVED.

"The Best Literary and Society Paper in America."

Its leading departments comprise Editorials on topics of fresh interest; Brilliant Romances, and Portraitures of American Life; Editorial Reviews of new events in the world of Belles-Lettres, Painting, Sculpture, Science, Music, and the Drama; Original Essays; Ample Excerpts from the best European Writers; Spicy Letters from Correspondents in all the great Capitals of the World; Copious Extracts from New Books; and racy accounts of sayings, happenings and doings in the Beau Monde; embracing the very freshest matters of interest in this country and in Europe—the whole completely mirroring the wit and wisdom, the humor and pathos, the news and sparkling gossip of the times.

SUBSCRIPTION.

Subscribers will receive back numbers when desired.

FREE OF POSTAGE.

The Home Journal alone, one copy, one year.................. $3.00
3 copies, one year...... .... 6.00
6   "   "   " 9.00

TERMS FOR CLUBS:

The Home Journal and any $4 periodical (either Harper's Magazine, Harper's Weekly, Harper's Bazar, Atlantic Monthly, Scribner's Monthly, The Galaxy, Lippincott's Magazine, Appleton's Journal, Frank Leslie's Ladies' Journal, Frank Leslie's Illustrated Newspaper, Blackwood's Magazine, Westminster Review, or any of the English Quarterlies republished here) will be sent for $5.25, the full price being $7. St. Nicholas for $4.50; full rates, $6.00. Littell's Living Age for $8.75; full price, $11.

Subscriptions will take date immediately, or at any time subscribers prefer. Address the proprietors and publishers,

MORRIS PHILLIPS & CO.,
No. 3 Park Place, New York.

ANNOUNCEMENTS.

THE HIGHEST HONORS
AT THE
CENTENNIAL EXHIBITION.

The Judges unanimously recommended the

MENDELSSOHN PIANOS

FOR THE
DIPLOMA OF HONOR AND MEDAL OF MERIT,

Placing them in the *Front Rank* without a *Superior.*

PRICES BELOW COMPETITION,
FOR STRICTLY FIRST-CLASS INSTRUMENTS.

$600 for $250.	$650 for $275.
$700 for $300.	$750 for $325.
$800 for $350.	$900 for $400.
$1,000 for $450.	

NO COMMISSIONS TO AGENTS.
NO DISCOUNTS TO TEACHERS.
NO DEVIATION IN PRICE.

THE MENDELSSOHN
GRAND, SQUARE AND UPRIGHT PIANOS

contain valuable patents and improvements never before introduced.

Mathushek's New Patent Duplex Overstrung Scale

is the greatest advance in the history of Piano making, producing the *most astonishing power, richness and depth of tone,* and a *sustaining singing quality never before attained,* being a "GRAND PIANO IN A SQUARE CASE."

THE MENDELSSOHN UPRIGHTS
are the finest in America.

They are pronounced the "Pianos of the Future."

Manufactory and Warerooms:

Nos. 490, 492, 494, 496 and 498 West Fifty-seventh St.,
Nos. 858, 860, 862, 864, 868 and 870 Tenth Avenue.
PIANOS SENT ON TRIAL.
Illustrated and Descriptive Catalogue mailed free.

MENDELSSOHN PIANO CO.,
BUSINESS OFFICE,
No. 56 BROADWAY, N. Y.

THE

SPUR OF MONMOUTH;

OR,

Washington in Arms.

A Historical and Centennial

ROMANCE OF THE REVOLUTION.

From Personal Recollections and Documents never before made Public.

By an Ex-Pension Agent.

Third Edition Now Ready!

BY

CLAXTON, REMSEN & HAFFELFINGER,

Publishers and Booksellers,

524 to 628 Market Street,

PHILADELPHIA.

SHORT-TRIP GUIDE.—ANNOUNCEMENTS.

HELMBOLD'S
TEMPLE OF PHARMACY,

CONTINENTAL HOTEL,

PHILADELPHIA, PENNA.

PRESCRIPTIONS

Carefully compounded with Pure Drugs and Chemicals.

IMPORTER OF

French, German and English Perfumery, Soaps, Pomades, Toilet Articles, &c.

COMPLETE LINE OF LADIES' REQUISITES.

Principal Agent of

ATKINSON'S, LUBIN'S AND LETCHFORD'S PERFUMERY.

Sole Agent for

GOLDEN HAIR FLUID,

L'AUREOLINE DE ROBARE.

Patronage of the public is respectfully solicited.

ALBERT L. HELMBOLD.

Principal Depot for the sale of Helmbold's Genuine Preparations

Helmbold's Extract Buchu,
    "   *Extract Sarsaparilla.*
    "   *Improved Rose Wash & Catawba Pills.*

OPEN ALL NIGHT.

SHORT-TRIP GUIDE—ANNOUNCEMENTS.

Travelers' Official Guide
OF THE
RAILWAYS & STEAM NAVIGATION LINES
IN THE
UNITED STATES & CANADA.

The only Guide recognized by the United States Government, and railroad officers, as the standard authority for time, distances, and other statistics relative to railroads.

PUBLISHED MONTHLY,

under the auspices of the GENERAL TICKET AGENTS' ASSOCIATION, and sold by all news agents and periodical dealers throughout the United States and Canada; also, at the various railroad depots and on trains. This is the best advertising medium in the country, and from its large circulation, affords unusual advantages to merchants and manufacturers.

PRICE PER COPY, 50c.; PER YEAR, $4.00.

For further particulars, as to prices of advertising, &c., application should be made to the

NATIONAL RAILWAY PUBLICATION CO.,
233 South Fifth St., Philadelphia, Pa.

"OFFICIAL TIME-TABLES."

A NEW MONTHLY PUBLICATION OF ABOUT 200 PAGES, CONTAINING, IN A CONDENSED FORM, TIME-TABLES OF THE RAILWAY AND STEAM NAVIGATION LINES OF THE UNITED STATES & CANADA.

The afternoon trains are distinguished from the morning trains by the use of a peculiar style of type for each. Telegraph Stations are designated, and the population of each place noted. A short description of each city, giving its business interests, lists of hotels, &c., is also incorporated.

A new, handsome, and accurate colored railway map is bound in each.

PRICE 25 CENTS PER COPY.

NATIONAL RAILWAY PUBLICATION CO.

PHILADELPHIA—233 South Fifth Street.

CHICAGO—96 Dearborn Street.

ANNOUNCEMENTS.

ZELL'S
ENCYCLOPEDIA.

Price, complete, - - - $37.50.

Also Sold in Nos. at 50c. each.

The shape of the book, type, plan of the work, &c., have been made to produce the greatest amount of matter in the smallest space, and at the lowest cost. The amount of printed matter is equal to that of the largest Encyclopedia published by an American firm. While every essential fact and date is included in each article, yet every subject is so condensed that our Encyclopedia has five times as many articles as the most voluminous ones.

This gives not only the convenience of compactness, but enables you to make references in so short a time that you are tempted to look them up when your interest is aroused, and they are thus fastened in your mind.

B. W. BOND,

No. 5 Beekman St.,

NEW YORK CITY.

www.ingramcontent.com/pod-product-compliance
Lightning Source LLC
Chambersburg PA
CBHW022138300426
44115CB00006B/240